Ever Your Loving Mully

**The Letters from Burma of Muriel Bowden
to her mother Alice Britten
in England
1922-24**

**Edited by Ann Bowden
and
Ian Adams**

For Susen -
With love

Ann Bowden -
June 2011

5, Shakespeare Mews, Titchfield, Hampshire, PO14 4DS.

1

ISBN 978-1-4092-5110-1

Preface

Valuable history is sometimes lost when personal accounts of past events are destroyed by the weeding of old papers by subsequent generations. The purpose of this work is to preserve a unique set of letters written by Muriel Bowden in Burma to her mother in England between 1922 and 1924. Muriel Bowden made carbon copies of her letters in three old account books in which she described her day to day life at Maymyo, Monywa and at her husband's camp sites in the jungle where he was foresting teak. Some of the letters, because of their age, and the method she used to record them, were difficult to decipher and were made more so by the fact that, like her mother, Muriel or Mully, as she signed herself, suffered from severe rheumatism which affected her handwriting. Her letters always began My Dearest Mother and ended Ever your loving Mully, from which the title is taken.

Mully was born Muriel Elizabeth Britten in 1892 at Tupsley, Herefordshire, the daughter of William E Britten, a land agent and surveyor and his wife Alice Ann Child. There are records of the Child and the Britten families farming in Herefordshire as early as the 1780s.

During the First World War, Mully served as a Red Cross nurse at the Military Hospital at Netley, in Hampshire. After the war she visited her cousin, Ethel Blackmore, who was married to a tea planter Sammy Blackmore and lived in Ceylon. On the boat returning from Ceylon she was introduced by Lieutenant Colonel J.H. Williams, Elephant Bill, to Herbert Frederick Bowden. Bowden, like Williams was employed by the Bombay Burmah Trading Corporation in foresting teak from the jungle forests of central Burma, on the banks of the Chindwin and Irrawaddy rivers. Muriel and Freddie were married in the autumn of 1920 and she joined him subsequently in Burma. In 1922, when the letters commenced her mother, Alice Britten was a widow, aged seventy-two, crippled with rheumatism and living in Herefordshire.

The Bombay Burmah Trading Corporation, which Freddie Bowden joined in 1908, was created in 1863 by six Scots brothers named Wallace, who settled in Bombay in the early 1840s, and formed a trading partnership in 1848 called "Wallace Bros. & Co." In the mid 1850s they extended their business to Rangoon, shipping tea to Bombay. In 1863 they floated a limited company "The Bombay Burmah Trading Corporation" (BBTC). Its shareholders were largely Indian merchants but the Wallace Brothers retained the controlling interest. In the 1870s it was the leading producer of teak in Burma and Siam and had interests in cotton, oil, tea and shipping.

By the 1880s Wallace Bros. & Co., was an influential financial house in London by virtue of its increasing interests and was in a position to provide the British Government with intelligence concerning Burma and to play on growing fears concerning French ambitions there. A crisis arose in 1885 at a time when the French were negotiating to build a railway from Rangoon to Mandalay. A fine was imposed on the BBTC by a Burmese court for under-reporting its extractions of teak from Toungoo and for not paying its employees and some of its timber was seized. The British Government believed the accusations were ill founded and the Court's decision unjust. It issued an extremely high handed ultimatum to the Burmese Government, the acceptance of which would have seriously eroded Burmese independence. As perhaps anticipated by the British, it was rejected out of hand, and Lord Randolph Churchill, Secretary of State for India, sent a British Expeditionary Force under General Sir

Harry Prendergast, V.C., [at that time a Major General] to seize Mandalay. King Thibaw was dethroned and exiled to India and the monarchy abolished. In January 1886, Burma was annexed and became part the British Indian Empire. A British military presence secured the state against resistance from the Burmans and a military style police force preserved the peace within its borders. There followed a period of peaceful occupation and prosperity until the late 1920s. Commerce with Britain blossomed and a number of privileged Burmans found their way to British Universities. Some aspired to participation in the political life of Burma.

Muriel Bowden's letters written some forty years after annexation, and shortly after a period in which the First World War had intervened, provide a fascinating insight into the social and commercial environment of the British in Burma in the final decades of the Raj. She described the lot of the wives who accompanied their husbands to this climatically hostile, but often rewarding, outpost of Empire. As well as detailing the methods used in harvesting teak, the letters reflect many of the contemporary attitudes of the British towards the Burmans and towards the Anglo-Burmese. Muriel Bowden was refreshingly free of 'political correctness' and, although she did not labour the point, she was well aware of 'the wind of change' that was blowing through the Indian Empire. She also understood that for her husband, employment in Burma represented financial rewards and a way of life which most middle class Britons were unlikely to achieve in their own country in the disastrous economic conditions of the time. She was well aware too of the damage being done to the health of her husband and to herself by his prolonged work in the jungle

During the early 1920s, the period in which the letters were written, Burma was administered as part of the British Indian Empire by the Imperial Civil Service under a Lieutenant Governor General. A garrison of British troops remained together with a military style police force. The first moves towards Burmese self-government were already taking place and a British Governor General was to be appointed under who Burmans were to be given ministerial responsibilities. Mully noted the foreboding with which long serving British residents received the news. This was the period when Eric Arthur Blair, better known as the writer George Orwell, served unhappily as an Assistant Superintendent in the Imperial Indian Police in Burma. His views on the experience and his distrust of autocratic government were reflected in his book Burmese Days, published in 1934. Muriel Bowden's letters emphasise the contrast in the life-styles, and social attitudes of the British in the centres of administration, with the much more primitive way of life, and interdependence of humanity, in the teak forests of the jungle. The letters also provide an insight into life at home in England at that time. The middle classes lived as best they could on what they had. Muriel's mother was an elderly and disabled widow who had lost two of her sons in the First World War and was living in reduced circumstances in a guest house at Ross on Wye. Modern generations expect social security benefits, an old age pension or invalidity allowance, wheel chairs, and free medical care provided by the state. For Alice Britten there were none of these. Freddie and Muriel Bowden were keen photographers, and took many photographs and a number of these, which illustrate their day to day lives in Burma, have been included. Mully mentions the difficulties involved in photography in the jungle. Unclean water, insects and grit tarnished the finished product. Modern digital imagery has enabled the restoration of this unique collection of photographs. Reference is made in the letters to numerous relatives and a family tree is included at Appendix 'A'.

The Brittens, Childs, and Turners from whom Mully was descended had large farms in Herefordshire and records show that their connection with North Herefordshire stretches back through many decades.

The last century has witnessed a period of dramatic change not least of which has been the revolution in transport and communication. From the pony and trap mankind has reached out to the space age and electronic mail threatens to replace the letter. Muriel Bowden's letters provide a unique window through which we may compare our present with her past.

Special thanks and gratitude are due to Debbie who after a long day's work arrived with her laptop and for many hours patiently helped to decipher the faded and difficult handwriting of the letters and also to relatives and friends who gave so much help and encouragement in the project.

A.H.B. and T.I.A.
July 2008

For Rodney
who would have been delighted to know that his mother's
letters written during her early married life are now
recorded for our family.

Ever Your Loving Mully
The Letters From Burma of Muriel Bowden to Her Mother Alice Britten in England
1922-24

Contents

Muriel Elizabeth Bowden

BOOK 1

Sabenago, Tuesday February 7th 1922

My dearest Mother,

I hope you won't mind having my letters in pencil from now onwards. Freddie has given me a topping book from the office in which I can write all my letters to you in diary form and get a duplicate written at the same time to keep, so you can never catch me out by saying I said something I didn't. I can now write a little each day and record all I do. I know how you love having letters, dear, so you shall have a good dose each week. Your efforts are splendid and knowing how you hate letter writing they are appreciated all the more. Yours of January 11th arrived the day after we got in from camp and was quite a surprise mail, and was brought in with our chota[1] which made it feel quite like home. Generally the mail comes in with a whole lot of official letters for Freddie any time during the day. Letters seem to take a shorter time to come now. Not a month, as when I used to receive Freddie's letters. I'm so sorry dear you have been laid up with a bad cold, and very wise of you to stay in bed. I am relieved to know you are in such good hands. I shall be most anxious to know how the treatment works and feel so glad you mean to try a course. I have not forgotten my little dollop of help, and directly things are straightened up in our accounts you shall have the promised little help. I am now awaiting my passbook which Mrs. Turner promised to send out at an early date. Needless to say I was overdrawn a small amount as I did not want to leave Hereford owing small accounts.

I see by the papers flu is very bad again at home. Funnily enough at the same time villages started the same out here. One near here had twenty-seven deaths. Hope all at Rosslyn have recovered. I am most interested in *The Hereford Times*, so do carry on sending it. Freddie is much amused at your thrills regarding the *Hay Case*;[2] he remembers our interest in the *Greenwood*, similar show, when at Bath.

What a pity it seems to send Goli to Lucton[3], changes always unsettle a kid, but they will love having him at Nunnington, where no doubt the kid will spend his holidays. You may have no fear as to my not taking care of myself. What I don't do, Freddie does, so all is well. I had my lesson in Ceylon, thank you, and religiously change after any exercise, though at present one never gets really hot. It is an awfully healthy life and I feel so fit. All morning and after tea I live in a jersey as the wind from off the water is so cold and at nights I am quite glad of a hot water bottle and three blankets. Freddie has a jolly fine vegetable garden which with dint of much trouble and watering he has every vegetable one could wish for; bunny's food galore, and we never have less than five lots of vegetables with our meat. The latter chiefly consists of chicken; generally two are killed each day and we see it served up in various ways. Other than what we kill ourselves no meat is obtainable. Mr. Hunt is a good shot and we often have Jungle fowl, snipe or gye, a sort of deer. All very good. My appetite is enormous. I don't turn a hair at eating two fried eggs and lots of ham for my chota. That meal is the same as our English breakfast and Freddie and I have it (when in Sabenago) in our little

---

[1] Breakfast

[2] R. v Armstrong (1922). The Hay poisoning case in which Armstrong, a solicitor at Hay on Wye was tried and executed for poisoning his wife with arsenic. There is in retrospect some doubt about his guilt.

[3] A preparatory school in Herefordshire.

hut at about 7am. He then tootles over to his office and leaves me to bathe in the tent adjoining our hut and dress at my leisure. The whole morning soon buzzes by; sewing generally. In the Jungle housekeeping does not come my way. Freddie gives out his own stores and the cook goes along his own line. At Maymyo of course I shall do my own ordering. My little 'boy' Bar Tai is still a great success, and making great strides in his English which I teach him each morning and talk to him whenever I have him with me. I have picked up a little Burmese, which is a pretty language. I can follow what Freddie says, but the Burmese gabble so. A Burman strikes me as quite a different man to the native in Ceylon. A Burman is very independent and believes in voicing his own opinion, which is generally of the soundest. So far I have not seen a Burmese girl to admire, which is disappointing after one's ideas of their beauty. My last letter was written from Gwebinmaw, in a 'tay' or hut surrounded by weird figures of Buddha. Nothing of the weirdness disturbed my slumbers that night, and I was quite ready to get up at the normal early hour of 6am. We had our chota as we always do in camp on a table outside by the log fire, while inside is all bustle packing our goods and quite near are the elephants being loaded up. We left them at their jobs while Freddie and I started off in the hired sampan, (small boat) as we thought we might vary our experiences by finishing our tour by doing the last six miles paddling up the Irrawaddy, and very nice it was too. We helped to paddle, for which I'm sure the two Burmans must have blessed us as the current is very strong. We hugged the bank all the way up, after making detours round a sandbank which was almost black with sand-martins migrating. At one spot we landed to see the workings of the queer fishing smacks which are very frequently seen along the banks, and always with the Burman's bamboo hut where he and his family live until the rains come and force them off elsewhere. Their idea of casting down a net attached to bamboo always reminds me of what one learns in the Bible, and I can quite imagine St. Peter etc., living and looking just like these men. The net stretched out and held by bamboos is lashed to a long canoe which is made firm to the bank. After a while the net is hauled up by pulling up the top end by a man squatting on the bank. If in luck the fish are pushed into a basket on one end of the boat and sufficiently covered with water to keep them alive until an opportunity to sell them, and so they go on. We were quite glad to stretch our legs as well as see the operations, and so was our little dog, 'Patch,' who by the way thrives well, and I'm glad to say Freddie is not quite so busy dashing after him to rub his nose in puddles. Freddie is splendid at teaching the animal to beg, etc. Before we finished our trip, the cargo boat (the one that brought us up here) passed us. We waved furiously and yelled, trying to attract the attention of our pal the captain, Mr. Lewis, but no luck. We arrived here just after the elephants and found Mr. Hunt already with his nose at office work. He had left camp early hoping for some shooting, but no luck. His sudden spurt of energy in the work line was due to a promise from Freddie to be allowed to go after a tusker if he had finished his job of making up the monthly accounts. At this time of year wild tuskers often become a danger in that they attack the female elephants at any of our camps and often run wild amongst them, or lead a female off into the Jungle, and of course she is seen no more. Shooting is the only preventative and Freddie says camps (with the elephants tied up) have at times had to be surrounded by men with guns to frighten the tuskers off. So yesterday, early, Hunt went off all agog. The only thing in his life is sport. Freddie finds him an awful nuisance in the work — no use at all, and is so dense that half of Freddie's time is taken up teaching him decimals and such like which of course he ought to have learned somewhere. I suppose Oxford doesn't go in for such teaching. We are glad he has gone anyway. The bungalow is so peaceful, and Freddie says his two clerks do twice the amount of work. Hunt owns up that he had no idea this job meant so much office work or he would not have joined the Corporation. We feel certain that his time is short out here. I often help Freddie with part of his calculations or accounts which keeps me amused and I am always ready to have my brain improved in some way or another. We came into Sabenago on Thursday 2nd in order to claim the money from the mail boat on the 3rd. Hunt went over for that at about 7am and had a pleasant hour waiting in the cold before the launch arrived to hand over the fourteen thousand rupees, which is about the amount which is sent up from Mandalay for wages etc., each month. The days at headquarters are much the same; Freddie busy in the office all morning, and I sew on the veranda. After tiffin[4] at 10am we generally lie down for an hour, tea on the veranda, after which, if work permits, we play tennis, which is often only singles for me. Freddie has so much to do in the office, and he is only too glad to get rid of Hunt who thinks himself rather good, but is like a whirlwind on the court and puts us off terribly. Sunday slipped by without us knowing it. I never do know the date or day. After being in the bungalow all day Freddie took me out yesterday hoping to shoot something. We were too late to get a hare and it was too dark to get the Jungle fowl which we could hear crowing and chuckling in the Jungle. A Jungle cock is just like a bantam.

The Government launch anchored just off our shore this morning and we have been expecting a man of sorts to put in an appearance. 'He' has landed and gone off shooting, so may appear later, especially if he has a thirst on him This afternoon this letter has to go, so will finish having come to the end of my news. Best of love dear, I hope this won't weary you.

Time your loving Molly

Sabenago, Wednesday, February 8th 1922

I only sent my mail yesterday, but will start my next letter, as a little written each day is easier. I felt awfully rotten from midday with a head etc., (which I've not had since I came out) so departed to our little hut to lie down leaving Freddie to finish tiffin alone, and thereby missing the great excitement of seeing a real live Englishman! A Mr. Petch, a Government Official, came up to enquire into trouble of sorts at a village near here. He arrived in the private launch earlier, and as he did not come up to the bungalow, as strangers usually do, I sent a Burman with a note to await his arrival on the shore asking him up for a drink, which accordingly he did at about 12.30pm. Freddie said he was quite newly out from Home and seemed very nice and to his astonishment rigged up like a perfect little gent in long grey flannels, tie and collar. Most go about in shorts and cricket shirt open at the neck. Hunt, much to our annoyance, plays tennis in shorts and socks. I'm afraid even you would have to become accustomed to men's bare knees out here!

I slept soundly the whole afternoon, and after Freddie had finished paying wages in the office we strolled out for a bit. The evenings are so lovely, wonderful sunsets over the Irrawaddy, and at present the nights are like day with the moon. In the evening the time is generally spent by Freddie lazing in a chair and me sewing in another. (Good of us to have separate chairs, isn't it). Each evening we try to bring ourselves to write the umpteen letters owing, but somehow they never get done! We have so much lost time to make up for, that I can't stick to anything really serious. Just as I was washing my dirty little self at 8am this morning, Freddie came dashing along to say the cargo boat was due at Male and as we had made up our minds to go aboard to see our old pal the skipper, I had to look slippy to dress in

---

[4] Tea

time. The Corporation provides a sampan in which we were rowed across, and arrived in nice time, in spite of being blown downstream by a strong wind which was causing a terrific sand storm about a mile upstream. This cargo boat brings up everything you can think of in the trading line. Burmans collect in crowds on the bank waiting to dash on the boat and be the first to trade during the short half hour allowed. On board were fourteen American tourists, and on looking up to the top deck we were faced with about the same number of cameras. It was killing to see one immaculate knut coming across the planks to shore in his perfect white flannels and brown brogues with a devil of a polish on them. The crowd was waved aside, and the knut picked his way on tip toe along the boards almost level with the water. Freddie did not see why we should wait in the smelly crowd for him, so proceeded along the plank meeting halfway. With our extra ton weight you can imagine the knut's shoes had some of the polish taken off them by the water. Mr. Lewis was waiting for us and we went along to his cabin for a talk. He is quite a nice man, and every time he goes down or up he hails us with long shrieks from the siren. We then came back in our sampan bringing various purchases the clerk made at the bazaar in the way of oranges, nuts etc. He also got us our mail, (not English) in which we had our first batch of papers from the Maymyo Club: *The Tatler, Bystander* and *Weekly Graphic*. Papers are put up for auction after the Club has had them for a week, and Freddie bid highest for those, so we are well supplied for a year at very reduced prices. After a rest this afternoon, Freddie and I had tea and then went out again, with a gun, but as yesterday, the Jungle fowl kept too much to the thick Jungle, so we came back with naught. I must now go and bathe and then have dinner. Always such a good feed too. Freddie is already splashing in his tub.

Thursday February 9th 1922

Nothing much doing today, except getting ready to go out to camp tomorrow. I always have my sewing machine in the corner of the veranda and find it most useful for running up things. Today I put a new canvas on a deckchair to take out to the Jungle. After tea Freddie and I again went out with a gun round about the bungalow but got nothing. The Jungle fowl are altogether too nippy.

Friday February 10th 1922

We were turned out of our beds at some unearthly hour with the boys claiming our sheets etc., to make up into the bed roll. Elephants all round the bungalow being loaded up, and after packing up all odds and ends in the bungalow, Freddie and I started off on foot with the ponies following with the Syce. Freddie again had his gun, and though we saw a lot in the way of birds, the Jungle was altogether too thick. Two lovely peacocks got up and we tracked them for a long time but no luck. Freddie walked the three miles to our camp at Nyaunggyin and I rode most of the way as we did not leave Sabenago before 9am and it was getting too hot for the walk along a very dusty road. Our camp is on the banks of the river where teak logs are lying in odd numbers waiting the floods to carry them on to the Irrawaddy. We are now under canvas with the usual log fire roaring away, and almost a full moon making everything almost as light as day. In no camp have I seen such a wonderful collection of birds and butterflies, all of the brightest of colours. After a snooze this afternoon we had an early tea and again went off with the gun to try our luck, but again with nothing to feed our tummies. Freddie and I had to be carried across the creek and I'd love to have a snap to show you with my arms around a couple of Burmans. (Not so smelly as they are at times). We enjoyed the walk through the village where we made the usual stir with its endless yelping dogs and kids scooting for dear life, only to be seen later peeping from out of their huts. This village is so pretty on the edge of paddy fields with the paddy just coming up in the brightest of green you can imagine. On our way home we saw a most wonderful meteor. I spotted this wonderful star shaped light going up in a curve and shouted to Freddie to look at the rocket, when he exclaimed: 'By Jove, it's a meteor!' It seemed to me so near as it curved down and out of sight and left a trail of sparks behind it. No sooner out of that excitement than, ongoing round a corner, we came across a young elephant, which are always rather fierce without their oosies[5] in attendance. A shout from Freddie made me take to my heels and run like mad and Freddie after me, and the elephant after us. Luckily the oosie5 was near and came dashing out and after much shouting and throwing sticks got the young beggar up into the Jungle otherwise we might have been a rather nasty mess on the road by now. I was scared, I can tell you. Well dear, this must do for the day. We have had dinner and Freddie is impatiently waiting for me to join him at the fire to have a good warm before turning in.

Saturday February 11th 1922

A mail arrived just as Freddie and I got into camp at Yenaoo, which I have mentioned before. We left Nyaunggyin about 6-45am and walked the first three miles hoping for a shot, and also to get exercise, as the early mornings are always so beautifully cool. We saw nothing, and after a time the ride became rather monotonous, as the Jungle in that part is very sparse and there is not much shade, so I was glad when we had finished the nine miles and sat in the 'Rest Bungalow' until the elephants arrived with all our kit and, at the same time, a messenger with the mail. As each mail arrives a man is sent out to whatever camp we are at, and generally with a basket of vegetables. We had our usual snooze this afternoon and we are now getting on with letters as the mail has to go tomorrow. Midday really was hot; first time I really felt the difference. I can hear the chicken for next day being killed in the background. We live on nothing else. Contractors seeing Freddie this evening brought their usual offering of eggs and fruit; twenty-six eggs altogether, and I don't mind betting that twenty-six of them are bad. Directly they hear he is in the district they apparently dash round birds nesting and bring what eggs can be found, never mind how near to being hatched they are. You would be amused to see Freddie. We often laugh at your dislike of his shaznbambees (we always call them shambimbos) and wonder if you would be flummoxed at seeing him sit down to his meals in them. They are so cool and I shall probably come to wearing them myself one day. Well Cheerio dear. I had quite a big mail this week. Emma Turner, and yours, and I want now to write to Aunt Mary. I am so sorry that your legs have again been giving you up and hope to hear soon that the treatment is doing good. Best of love.

Camp, Sunday February 12th 1922

It does seem so queer to think today is Sunday — 6pm. You are probably now sitting down to your round of 'good old English beef' after, I hope, going to church this morning to listen to another weary effort by Mr. Ledger[6].7 Our day is very different out here and but for my diary I'd never know today is the Sabbath! Once more we got up just at daybreak and started the great ride at about 6-45am. For the first time we allowed our little 'dawg' 'Patch' to come with us. Up till now he has always been left behind. He was yelping like mad as he saw us disappear and was later brought along by one of the men perched on top of an elephant. 'Patch' seems none the worse for wear so I expect from now onwards he will always accompany us. His long curly tail is becoming an awful 'give away' as to his parents! I fear a large amount of 'pi' is in him. However his temperament is all that it should be. His tail apparently is a great eyesore even to himself as so often he twirls madly round and round, and is not happy till the end is in his mouth. The march was very much better than yesterday, flat through Jungle for the first two miles and then a steady climb up a rough path, which was

---

[5] Elephant riders
[6] The Vicar of Tupsley

all done on foot, also down the other side making about four miles in all. We crossed a very pretty creek at the foot, with odd teak logs lying high and dry awaiting the rains. This creek is very poor for floating the logs; there not being sufficient water, and at the mouth logs have to be carted some miles to the Irrawaddy. Some logs take up to six years to get down a creek. We then crossed a number of paddy fields all dried up and brown, and so into Pinkan village where we camp at the forest's rest bungalow until tomorrow. Hills are all around, covered with trees of course, and away up to the right the hills are 6,300 ft. high. Mr. Hunt has not turned up yet. He camped here, as arranged, to meet us yesterday after chasing a tusker for six days. The tusker evidently is a cute one and gave him trouble and up to this morning he had no luck. Hunt is such a keen sportsman, and so fearfully energetic that his knees will be the undoing of his health one day. This is an awfully nice large bungalow with a wide veranda, where we are now sitting with a lamp, and Freddie at some office work. Air full of night sounds and those of the elephants feeding near. I am now going to sew at one of the curtains I am embroidering on that Government linen for our Maymyo drawing room. The road from Pinkan to Kankmaw was quite the best we've been along during our travels. This part belongs to a Rajah or Sawbwa[7] (he came up from Mandalay on the same boat as we did after he had been down to see the Prince) and this road he made purposely to travel along at the time of his visit to the Prince. The D.P.O however did not come up to his expectations of finishing the road outside his area, so it all came to naught, except for the benefit derived by all travellers in having a jolly fine road curling around the hills almost at a dead level. The banks and trees are wonderful on the sides of the road as it is always more or less in the shade and very much greener than in other parts. At Kankmaw we camped under canvas in dense Jungle, teak trees with their large leaves giving us splendid shelter. In the evening I went with Freddie and Hunt while they looked over a few logs in a creek nearby. These logs were found in an area declared finished by Freddie's predecessor, which shows careless work on someone's part. When an area is declared finished a forest inspector tours through it, and should there be logs or girdlings left or logs found burnt, there is the devil to pay. Freddie is finding a lot of these sort of things to clear up in the district.

Tuesday February 14th 1922

This day started badly by Freddie suddenly having the most awful pain across the pit of his back. It caught him just as he stepped over a log before leaving camp. I'm afraid he had it all on the march to Werboung and the riding did not seem to help. I'm sure it's lumbago, and as the poor dear has never had it before he can't quite make things out. The road was nice and shady and not more than six miles. The march up to Werboung is always a weary one and rather a waste of time for Freddie as it means five days travelling and no work until he gets there. This area is left in the hands of a Eurasian, Mr. Partridge. There have been awful muddles as he is only two years at the job, but Freddie is gradually licking him into shape. Last evening we sat in our little 'tay' while Freddie and Mr. Partridge talked 'shop' and I sewed, with our usual log fire roaring away. I had great tussles with Freddie during the day as he would not let me rub him with Elliman's.[8]9 However, I won the day and I think did him good. Hunt went off shooting again all afternoon and brought in five Jungle fowl. This is a wonderful area for all sorts of game. It is still awfully cold at nights and my three blankets are none too much.

---

[7] The hereditary ruler of a district.
[8] Elliman's Universal Embrocation for pain relief.

Wednesday February 15th 1922

Lordy! How we slept last night and were almost too ashamed to call the boy on discovering it to be 8am! Freddie did not have a very good night and was restless; so that's our excuse. However, today we do not move camp which is a nice change, so a late hour does not matter. Freddie's back is better, but he still looks like the advertisement for backache kidney pills!

Thursday February 16th 1922

Instead of moving camp today Freddie decided to spend an extra day in order to go further into the work with Partridge, as Freddie will not be again in this district before September, and incidentally, the rest will do his back a lot of good; in fact it is already a lot better. I think iodine has done the trick. While sitting at tea yesterday a couple of men brought in such a topping young gye shot by one of them with Freddie's gun during the afternoon. A gye[9] is rather like a young stag with a brightish brown coat. It seemed such a shame to shoot such an animal, but it comes in very useful to vary our menu from the everlasting chicken, though personally I never tire of that diet. We only had a small quantity of this gye and the men were delighted to have the rest. After tea Freddie and I walked up to the village pagoda perched on a hill where we saw the most lovely sunset and all the country for miles around was one sea of trees. It is a wonderful sight. When we got back I had a tub and a change while Freddie had Partridge up. I could hear fur was flying in all directions as the wretched man had shot a tusker without a permit and the police heard of it. Directly Partridge saw there was a row about it he wrote off and sent the tusks to Freddie hoping to hide behind him, and the fact that Freddie had a licence to shoot a tusker. Freddie is awfully fed up with the underhandedness of it all and is leaving Partridge to fight it out himself. This morning, while still at our breakfast out in the open by a fire, elephants belonging to this Camp were brought up for inspection, including one with her baby of two months. They are always rather upish then and the oosie had to keep her in order with a spear. Freddie got her plus the baby to go across the creek in the sun and took a snap. I hope to send you some soon. During the inspection Hunt came slopping along and I could tell by him having his pyjama coat under a sweater that he had only just tumbled out of bed and then his tale of woe was told; how he was burnt out of his tent during the night. The silly ass must have gone to bed smoking a cigarette, or on putting on his clothes on top of him to keep himself warm, part of the cigarette must have got brushed off. Anyway, in some extraordinary way the man went on sleeping and woke up to see his mosquito curtain just burst into flames, and found the bed canvas, and green mac on top of that, sheet, blanket, pillows, and two coats and a sort of eiderdown smouldered almost to nothing! The smoke must have sort of drugged him, and his belongings are now looking a sorry sight on the ropes of his tent. The tent also had a big hole burnt at the side. Hunt is a queer bird altogether, and we spend our time trying to teach him manners! He will come flopping into tea with only a sloppy pair of shoes, no socks, his pants coming, somewhere round his chest, and his trousers well below his middle! Rumour has it that a tiger is prowling around after the baby elephant, and one elephant has already been attacked so Hunt will be off stalking that tonight. Whenever will he settle down to do a 'spot' (his pet expression) of work, goodness only knows I am sure I don't. Freddie and I have just been over to see Partridge's compound. Thanks to Freddie he now lives decently, instead of like a Burman, and has a good vegetable garden in front. Freddie and I are spending the morning writing in our little tay.[10] Freddie is making out his working statements for next year.

---

[9] A Barking Deer *(Muntiacus muntjak)*.
[10] Grass hut.

Friday 17th February 1922

Left Werboung this morning Walked the first five miles up hill on a rough path. All three ponies cleared off at once, much to Hunt's disgust, and then were rescued. The reason for so many wild elephants around here is because within a few miles there is a kedda where elephants are being driven from the Jungle to be caught and trained. A mail arrived today but no English one yet.

Toodleloo for another week dear. Keep cheery and always let me have a line to let me know how you are. Best of love and from Freddie.

Sabenago Wednesday February 22nd 1922

I have not religiously written every day since the sending off of the last mail as we have been kept on the go, and getting here again always means odd jobs and a disinclination to settle and write. This evening Freddie and Hunt are pen pushing like mad in the office to get the monthly accounts finished, so we had to do without our usual after tea tennis. Poor Freddie has an awful time with Hunt who cannot keep his accounts right and is like a brick wall to din anything into. Tonight Hunt is like a kid with the sulks as he is made to go without his spot of tennis. Must get back to Sunday last when I sent my mail too early really, as Tuesday is the down mail. We got in here Monday but I was afraid that something might keep Freddie out an extra day. Sunday we had a long hot and rather tiring ten miles to go to Twinge where we found the forest's bungalow where we stayed before with the roof off and undergoing general repairs, so we had to camp under the solitary tree on the large flat space leading to the Irrawaddy, and which is covered with six feet of water during the rains. All the huts in the village are built up on posts and folk go about in boats when the river is up. I forgot to tell you Saturday's march was Poungsho to Chaukpyn, the first three miles I tramped with others down a running creek to inspect where a few logs were lodged, and for Freddie to have a rough idea of the country on either side, which is being opened up next year. It was a case of paddling from start to finish, which I much enjoyed, and my boots seemed none the worse. Hunt had a shot at two of the four gye we saw but all too nippy for him. We rode the remaining four miles to Chaukpyn where we camped on the edge of paddy fields. During the march next day we were overtaken by a whole cavalcade of men and ponies and a Mr. Wycombe, the W.P.W., bringing up the rear. Of course a white man is hailed with great excitement out in the Jungle, so the three men had a 'buck' at the point where our roads divided. A great huge man who looked as though he would burst at any moment, in riding breeks tight at the knee, buttoned up shirt, collar, and bow tie. *The perfect gent he looked, 'e did.* He was out inspecting the road to Thabeikkyn, the first time, and we came to the conclusion he must be quite fresh to the country and its heat. I bet he will soon take to bare knees and bare neck. It was fearfully hot at Twinge. The coming home of the endless cows and goats along the sandy track just behind our tent did not improve matters. I had a very amusing time to start off with, by acting the barber to Freddie who had several weeks' growth on his thatch. He bore up bravely and the result really was quite good, though the neck where I started looks rather like a beach which has been left in ridges by the sea. On Monday we left Twinge and finished our tour by doing the last seven miles in a sampan down the Irrawaddy. We hoped for a breeze to sail but nothing doing. Everything was the same on our arrival, and so we got all our kit sorted out. Sabenago is in what they call the dry area and we found it a jolly sight hotter than the Werboung Area from where we had come. It is getting hotter every day, 89° in the dining room and I fear my days here are coming to an end. How I hate the thought of returning to Maymyo. Freddie will pick me up but will only be able to spend about a couple of days, as elephants are now at their rest camps and need so much supervision and apparently the tourungs (men who look after the elephants) are awful blighters and neglect the beasts. This morning Freddie had to shoot off early to inspect an elephant about six miles off which has been thoroughly overworked and he was afraid couldn't recover. The up mail arrived today and I was so pleased to get your letter, also ones from Aunts Mary and Bea.[12] I do think they are sweet to write. And I love hearing all the news. Freddie is awfully worried about our two ponies which still have dreadful coughs. The bally Syce gives so much trouble. He says he is overworked and is always demanding a rise. Servants in this country are the limit. All the world over apparently! Having to keep up two establishments will mean living above Freddie's pay per month. It is just as well he has been so careful in the past. Next year things will be better. Freddie will be acting manager and will be at Mawlaik, a very much cheaper place for living and with luck we will not have so much Jungle work. My tub is ready dear, so farewell for today.

Sunday February 26th 1922

Nothing of importance has happened since I last wrote so it hasn't been written (wise remark!). It is getting very hot now; registers about 86° per day in the dining room. Freddie has sent to Mandalay for fans which will be a joy. He has tinkered up a table fan driven by hot air by means of a small methylated spirit lamp underneath it which revolves the fan and makes a topping breeze for me when I lie down in the afternoon. The flies are such a nuisance and I am one mass of bites. Mosquitoes are not very thick yet. Jungle fires have started and all the hills around are obliterated by a thick haze which is smoke. Freddie is awfully fed up as a message came to say that in the fire logs had been burnt, having been left. Instead of doing the usual fire protection of clearing everything for twelve feet around the men had left it too late. This is the first time this has happened during his fourteen years out here and he is naturally annoyed, and another thing to upset the poor thing was the death of an elephant. Freddie is not to blame for that as the elephant was very much overworked before Freddie took over this district. We still play threesome at tennis. Hunt is gradually sobering down and is not quite such a whirlwind on the court. Lord only knows how these two men will get on together when I've gone. Hunt is a most annoying ass and Freddie finds it a great strain not to tell him so. As it is Freddie is constantly taking the young pup down a peg or two. I often wonder how long Hunt will stick this job when he gets so fed up with the office work, and is like a sulky kid when Freddie makes him work after tea to finish the accounts which have to be in every month. Freddie's boss Mr. Street is coming with Mr. Agar on the 28th for a few days. The former is going home on leave and is handing over to Mr. Agar.

Tuesday February 28th 1922

I suppose Princess Mary is beginning to feel a bit squeamish if they keep the original plans for her to be spliced today. I should think the poor girl will be thankful when the whole show is over. This mail must go today. Street and Agar are expected any minute and I have been shooting round to see the bungalow looks more or less respectable. Last night I had a great time making sweets, peppermint creams and walnut fondants. They really are a great success. It was great sport making them with Freddie and Hunt playing the giddy goat, to say nothing of a run of rude remarks to one another. My small boy Bar Tai would have wondered what would be the outcome had he known English. Last week I also made a whole lot of marmalade from fruit that grows wild in the Jungle and is a cross between lemon and orange. That also has turned out alright. We still get quantities of vegetables from the garden. Owing

---

[11] Elephant keepers.
[12] Alice Britten's sister-in-law Mary Child and her sister Beatrice.

to the need for constant watering and the water having to be carried half a mile we have not gone in for flowers, except a few beds of different coloured balsam in the front. Freddie is so killing about me meeting Street, even to ordering out of my clothes and has chosen a cretonne overall Edith gave me to wear in the day, and a band round my carroty topknot. (He always imagines that helps me to look more presentable). I always thought husbands took no interest or notice of one's clothes, but Freddie must be the exception to prove the rule! I am so sorry dear to hear Dr. Pope holds out no hope for any cure to your knees. To me you are still a jolly sight younger than most of your age and so long as you are not prevented from moving about and the rotten rheumatism does not get a hold of you in other parts I think there is a lot to be thankful for. Medicine to keep the blood in good order is now about the only thing you can do and I do hope the different concoctions will keep you free from pain. Hunt was out yesterday shooting to replenish our larder for our visitors. He brought home snipe and Jungle fowl, these plus a peacock Freddie had as a present ought to keep us going. Worst of it is these hot days game will not keep and the other night the smell of a peacock cooked for our dinner fairly bowled us over so Mr. Hunt, who is the biggest glutton I have ever struck, lapped up quite half of the breast. Freddie and I were wiser and got out a tinned tongue from the stores. Well dear this must end. With lots of love and do write, even a tiny scrap to let me know how you are, and also send any letters from other members of our scattered family. Have not heard from Edith or Mary since I came out. Perhaps they look on me as the guilty one as I'm afraid I've not written to Edith yet. Give her my best love. I really will make the effort sometime but you always drain me of all the news. Best of Love.

Sabenago Tuesday February 28th 1922

Here goes for another mail. After waiting for Street and Agar they didn't appear for the meal after all. About 1 pm we heard a great tooting coming downstream and soon spotted the B.B.T.C. launch which tied up close to the bank below our bungalow. Freddie, Hunt, clerks galore, bullock carts, and endless Burmans went down expecting Street and Agar plus the luggage to come to the bungalow. Not a bit of it. The clerk went on board and found them both asleep and on awakening Street got something for his trouble. Street shot up and said: "Who are you?" "I'm the clerk" he got in answer. "Well clear out, can't you see I'm asleep?" And that's that. However, Freddie braved it all and went in to have a buck. Street and Agar decided to stay their three days on board, for which I was thankful. According to their time we were one and a half hours slow, to be like the 'daylight saving hour' coming in. Street and Agar arrived in the early afternoon and found us all, in our turn, in bed. After a hasty tea Street went off shooting with Hunt and I had tea with Agar and Freddie who are great pals and wanted to talk shop in preference to shooting snipe. We wandered off for a walk before it got dark. It was a great pity we had no gun as we saw a whole lot of Peacock and Jungle fowl. Agar expressed concern about his weight. He had been for a cure which consisted of hot water and salts. This brought him down several stones but left him such a worm that he says never again. These two men and Freddie have always worked together. Street I am not particularly keen on. Freddie's boss in the past has not always played the game. However, of late he has improved and this trip he couldn't be nicer. Whether that was because I had acted as a sort of umpire or the fact he goes on leave at the end of the month to join his wife who went home in December. They were married out here just before we were. Both men came to dinner Tuesday night. Street knows the Tusons very well and says Nora was staying out here with his sister Babs at his brother's place.

Wednesday, March 1st 1922

The whole morning was taken up with Street and Agar in the office with Freddie while I sewed on the veranda. They did not stay for tiffin. I think they've found our quarters rather too hot during the day. On the water in the launch there is much more breeze going. Street is mad on shooting and again went off after tea with Agar and Hunt. Freddie had so much correspondence to do for the mail the following day that he could not go, so we went for a walk together later in the evening.

Thursday, March 2nd 1922

Still more office work, Street monopolised the bungalow so I sat down in our hut all morning. It got frightfully hot midday 96° in the dining room. A terrific wind gets up midday but as it only brings hot air is not much use. Freddie joined them in the shoot today though he needed a bit of pushing on my part to get him to go. He hates having to borrow cartridges. It had to be done as though ordered last April he has not yet obtained a certificate to buy any. Freddie has bought a new gun from Street, having sold his old one to a Burman. He seems pleased with his new purchase and got several snipe that evening. Hunt, suffering from a bad bilious attack, did not join them. I sauntered off on my own for a walk along by the river. The two men again came to dinner turning our early evening into an 11-30pm touch.

Friday, March 3rd 1922

We are once more our usual small party. Street and Agar came up early, inspected all the compound with its numerous huts, blacksmith shop, and stores etc., and then we all walked down at 9am to see them off in the launch. The Minthance (Princess), a topping little steam launch, and I wish I was allowed one for our use up here. The remainder of the day we all felt good for nothing. Poor Freddie felt sick and I was too sleepy for any good. Late hours, too much game eating, and visitors, proved too much for us. However, sleep and then tennis after tea did us all the good in the world. On Wednesday we got English mail and again your welcome letter of February 1st and The Hereford Times. So once more I was kept interested in the exciting Hay case. The only letter this week but I had a short one from Ethel yesterday. She had just returned from a trip to Trimcomalee. She wrote to say the money I sent early in January, in return for what I owed her, had not arrived. Can't make it out, but I suppose Rangoon office mislaid the letter. I am so glad Maymyo letter was received alright. You now get my weekly efforts more regularly. There is a possibility of us having to turn out of Glenside to the bungalow in the next compound after all. It really is rotten and all caused through Rangoon office making a hash of arrangements. In any case we shall only be in Maymyo until the end of October as then I can return to the Jungle. The mosquitoes are not very bad here yet. But eye flies (tiny little black things) are the very devil. The bites arrive so I am everlastingly scratching.

Monday March 6th 1922

It has been awfully hot last two days and instead of stewing in our hut or the bungalow I now have long chairs under the bungalow where there is deep shade. Between 1pm and 3 pm it is like coming out of a furnace sometimes but I don't mind lying in a kimono writing as I am now at 9am, and it seems impossible to believe it will be so awfully hot in about two hours time. It always registers 100° in the shade of the veranda. Drinks are kept nice and cool by having a box bored with large holes all round, filled with straw and into which go the bottles and the whole thing is slung up on a bar under the bungalow with a boy constantly saturating the straw with water and swinging the box. We still get good vegetables from the garden and have lettuces for chota and tiffin. Jungle fires are now a grand sight at night. Hills all around with large fires creeping along and in the day heavy smoke hides the hills altogether. This morning Hunt went off on a tour of fire inspection and will be out several days. He has thoroughly got the wind up because Street insists on him going in for his Burmese exam at the end of April. He is such an awful slacker. Instead of swatting the language for at least two hours a day he does nothing but dreams of shooting and goes to sleep after dinner. It is just as well he is being chivvied up a bit. The pony's cough is much better and we now hope I will be able to ride him on our tour in about a week's time. I want Freddie to get rid of my pony. It is such an expense and I don't mean to ride in Maymyo. Until this rotten job of having to keep up a double establishment is over we shall have to cut down expenses in every way. Nearly all one's pay goes in paying out to servants. Last week I received my Red Cross Nursing Medal sent on from Nunnington. It is quite a nice thing , a piece of gilt metal, about the size of a halfpenny, with white ribbon and bar above. In spite of all the heat I feel extraordinarily fit and I think look even better than at home when my mug certainly looked like underdone suet pudding, at times. My hair does not come out so much, which is a blessing. Both Freddie and I cannot afford to become any thinner on the thatch. I wonder when you will go to stay with Aunt Minnie. I'm sure she wants you so don't put her off. I expect she will find life very lonely now Helen has decided to go to London.

Tuesday March 7th 1922

This must catch the mail today. Yesterday was not nearly so hot. Freddie had office work to do all the afternoon so I spent my time under the bungalow in my kimono reading the *Daily Graphic*, a bundle of which we have from the Maymyo Club every week. At tea time we had two women and one man caller! All Burmans of course, all bringing an offerings of sorts. One was the girl whose finger I doctored when I came here first. The finger is now quite healed and she brought some very nice fruit, as a thanks offering I suppose. We had some fish from the Clerk's wife and a contractor brought Freddie twenty eggs and me a lovely bag made by Burmans with seeds and large blobs of silver for decorations. All the jewellery one sees on women out here is made out of pure gold and silver and made up very cheaply by Chinese or Burmans. They never seem to have anything but pure stuff. Freddie and I went out after tea for a walk and hoped for something to pop at with his new gun, but no luck. Shooting time is getting short as it is close season for everything sometime in this month. Unless the *Overseas Daily Mail* is ordered don't bother about it. Now we get the *Daily Graphic* we get about as much as we can digest. But doesn't matter if the order is given and they won't cancel it. Will you please forward the enclosed to Edith. I don't know where she is nowadays. Sorry I have no English stamps to put on. Cheerio dear. The best of love to all the Rosslynites when you see them.

P.S. Will you ask someone to get me a packet of Greenland's fine darning needles and enclose them in one of your letters. Needles out here are hopeless. You had better start a little black book against me.

Sabenago Thursday March 9th 1922

The Dickens of a wind is blowing and everything on the writing table is flapping. Every now and then I have to make wild dash to stop a paper or book from being blown off altogether. The table looks rather like a beach at present with about a dozen large stones acting as paperweights. At present, 11am, the wind is nice and cool but gradually this becomes hotter until it is rather like being left in an oven. I think my last life must have been in a very hot atmosphere as I don't really mind heat which does not leave me feeling a wet rag. Life is so much more peaceful with Hunt still on tour, extraordinary what a disturbing element he brings with him and often I'm on tenterhooks as to what Freddie is going to say by way of a sound telling off. I begged Freddie to do his training when I am out of hearing. Yesterday Freddie and I decided to go across to Male to nose round the cargo boat and also pay a visit to Mr. Lewis. Generally Mr. Lewis tootles with the siren as he comes round the corner of the river as a warning. This time he forgot and suddenly a tremendous yelling from the shore and we looked up to see the old launch almost level with our bungalow. I had only just finished dressing and I was busy darning a huge hole in my stocking. Couldn't stop to make myself any more respectable but dashed off with Freddie down to the shore, with 'Patch' bringing up the rear. We meant to leave him on the shore as he is such a nuisance in a small boat. However, he thought otherwise and we had no sooner cast off than, with a fearful yelping, 'Patch' plunged in *after* us. His first ducking! We dare not let him go too far as the current is so strong. So in 'Patch' was hauled by one of the men. Here the river is quite half a mile wide, so we had to nip across pretty quickly and scramble up the side of the launch to save going across the plank with all the Burmans. 'Patch' cried his heart out at being tied up in the boat. The smell of the crowd was too much for us so we retreated to Mr. Lewis' cabin where he was in the middle of having his breakfast. He made us go and sit down and after a good drink of shandy gaff and a 'buck' we left with our usual cheerio played on the siren. About half an hour after leaving the bungalow the clerk appeared with our mail and your letter of February 8th. Dear, I'm so sorry not to have commented more upon your letters which have all arrived most regularly. The early part of my life out here was so very rushed it was difficult to say much more than 'I hope this will find you as well as it leaves me at present' in the pink sort of thing! I love getting your weekly letter dear, so please do carry on. You are the only one who does honour me. Edith and Mary seem to have disappeared. I'd like to have Jeff's letter sometime. I expect the Turners love coming in to have a chat with you, do give them my love. Mary had better have a brass plate outside her gate: - Court Dressmaker. I'm glad she still does odd work for folk. She always seemed much happier with the idea of making something, to say nothing of making a little money. I doubt if you will ever be able to make a silk jumper dear. They are dreadfully hard as the stitches will slip off. Aunt Bea writes that she had attempted to make one but gave it up. However, from experience I know what wonderful things you do turn out so no doubt Mary will get her silk jersey. All the things you made me are so useful, especially the grey scarf. Before the hot weather I wore it every day and lived in two jumpers on board. I forgot to tell you I received my Red Cross medal about two mails ago. Quite a nice medallion about the size of a halfpenny in gilt metal with white ribbon and gilt bar at top. I am glad I have something and this wasn't given without a struggle on my part to get it. I am making more marmalade as Freddie liked the last lot so much and we have been able to get more fruit from the Jungle.

Sunday March 12th 1922

The past few days have been very quiet but they seem to buzz by before we know where we are. Last Thursday Freddie had to go off immediately after tiffin to Oombein about eight miles away to see an elephant. This elephant some time ago had torn one pad nearly off while at work in the Jungle, leaving a great open wound. On leaving the Jungle rest camp on the Irrawaddy the poor wretched beast lost its balance going down the slope and fell. Not able to get him up the men came to tell Freddie, who on seeing the elephant found him to be in an awful state and quite unable to go on. So arrangements were made for him to remain there and another elephant brought back as a companion. I don't suppose the elephant will ever be fit for work again. At this time of year it is so difficult to heal wounds in animals. Flies are such a nuisance and, if in the water, fish come and have a feed. I started off to meet Freddie about 5-30pm with a boy following up. Freddie's warning to never go on a walk alone is quite correct. Not having a gun of course we saw no end to shoot. About eight peacock strutted across just in front, no end of Jungle fowl and a gye (barking deer). We walked on to Nyaunggyin and it was then 6pm and getting dark and I thought time to turn back, which I did, and reached home before Freddie arrived. Directly his boy arrived saying something in

Burmese and shot off with a bottle of water and a tumbler. Immediately I got the wind up that Saoo, the boy, had heard Freddie had collapsed on the roadside or something, so I called up the clerk who speaks English and who explained Saoo had only come to meet Freddie and knowing the long way he had ridden thought Freddie would like a drink. I am afraid such kind thoughts did not enter my head!! The Jungle fires that night were such a lovely sight all round and opposite our bungalow. Huge lines of fires creeping along making the air very thick and hot. There is not much office work to do just now so I see more of Freddie. He comes up to the bungalow during the morning and we each drink each other's health with a nip of stout. This I had better add is an occasional treat. Friday evening we went out with the gun and last night practised golf strokes in the front. We had no sooner shown ourselves than we were surrounded by children in their scanty garments. They proved most useful in fetching our balls and we were struck by the quickness and the knowledge at placing the ball on a nice little tuft of grass ready for striking. It came out later that Mr. Heath who was here before Freddie used to practise also. Yesterday we got the one punka [13] up in the dining room and it makes such a difference when we have our tiffin. Miss Pringle, a girl I was pally with on the boat, writes from India, very fed up in bed with colitis. She is coming to stay with me in July at Maymyo on her way home. I shall love having her as all July and August Freddie will be too busy to leave Sabenago and I can't possibly be with him.

Monday March 13th 1922

Oh dear! We had such an ordeal yesterday. Since we have had *'Patch'* his tail has annoyed us growing almost the length of his body but we have never had the pluck to cut it off. Yesterday we determined to have the deed done as Freddie came to the conclusion *'Patch'* could not possibly reside at Glenside looking like a 'pi' dog. [14] We shaved a circle round the spot and then fled off for a walk leaving the boy to do the operation. I kept thinking I heard yelps but Freddie dragged me on and we were away about an hour and returned expecting a very sorry sight. Not a bit of it, when we called, *'Patch'* came dashing down the steps wagging the whole of his back parts having only a nice little stump left. I was so pleased and today he seems none the worse and has not even tried to bite off the bandage. He now looks quite respectable and will return to Maymyo with me. You must think us cowardly running away but I really feared the possibility of too much yelping. It is quite a sight now with the Jungle the other side of the river burning such a glow at night, which we watch from our veranda. Trees are now quite bare and give a resemblance to winter at home, except in parts where certain trees look on this time of year as their Spring. Teak drops its huge leaves. Some predecessor of Freddie's planted a line of them behind this bungalow. Silly trees to have as they give no shade in the hot weather and take years to get to any size. This bungalow would be perfect if someone had had the sense to plant evergreen trees in front as we get all the afternoon and evening sun. I believe Hunt will be back from tour today. Awful trial as it is so nice to have the place to ourselves.

Tuesday March 14th 1922

Another mail day so this must stop. I can see Freddie sitting in state surrounded by at least a dozen Burmese girls, got up in their best bibs and tuckers, having come with gifts from a village near here. It is some sort of feast day and they come at the end of such parades with a present for Thakin,16 [15] otherwise Freddie. The Kin looks thoroughly contented though with rather a bored air as he lolls back in his chair smoking a cigarette. The colours of the

---

[13] A fan.

[14] A wild Asian dog which runs around a village in a pack.

[15] Master.

22

girls' costumes arc very striking, shades of pink predominating. Hair done high up on the head like the Chinese, swathed and plastered down in a circle, making it look like a rather smooth black pill box hat perched on top of the head. Garlands all round them and out of the hair. They wear a fine muslin sort of Eton jacket loose to the waist and lungi[16] or cloth twisted round their middles to the ankle, always of the most beautiful thick silk, and then wooden sandals on their feet. I've just had an awful shock as they all came parading out of the office and I yelled for Freddie to come to my rescue thinking they were coming up on the veranda. However, I was saved that, and watched them go off from the window. Hunt arrived in this morning. He is a stuffy old thing. After doing a march of about six miles he went straight into the office, pretending to work, instead of bathing first. He might at least think of Freddie. Mosquitoes are beginning to discover I'm a fresh piece of meat out from England and have a great liking for my beefy legs. In the evening I now sit with long boots on belonging to Freddie and have much more peace. My next letter will be sent with us on tour. Freddie has to go round to all the Elephant Rest Camps before he takes me up to Maymyo at the end of the month. Bar Tai is just supplying me with a coconut drink. The fresh coconut milk is awfully refreshing and beautifully cool. It is much cooler this morning. Last night led us to expect rain which is badly needed. I have seen no rain since I came out here. The river has already started to rise from the snow water, away up in India. It makes a vast difference to the temperature of the water of course and we always welcome it when the wind blows from off the water. I'm quite sure Ethel would have bathed had she been here but I daren't risk it. Have had no news of the Ceylonites for ages. This area is very unhealthy and men are always going down with bouts of fever. Mr. Partridge, the Eurasian in charge of Weboung came in today on his way to Mandalay for a holiday. Directly he went into the Dry Zone (Sabenago) he went down with fever. Freddie and I had tremendous discussions as to the various ages of our numerous family last night. I made Edith forty-two, which makes George younger than Freddie, and then we couldn't wedge in the others of us between George and me. Do settle it and give me a list. Toodleoo, dear. It is so nice to know you will be reading this in April when I hope it will be nice and warm for you to toddle out occasionally. Best of love.

Sabenago c/o Messrs. B.B.T.C. Ltd Maymyo
Friday March 17th 1922

We received our English mail on Wednesday the 15th and I had a lovely bundle. Yours of February 15th. It took exactly a month to the day. Yours from me arrived earlier no doubt, as mine have to be addressed from Rangoon. In future will you please address as above. It is safer to send there. The office then redirects it to Glenside. Letters addressed to Rangoon will reach me alright but at a later date. I also heard from Ethel, Stella Middleditch, Dorothy Brooksbank and Annie Bowden. All seem to have had flu to deal with. I do hope you and all the nunnery will escape. Plague seems to have taken the place of flu out here and is very bad in Mandalay. On Wednesday's cargo boat a man died from it soon after leaving Mandalay and was thrown overboard, another was lying dead in the boat and hidden away for fear the captain would know and forbid Burmans off the boat to do their shopping at the Bazaar. Awfully dangerous thing of course as bugs from these cases might get about and infect the whole boat. Servants here who were anxious to return to Mandalay to their homes are now only too anxious to remain on here. Ethel wrote me such a depressed letter and fed up to the teeth at being on Carolina[17] alone; Dorothea[18] having gone up to Nuwaa Eilya to

---

[16] A length of cloth draped around the lower half of the body.
[17] Sammy Blackmore's tea plantation in Ceylon.
[18] Sammy and Ethel Blackmore's daughter.

play in a tennis tournament. Ethel does not seem to buck up and take an interest in anything and, as she says, has no resources of her own to fall back on. I was so pleased to have the enclosed letter of Aunt Helen's. She is like you in letter writing; gets so much interesting news down in a small space, very different to my efforts I'm afraid! I'd like to have Jeff's letter sometime. I'm glad Mary has somewhere to lay her head, pro-tem at any rate. I wonder where the flat is. It is splendid your being able to relieve your rather monotonous life by playing bridge and so meeting old friends. Violet Mac's remark about Freddie made his few remaining hairs stand on end! Tell Vi I suspect what went on between the two of them when Freddie called at her studio re my photo!! I will certainly send any heads of seeds I come across. One sees nothing of that sort out here. Berries in the Jungle are often very pretty but too hard to thread. I hope the mother-of-pearl necklace bought at Port Said has arrived. Annie Bowden wrote that Dora is such a good sort. The temperature is steadily warming up and registered 102° on our veranda yesterday and so under the Punka is a perfect joy. One was put up in the office yesterday. I should think that is badly needed to cool Freddie's heated brow and the fag of trying to din something into Mr. Hunt's head. Hunt's latest craze is to go down and play footer with the villagers from about 5-30pm and then charter the corporation's sampan and be rowed out to midstream to have a dip. He is consequently so sleepy after dinner his 'spot of Burmese' has to be given up. Don't wonder at his dread at the exam coming off in April. *'Patch's'* tail is splendid now. Quite free of bandages and as the tail does not look so depressed as at first he is quite a good looking dog. Freddie and I have been playing singles last two evenings, which is jolly good practice for me. From the Syce downwards all come out to field the balls for us. This morning Freddie was out early measuring, classifying, etc., about a dozen elephants here in the compound. I managed to finish my tub and dressing to see several including *'Pedouk'*, a traveller of Hunt's who to everyone's surprise has just produced a baby. On our last tour I said to Freddie. "I'm sure that elephant is going to hatch." Freddie seemed to think not and I took it his experience with elephants in the past must prove him to be correct. However, the argument was settled in my favour by *'Pedouk'* producing her calf about three weeks later! Descriptions of all the elephants have to be reported; height, girth, any defects, i.e. toes missing, blind eye, holes in the ears. Freddie and I took several snaps which will be sent you in due course. I was rather amused at Mrs. Luard's account of her visit to a coffee plantation in Mysore in last week's *Hereford Times*. I could write of a few more excitements other than the post being held up by a tiger and she herself seeing the pad of one behind the bungalow. A tiger prowls around this village every night and nearly every time we go shooting pad marks are seen in the thick dust on the road behind our bungalow. Since I have been here Freddie's one clerk has shot two tigers in the next village. Tomorrow we go on a four or five day tour visiting elephant rest camps. There is a Kedda[19] not far from these parts and wild elephants have been driven into a small area and have proved an awful nuisance to our elephants. A man came in for the Corporation gun as an extra protection. Touring at this time of year will mean starting about 4am so as to reach next camp before it is too hot. Camp Waygu,

Sunday March 19th 1922

Freddie has just told me a messenger goes to Sabenago early tomorrow so I must buck up with this. Freddie pays out ages to tour-goers and contractors to say nothing of subsidising them and their ancestors for generations back. These men are such blighters and are always demanding advances. If that is refused they refuse to work and so debts accumulate and sometimes into thousands of rupees, which the Corporation has to write off and sack the man; who is quite capable of abandoning his elephants and buffaloes. On Friday Freddie had an

---

[19] Elephant trap.

awful time with some of his Oosies. In the morning they brought in all the travelling elephants and much to our surprise we heard all of them again after tea. Presently three Oosies presented themselves in the office and I heard partial altercations going on and saw the Oosies backing out of the office with Freddie following them up shaking his finger and bellowing out in Burmese at them. My surmise of trouble proved right as the blighters had brought in the elephants to hand them over and refused to go on tour next day as they wished to go to a pive (play), at Nyaunggyin a village near Sabenago. Freddie would not, (could not, after their threat) alter his plans as we have to be back on the 24th, so Freddie threatened to call in the police and hand them over. We packed up that evening but were not at all certain of starting in the morning. However, at 4 am we heard the kyloks[20] and knew the elephants to be on their way. Up we got, had our chota. It was still dark, and by 5-30am we were on our own way to Twinge where we stayed in the nice bungalow perched on a hill which overlooks the village and the wide plain reaching down to the Irrawaddy. After starting a such an unearthly hour I made up for lost sleep and the hot hours of the afternoon were soon gone. That night we had our beds out on the veranda, which was perfectly lovely. Up again at 4-30am just after Pongyi Kyang is sounded. That is a very deep sounding gong which each village has sounded at dawn and sunset. Pongyi Kyang is Burmese for monastery, where the gong is always kept. It is a weird sound which is extenuated by every dog in the place keeping tune and time with the gong from start to finish! We left Twinge this morning at 5-30am leaving the elephants around the bungalow collecting the kit. Our way lay along a dusty plain which is the bed of the Irrawaddy, now a flat plain with quite good grass and thick bushes growing. Thousands of meagre cattle graze. Why cattle are kept I can't think. They are never killed for eating purposes and milk is almost an unheard of requisite. During the rains the Irrawaddy brings down very good soil and when the waters subside the ground is good for cultivation. Burmans then come to peg out their claim and grow beans, Indian corn, etc. This year everything is a dead failure owing to the lack of rain. The usual rain that comes in February has given us a miss. About a mile from Wengee we stopped to take descriptive rolls of about a dozen elephants which sat in the shade of a small hut made of the tall grass which grows in abundance all round here. In this shakedown the Burmans in charge of the elephants live until the rains. Elephants are then taken back to their respective districts for Jungle work. Before I had been there a quarter of an hour women and children came all round me chattering, and quite happy to do so, without any intelligent reply from me. Burmans are as a rule very uninterested in one. On coming to a village they generally chivvy into their huts leaving the dogs to yowl at us as a welcome. But I must say they were most awfully generous and showered on us fruit, eggs, and this morning one old woman presented me with a packet of cigarettes and a box of matches. I hope she was not offended that I did not smoke. I happened to be looking at the *Daily Graphic* with pictures of the Prince, at Mandalay, at which they were quite thrilled. We finished up by walking to the camp. In fact I walked the whole five miles from Twinge as it was so nice and cool. We are still in the bed of the Irrawaddy covered with high grass on which the elephants feed. Our tent is under a huge 'tay', a shelter made of bamboo poles and grass. Except from 11am -11pm it will be nice and cool. Between those hours it is awfully hot. I just stay in my dressing gown and sleep the whole afternoon. I've got a rotten head tonight so I'm going to take a pill and go to bed! We are staying here three days as there are so many elephants to inspect. Best of love dear. I so look forward to each mail bringing your letters. I often long to pop in on you and see you sitting peacefully by the fire knitting.

---

[20] Elephant chains.

Sabenago Thursday March 23rd 1922

I have just finished having a tub and change after our very dusty and rather hot ride from Twinge this morning and I feel more inclined to settle at something. On Sunday last my mail went in to catch the following Tuesday's mail. Much to my surprise the messenger arrived on Monday while we were at tea bringing your letter and newspapers. Freddie had to send a telegram from Thabeikkyn on Sunday and these letters were given to the messenger, otherwise the mail waits there and comes up by boat on Wednesdays. Poor Mary does have a rotten time with John. How much better the kid would be living out in the country. I hope all her troubles are over, kid well, an found a house. Mary had better take up moving and settling furniture etc., as a trade. Se has had plenty of opportunities to become an expert. Mr. Davies is the only on who apparently holds out any hope for you to benefit by treatment to your legs. I do so hoe this will do good and you must not worry about expense to keep you fit and free from pain and the chief thing to be remembered. I was very interested in the cutting about the Masters! What a little beggar Freda is but she has now done herself very badly and she as no money of her own.

We stayed at Wergee three days. Fearfully hot in the afternoons, and all wind seems to die down until about four o'clock. My days were very quiet and I scarcely left the camp. Freddie would be up and off before 6am and as I didn't see the sense in getting up to be alone, stayed on in bed and had breakfast about 7-30 am. All round this camp is quite useless for walks, nothing but sand dunes which are covered by the river during the rains and further away miles of high grass growing to about eleven feet, which is about all the elephants find to eat at this time of year. Just below our camp is a huge lake, the Irrawaddy leaving a sufficient depth of water to last until it is joined up with the river itself and which goes back about three miles from its present course. Every evening elephants are taken down to the lake to have their daily bath. One I watched hated the water and dashed up and down trying to pass the Oosie who waved him back into the water. Others loved it and one would go right in with the Oosie standing on its back until one would think the Oosie stood on water, until after a time the elephant heaved its great body up out of the water. After giving the beasts a good scrub down with a stick the Oosies take the elephants back. After tea I would join Freddie at one of the elephant camps where he was taking descriptive rolls. Every detail of an elephant has to be kept in case the animals wander off and a large C is branded on their hindquarters. Several elephants had young calves which are very mischievous and dash round and round trying to butt anyone they comes across. During the examination of the mother the nurse elephant has to stand by her side otherwise the mother is restive and won't allow measurements etc., to be taken and when finished all then go marching off together with the young 'butchar' trotting between its Ma's hind parts. She must find it jolly awkward and yet you never see her touch her calf. Wild 'tuskers' and tigers come to these Rest Camps and have to be chivvied off. One evening a cow was killed by a tiger so the next afternoon Hunt went and perched up a tree by the remainder of the cow carcase but as the Jungle fire was burning near at the time the animal was probably too scared to return for his feed and Hunt had the joy of remaining up the tree for five hours with no luck. On Wednesday we left Wergee in the very early hours of the morning and walked the twenty-three miles to Sherdar where in the rains there is a small village right on the edge of the Irrawaddy, so you can tell the immense flood of water the river recovers. Freddie found several logs high and dry near the village being left from the last rains. These will be polled or rafted into midstream and sent on their way down to a rafting depot this next rains. I've never had such a night as we had at Twinge. The bungalow is perched on a hill and the slightest breeze makes it quiver and this night we fairly got it in the neck. Talk about equinoctial breeze, it was a prize one that night. Our beds in front of the open space leading to the veranda we quite thought would be lifted and of course mosquito curtains were up in the rafters somewhere. Thunder and the most awful lightning and I don't mind owning up that I was scared stiff. Our sleep did not amount to much more than a couple of hours that night. Our ride into Sabenago was rather hot and fearfully dusty, chiefly sand and still a good breeze a-blowing made almost a sandstorm. It is so nice to be back in our bungalow once more. I feel very sad to think this will be my last tour for some time. However November will soon be here and everything will be quite fresh and as interesting to me.

Friday March 24th 1922

Golly! What a torrent we had last night. Another awful storm and our little thatched hut leaked horribly. So in the middle of a terrific thunderstorm Freddie and I had to get up and try and find a spot where puddles from above would not be made on us in our beds below. We did not know which was the lesser of two evils: To remain in bed and get wet or get out or run the risk of being covered with fleas. It is apparently the time for such cheery companions to show themselves and they choose the floor of our hut as a breeding ground. We enjoyed the game of catching them on my white stockings. After a thorough cleaning and the place soaked in water things are not so bad. It is delightfully fresh and cool this morning after the rain. If it keeps cool I shall stay on here longer. A Mr. Agar is coming here tonight en route to a district further north. He is Freddie's temporary boss.

Saturday March 25th 1922

Freddie and Agar are bucking to their hearts content u on the veranda so I have left them at it and come to write in our little thatched hut. These two get on very well together and Freddie is delighted to have someone with who he can talk shop. The Corporation is causing so many grievances these days as there is so much favouritism shown towards the Rangoon staff and up-country-staff who do all the dirty and more important work in the Jungle don't get a look in. They are not on the spot and don't come in for quick promotion and fat bonuses as those in Rangoon. During the hot weather Rangoonites take leave in Maymyo taking houses which really are only for up-countrymen; all free of course. Men of twenty years service who have had to leave on grounds of ill health are given £1000 as a parting gift and told to buzz off! Men of fifteen years in Steeles, (Another, and the only other, teak firm in Burma) get £14,000. The chief reason as far as I can see is that the big bugs who have mostly retired hold the shares which pay 28 per cent and say their expenses only amount to 20 per cent more than pre-war days! To keep to this record they cut down pay and bonuses as much as possible. Dirty dogs! Although Freddie gets paid equal to his service, he has been kept back and is still an assistant simply because he is able, and will stick Jungle work, and pull up any bad work better than the others. However, we can count the months till he is acting manager and so many months on end in the Jungle will be at an end. Agar arrived by the mail boat last evening. We waited dinner but he had had his on the boat. Street has left, bequeathing his three spaniels to Agar, who is rather fed up having so many and would be only too thankful for us to have one. I would love to and then 'Patch' can remain here with Freddie. I couldn't really be on pension with no dog as a companion. I had a letter from Ethel last night after one not so long ago in which she was feeling too ill and fed up to do anything. This letter was full of a visit to Colombo, a coming tennis meet and the great festivities in communication with the coming of the Prince at Kaudy, came as rather a surprise. I'm so glad she is better. Ethel says nothing about going home this year. Dear, it is 1924 we shall be home. From one of your letters I gather you thought it would be 1923. That will be here before you know where you are and will give you extra time to become really free from your rheumatics and able to join us at the sea or whatever spot we hit on. It seems so queer to think today is Sunday. All days are alike here as Burmans do not keep Sundays. Agar went off in the early hours this morning leaving one black spaniel, 'Twinker', in my charge. The other two are lady dogs which I thought would be an awful trial to look after! When the liver and white one hatches I have been promised a pup as my own. We had quite a good day yesterday. At 4 pm set out for Nyaunggyinabout three miles from here to shoot snipe. The beaters went right up to the village and drove the birds towards the three guns all across the paddy fields now under water. The paddy is about eight inches high giving them the usual beautiful bright green. There were plenty of birds and Agar, Hunt and Freddie shot twenty-one between them and going home a pretty sight, having sunk up to my knees in the muddy water. It was most exciting to watch. After dinner we went out again but after hares this time. The Burmans have a most ingenious way of killing these animals. One man goes ahead with a tin with one side opened out and any old oil lamp flaring inside. He holds it well in front and at the same time jingles a couple of wires on which are a lot of small square pieces of metal at the end and when shaken make a noise not unlike castanets. Behind this man is another with a long bamboo pole and knocks the animal out. One hare gave an exciting chase as the one blow was not sufficient but the poor thing could not get away from the dazzling light. It really was a most queer show and we walked about a couple of miles through short grass, quietly following up this queer procession. We only brought home two but put up six hares.

Tuesday March 28th 1922

Golly its 'ot! And registers 90° on the veranda. After a very still and hot night a terrific south wind got up this morning and is now blowing a regular gale. The river is quite like the sea with its white horses. This time next week I shall be packed up ready to depart for Maymyo. How I hate the thought of going and Freddie will be so fed up having to return here alone. The poor thing is so worried just now over the work. A 'tusker' has just died through sheer carelessness and neglect which makes the fourth this year. This elephant tore half his foot away during the work in the Jungle and the 'touroung' is such a rotten man and did not look after the poor beast properly. And yesterday came the news that a contractor who is heavily in debt has decamped with ten buffaloes and is nowhere to be found. They are such blighters and know they have the upper hand in that an advance has to be given in order to start the man and which, of course, should be worked off. Some do but the majority keep demanding advances and do no work. If the advance is not forthcoming they either decamp or let starve the whole of their Corporation's buffaloes or bullocks, whichever they work. If the man is traced and taken to court, the Corporation has to pay maintenance during his imprisonment. I do so dread that this continual Jungle work, and worry will play 'old Harry' with Freddie's health. He frets terribly that other men who have relations of influence of some sort with the heads of the Corporation have superseded him. It is all horribly unfair. And when his managership does come, half the energy for that work will have gone from living this rotten life for so long. The man of today doesn't see joy in this life and won't stick it. Several new men have left owing to what they think an impossible life and not good enough retiring pay after twenty years. Yesterday I got such a pleasant surprise by receiving your mail of March 1st two days earlier than usual. A messenger returned from Thabeikkyn and they always bring anything from the Post Office which waits there for the up boat on Wednesday. I see an English mail of seven bags has been destroyed by fire, coming from Calcutta. I wonder if we shall be affected. Hope not. I just love *'Twinker,'* Mr. Street's dog. Yesterday when out for a walk he put up no end of Jungle fowl and three gye. The two curtains I embroidered are just finished and really look quite nice. I am making up another design for another one by enlarging one of Liberty's patterns. Best of love dear. I must write other mail letters. I do think you are wonderful and both Freddie and I think you knock spots off many writers 50 years your junior.

Sabenago Sunday April 2nd 1922

I've not started my letters this week until the day before mail goes. Nothing very much to say being the chief reason I think, and also I was very anxious to finish embroidering my curtains before we leave for Maymyo tomorrow. That deed is done, also most of the packing. It is wonderful sight to see the amount of kit even one traveller takes and we shan't have much under twenty packages tomorrow; bed roles, stores, clothes, etc. The blacksmith carpenter combined who does all the repairs to buffalo carts etc., and has his premises in the compound, has made me such a topping box for my sewing machine. I shall line it sometime, but anyway the machine is safe for any amount of travelling now. Teak boxes with stores in etc., are often being sent up from the mills at Rangoon and come in most useful as it is really good wood. The carpenter is also knocking me together a bookshelf. It is getting very hot and now anything from 100° to 104° on the thermometer around noon, and now 96°! It would burst the thermometer were it much in the sun. Hunt went out on tour [remainder of paragraph missing]. The little thatched hut was warming up and the number of sparrows with their nests of young ones finally drove us out. We now sleep on the veranda which is about the coolest spot. This country possesses very many more birds than Ceylon both in the way of songsters and brightly coloured. Of course the sparrow and crow predominate as in other countries. A bird, rather like our pee-wit, is very common also goes by the name of "Did 'e do it" (even Burmans call it that as its call is those words so very clearly). One means "did 'e do it over the hedge?" "Yes Mama" from the partridge. (Dirty dog for telling, I say). Parakeets are round and round in clusters in the evening, rather after the style of swifts. Green pigeon is also a pretty bird and very good for eating, Jays all blue, or black, and red or green birds also show up at times.

We were very surprised yesterday morning to see the river had come up over four feet during the night which makes a difference in the outlook from our bungalow. Many storms and the melting snow in the Indian hills being the cause. Pretty heavy, whatever it is, to make the appreciable difference of four feet in a river which is over half a mile wide. All day the water is thick with rubbish being brought down and logs left on the banks are brought down by the early rise instead of being collected and rafted. The B.B.T.C. has the monopoly of collecting all logs in the Irrawaddy and logs belonging to all. Firms have to pay the government three rupees per log found adrift and the B.B.T.C. receives three rupees per log collected, so their gift is a washout. At certain points of the river contractors are given eight annas per log which is salvaged. This was going on all day yesterday. A couple of men in a boat go out midstream, attach a rope to any drifting log and paddle it in, one man at the end of the log and t'other in the boat. These are collected and tied together close to the bank. Pretty hard work when a log may weigh anything from three tons upwards. Our *"tum tum"*[21] pony was taken up to Maymyo by the Syce last Tuesday. We go down by the mail tomorrow, leave here about 3pm, tie up somewhere between here and Mandalay for the night, and arrive Mandalay early morning. We shall catch the midday train up to Maymyo. We have been taking quite a lot of photos lately so hope to send some to show you our bungalow etc., sometime.

Glenside Maymyo, April 15th 1922

It just seems years since I last wrote and I only hope no mail has been missed. Life lately has been such a flotsam and jetsam affair that I don't seem to have had a second to sit down and write. My last was posted in the mail boat the day we left Sabenago. We had quite a good trip down. Several other passengers on board, chiefly Globetrotters who don't seem to

---

[21] Pony and trap.

mind seeing the world with the temperature well over 100°. The breeze was glorious and we thoroughly enjoyed going down and to feel cool once more. We arrived at Mandalay about 9pm, an hour earlier than expected, so no one awaited us in consequence. However, we got a 'gharry'[22] and went along to the B.B.T.C. office and then on to the club. We filled in an hour having lunch before catching the 1-30pm train to Maymyo. It was awfully hot in Mandalay and the train very crowded. We got in with a couple of men. Scarcely room to sit for luggage, which is piled up in the carriage to save expense as each package in the guards van is charged for. A few stations on our journey we got out and went along to the tiny restaurant car for a drink. We spun out the time as much as possible and on returning to our carriage found it full up with Eurasians and four kids. We looked and they looked and then pointed to a ticket on the door to say the seats were booked. So there we were! The man was very nice and insisted on clearing out to give me his seat and he did the trip up to Maymyo on the engine! Freddie and I managed alright and arrived at this end about 6 pm. The boys brought along endless packages and we drove to our little home in the *'tum tum'*. The Butler Daniel who had been left in charge while we were in the Jungle had got the bungalow very nice. Flowers everywhere and things are looking most spick and span. And now I am a lone grass widow once more feeling horribly lost without Freddie, who left for Sabenago on Thursday last. The heat up there now, of course, is terrible. As the month of May consists only of office work Freddie is bringing up his office plus one clerk to work here. So with luck he will be back early next month. He was splendid of course in trying to settle me in, comfy like, and leaving servants etc., working satisfactorily but it was all a mighty rush during the short week. Then the hopeless job of 'calling' had to be done and every evening we sallied forth in our best bibs and tuckers in the *"tum tum"* to shoot cards into little boxes. Two evenings we played tennis and one golf, and whatever the programme one always finishes at the club to meet endless people. There are crowds up here at present for *'The Week'* which starts on Monday and for the following six days there is a pretty hectic time. I will enclose the programme and next letter will tell of all my evil doings. Without Freddie all the festivities leave me quite cold, but this simply must be got through as social life and a man's job in life seem closely connected out here. I don't want to be a dud for Freddie's sake! I have watched the polo several times and there is always dancing at the club when it is too cold. There are chairs to sit on the lawn which is in front of the club and where all the lads and lasses collect, drink one another's health and strip various wretches of any good reputation they might possess. I have met some awfully nice people but I feel so beastly shy and now Freddie is not here I fly from people. However a Mrs. Barton is now staying with me which makes life much nicer. Mr. Barton is in the same show as Freddie and was married end of last year. She is to have an infant in August. Pakkoku, their district is so terribly hot they asked us to take her in and she will pay her share. Mr. Barton departs this evening leaving two lonely *'widdys'* to console one another. I am thankful to have her - very pretty little thing, only about twenty-three and as nice as she is pretty. We are both keen on sewing and not too much gadding so will shake down together alright. The menage is gradually sorting itself and now the curtains in the rooms are quite nice. Awful tussles with the servants, the dirty dogs. Our Jungle cook gave so much trouble and seemed to be overcharging for everything so we changed on Thursday. I think the present old Butler will do. The Butler is good but I don't trust him a yard. My little Burmese boy Bar Tai is here and is the one happy link to my topping free Jungle life. Every day the cook tramps down to the Bazaar and does the marketing and presents his bill daily and this is where all the trouble comes. They depend on making 'bucksheesh' on this and if one cuts them down too much they leave. I shall find my feet alright in time of course. I have my little home. Haven't nearly finished it, cushion covers etc., to be made. The Jungle

---

[22] A horse drawn cab.

curtains are up and look quite swanky. This must go dear. I'm so sorry to send such a rushed letter but now I have more time I will start again writing a little each day. I received your letters of March 7th and 14th alright. Thank you so much. I ought to receive another mail today. I do so look forward to letters. One from Auntie Bea last week. She is so good to write so often. Will address this to Malvern. I feel so glad you are now with Aunt Minnie and I hope she is not corrupting you in your old age!! Give her my best love. Your *'Daily Liars'* are much appreciated. I don't ever remember anything about the Mr. Johnson of Geneva account and I feel certain all accounts were settled before we left Suisse. I suppose there are no receipts amongst yours at Rosslyn? Anyway after a lapse of three years they cannot make you pay and I certainly don't think you should. Let me know what happens. Lots of love dear.

Glenside, Maymyo Tuesday April 18th 1922

Mrs. Barton has gone off to her shut-eye so before doing the same myself I will start my letter to you. m sitting in our drawing room by the open window. There is a lovely breeze and all the bungalow is shaded by several large trees in front. We have taken tiffin at 12 o'clock and from about 1pm till 3pm the whole place is peaceful as the servants go off for their meal. Such a joy when they are away too. One cannot get away from the incessant chatter. At the back I have had fearful games with them all since my last letter. I have just finished having a council of war with three awfully nice men in the bungalow in the next compound. Two, Mr.Phillips and Mr. Burke are in the B.B.T.C. and will do anything to help. Our wretched Butler seems to upset everyone including the Syce, who is an awfully hot tempered man, and apparently when I was out last evening they came to blows. Daniel (Butler) I didn't trust a yard and feel sure he orders the other servants about too much. He has also got the daughter of another Butler near here into trouble and also I am certain that he sneaks about to hear what we talk about. I feel Daniel won't be much use to us. However, he must remain until Freddie returns. The Syce has for sometime wanted to return to the country, Manipur, so for peace and quietness I'm sacking him directly. Another is forthcoming. The Mali[23] and sweeper both went on strike one day because they were forced to go to other quarters to sleep but returned next day after being told they can stop away minus a month's pay, which we always keep in hand. Daniel even upsets my poor little Bar Tai who I know gives no trouble. On hearing a fearful din outside this morning I went out to find my brass Buddha (you remember the one given me at Gloster) being thrown at the sweeper's head and Bar Tai in floods of tears! *I scattered 'em all right.* The less said or listened to from these blighters I find to be the best policy. Mrs. Barton's maid kicked up a dust too. She objected to sleeping between two men at night. We made no objection to that dust up and have now given her a bed elsewhere. My cook Valog is much nicer than the other one and, as he speaks English, I find the housekeeping much easier. I now have my storeroom more or less fixed up, and give out stores each day and that also makes life more simple. I hope to have the ménage running quite smoothly by Freddie's return when he will really be able to enjoy his home. I think it has been one long worry with servants. Their wretched castes make so much trouble; one looks down on another - sort of thing! Well to the lighter side of life. I just love having Aida (Mrs. Barton) with me. She is a delightful visitor and it's so nice to have a girl to talk things over with. Her husband returns to Pakokku on Saturday evening. Sunday (Easter Day) I drove to Kirk and went to 8 o'clock service. Church packed. In the evening Aida and I walked across the links to the club, watched the tennis for a bit then walked home again. Maymyo is full to overflowing now. All the lads and lassies sporting their best bibs and tuckers and the residents wishing 'The Week' over so as to settle down to the quiet yet quite gay enough life. All yesterday morning we were down in the Bazaar and I managed to find a

---

[23] Gardener.

bookmaker who will make me a pair of shoes to wear at the PWD fancy dress dance tomorrow night. At 3-30pm a Colonel Loch came up for me in his little car and drove me down to the club where we joined his wife and then on to watch the first two matches of the polo tournament. Mrs. Lely called for Aida in their car and joined us later. Most exciting games and the ponies were wonderful. The native players in the police are such good players. After a short time at the club Aida and I came home in a gharry and she helped me to don my best for the dance at Government House. I wore the white frock Mountstephens made for me, after titivating it to hide the fashion of 18 months ago. I dined with a party of ten others at the Williams'. Colonel Williams,[24] otherwise 'Stonker Bill' was on the same boat when I went home from Ceylon and incidentally was the one to introduce Freddie to me. Very cheery dinner and I was later driven to Government House where we had a fine old bun struggle of two hundred and forty people. The place looked so topping. Whole of the huge bungalow illuminated by electric light inside Chinese lanterns. The Governor and Lady Craddock stood in the large hall and as each name was bawled out we filed past shaking the poor weary looking things by the paw. They are pretty ancient and looked bored to death. Lady Craddock holds her head at an angle of 45^0 and is never still. Her head waggles the whole time and it is most tantalizing when talking to her. A lot of people cleared off to play bridge and the dance was not at all crowded. I managed to dance all but one. Besides every drink and refreshment one could wish for we were fed with a most scrumptious supper before departing. It was such a pretty sight with all the different regiments' mess kits.

Friday April 21st 1922

It is actually raining. First rain they have had in Maymyo since before Christmas and were badly needed. I feel so fed up about my mail; no English letter for two weeks. It's the fault of the office somewhere; probably sent them up to Sabenago. Aida and I do nothing but look for the postman and she has had much more luck than I up till now. Only the letter from Freddie written on the boat so far. I have had more trouble with the Syce so have given him the chuck and he departs in a couple of days. I didn't want to until Freddies's return but peace at any price and as he and the Butler are always coming to logger heads, the sooner one or other goes the better. This week has been very gay and we had quite cheery times but always shall think them wasted without Freddie as an escort. Tuesday Aida and I drove out to pay off some outlandish calls. Maymyo is a large place and the regiments' quarters are a good drive out. It is so nice having the *'tum tum'* and I love driving. The rides are jolly fine up here too; tracks cut right through avenues of trees and scrubby sort of country. The dinner and dance Mr. Burke and Phillips gave at the club on Tuesday was a great success, thirty-six altogether, and to digest the umpteen courses more easily we danced in between. Round and round the long table until we spotted the next course was ready, and then made a dive for our seats. Aida and I left early as an evening outing is quite an event for her. On Wednesday we watched a polo tournament again and went to the fancy dress dance at 9-30pm given by the PWD. I first of all dined up at Candacraig (Headquarters' of B.B.T.C. men on leave) and then was driven down to the club. A wonderful lot of costumes and the mass of colour with the beautiful flower decorations was a sight. Over three hundred guests and all in fancy costumes. I wore my Dutch and the man in the Bazaar made me a topping pair of sabots which were quite comfortable enough to dance in for a time. The scrummy sit-down supper was served in marquees outside and the grounds lit up with electric lamps. I stayed until the bitter end and got a lift home in someone's car at 2am. Yesterday, Thursday we watched some very good tennis. Military versus Civil.

---

[24] Lt. Col. J.H. Williams, the author of *Elephant Bill.*

Saturday April 22nd 1922

This must be posted today as the English mail goes a day earlier than usual. It has suddenly turned so cold and I am once more in wintry clothes. Aida and I have just returned from a drive to the Bazaar. The crowd in the streets is always so difficult, men slouching about and will not move. Bullock carts that creep along, and having no shafts, the Bullocks suddenly swish out and get the pony one in the eye. The people are very interesting with all their different costumes and mostly wearing huge shan hats. Last evening Colonel and Mrs. Loch and their nephew Captain Loch came to dinner. Then we all went off to the concert at the club. My first attempt at a dinner party went off ok and the table was so nice, with your four candlesticks and many of the old home touches. The concert was awfully good once it started, after a delay at the beginning owing to His Honour and Lady Craddock being late. He came in and looking thoroughly overfed, so that was probably the reason why we were kept waiting. The first part consisted of songs etc., and the second a short play. It was awfully amusing; a skit on the present attitude of servants demanding nights out for theatre going etc. All parts taken by Maymyo residents who looked perfect sights when made up as a kitchen maid and a tweeny etc. Tonight I am dining at the club with a dance after. I still have no home letters and none from Freddie which was due on Thursday. I expect he has got his nose too much to the grindstone to write. Farewell dear this week. I feel so lost with no home letters for so long and none to answer. Lots of love. I'm beginning to lose some of my horrid lost feeling but still count the days till Freddie comes back.

Glenside, Maymyo Thursday April 27th 1922

At last I've got a letter from you. The silly asses at Rangoon office had taken no notice of Freddie's letter asking for all my letters to be sent to Maymyo. I was so glad to have news of Edith. Do send me on any other letters. Except for your weekly and very welcome letter I seldom get any home news. My Netley pals have not forgotten me but sisters seem to have done so. I really get very little time for letter writing. Now that I am becoming more accustomed to the life and grappling with the servants, and the ménage generally does not sit so heavily on my chest, I may turn over a new leaf and pick up my pen more often. How splendid your knees being so much better. I am so glad. And now with the summer before you life will cheer up for you. You always speak of your hand being so painful as your writing denotes. Not a bit of it. Freddie and I always remark how extraordinarily clear and even it is, right up to the end. You have more difficulty reading my letters than I do yours. I am glad Aunt Mary[25] is getting about again. What is uncle Jim[26] doing these days and where does he live? Life up here is still going very strong though visitors begin to go down to the depths below where I hear it is terribly hot. Poor Freddie hates Sabenago more than ever. He says there is even no hot wind now and he seems to sit and sweat through one shirt after another. He was just off on tour, when he wrote his last, to the elephant camp where another is about to peg out much to his disgust. He certainly has had awful bad luck with his animals since taking over Sabenago. With Luck Freddie will be up here in a week's time. He and Hunt and one clerk bring the work to Maymyo for the whole of May. 'Aintree', 'a corporation chummery', almost next door, has a lot of spare rooms, so Freddie proposes having one for his office. Hunt will be overjoyed at the prospect, being a *'gay dawg'*. Too much Jungle work does not suit his fancy. It will be topping to have Freddie again and we shall squeeze in as much tennis as possible. I've had quite a lot lately. Aida and I were

---

[25] The wife of George Child of Nunnington, Alice's sister-in-law.
[26] James Turner Child, Alice's brother.

thankful to have a fire but the rain has departed now leaving it once more beautifully sunny and a nice cool breeze. The races are on this afternoon, the road leads past here to the course. They don't interest us at all so don't intend going. I hate all these public shows without Freddie to help me round.

Saturday April 29th 1922

I've received your letter of the 4th and just can't write about the sad news you tell me. Poor dear uncle George. He was just one of the best and as you know I loved him as a father and I can't realise we shan't see him at Nunnington when we come home. I always feared something of this sort would happen. Uncle George was always so thoughtful for others and never regarded his own health. Oh dear, it is so sad for us all. He did so love his relations and all they had to say. I know dear how very very much you will miss him too. I keep thinking of the day he saw me off at Birkenhead. I was a little sad as he said he did not know whether he would still be here when I returned home. It has always been that, bless him! Poor Aunt Mary is by no means strong enough to have such a shock and do hope she will keep up alright. Mother dear I can't go on writing more this mail. I feel it can be only on one line and after all that won't help you in what I know is a very sad time. Lots of love. I do wish I was nearer you all.

Glenside, Maymyo, Sunday May 7th 1922

My mail is being started very late this week, and I must buck up as this has to be posted today. I have just received yours of April 11th. It has scarcely been digested yet as I've had so much worry with the servants this morning. At least with Daniel the Butler, who thank goodness has departed altogether with the police on his heels for having stolen a hundred rupees worth of material belonging to a man near here. Daniel has proved what I always felt him to be, an absolute blackguard. This wretched woman he got into trouble disappeared, and Daniel said he knew nothing, and then last night Freddie happened to go round the back and discovered both of them in the store room where all our packing cases are! And my dining room cushions for their bed!! We may be poor but we do have excitements. We have chits for another Butler so hope to be fixed up soon. In spite of this, life is very nice and Freddie is once more here. He arrived last Wednesday, wrote that it would be by the usual evening train, and behold he caught us on the hop just as we were going to go down at one o'clock. He and Hunt went from Mandalay giving them a whole extra afternoon. Last Tuesday Major Crump gave me my second anti-typhoid injection. I expected it would make me feel rather dickie as I chose to have two injections in one. However, other than a tender arm, I felt none the worse. Monday I had some awfully good tennis with the Wroughtons and Mr. Cleaver, all B.B.T.C. men; the former in the next bungalow for a couple of weeks. He is top dog in Rangoon and both topping good sorts. They are the sort to pop in after dinner and Aida and I often go in to see her. Last Tuesday morning was the big Bazaar when Burmans, Shans and natives of all sorts come in from miles around with their vegetables and fruit, fish, pottery, and every imaginable article to sell on their stalls in a large market sort of place. They pass here by the score with their large Shan hats, a pole over the shoulder with a large basket dangling on each end. With different coloured lungees[27] it gives a very pretty picture. Aida and I prowled into the Bazaar but would have fled from the hustling and swelling crowd had it not been for Mr. Chesham, IES who believes in buying his own fruit and I trailed round with him buying vegetables etc. Strawberries are now over, worse luck, but we get mangoes and apples, and various other kinds of fruit. I saw in the paper the other day strawberries at six shillings each. We have fed on the most luscious ones

---

[27] A type of skirt worn by men and women.

since January. I expect you're getting them at home now. There seem to be a whole lot of Freddie's pals in here on leave just at present which makes it nice for him and we get good tennis. Freddie looks fit and I think is naturally very bucked at being home again. Sabenago office used to be up to 115° midday when he left. Work worries him a good deal. Drastic steps for economy are the order and he has great difficulty in curtailing expense without extra work and touring for himself, which he is quite unable to do now during the rains. After fifteen years of it he finds his health won't stick it. However, Sabenago won't have him for many more months. Mawlaik ought to be better. Freddie and I went to a very nice dance at the club on Thursday. Lordy! It does make a difference having him to sport me around. Friday afternoon I made sweets for a Bazaar the next day, and then Freddie and I went out to tennis. The bazaar yesterday went off very well. Mrs. Roberts (her husband is Freddie's first manager) asked me to help with her 'bran tub'. Before the Bazaar was opened by Lady Fane we had a whole queue of small schoolboys with their arms bared ready to dive in to get their parcels. Within half an hour we were sold out and finished up with over eighty rupees. Had we the parcels we could have made many times that amount. Freddie and Aida came down later in the 'tum tum' and after tea, all together, Freddie and I left for tennis with Mrs. Lely. Saturday we were very much surprised by Harry Van Someren rolling up. He is a cousin of Freddie's and we stayed with them in Rangoon. We quite thought Harry had gone home with his wife. The business kept him. He hopes to follow her next month. Harry came in for dinner last night. Freddie has a room in the bungalow belonging to the B.B.T.C., in the next compound but one to this and he goes over every morning and does office work. There is not much in the garden these days. We don't intend doing much as it was in a poor state when we came and don't see why we should do it for those who come here in November. I had a letter from Miss Holmes today enclosing one from Dorothy. She is most anxious to know where Granny Britten is, so do write to her. No one ever mentions B. Is she doing anything with her massage? Goodbye dearest. My very best love and from Freddie to you and tell Helen her lampshades have often been admired.

Maymyo Friday May 12th 1922

This will get you at Malvern I suppose. I do hope you and aunt Minnie are enjoying yourselves and not being too vulgar together. The change will do you a lot of good and if only the weather is nice you will love sitting out in the nice garden. I have a very tender spot in my heart for Birchwood and all it contains. It takes me away back to my Worcester days when I used to blow over to Malvern and let fling my pent-up bad behaviour of the previous two weeks! I'm starting my letter before lying down after tiffin as I generally do. Freddie is already well away. He is not at all fit and this morning I chivvied him off to see Major Crump, Indian Medical Service. He puts it down chiefly to the change from Sabenago and general sort of debility. Maymyo does not suit everyone by any means. I have been among the many who have suffered from 'Maymyo trots' the last few days! You can guess what that particular disease is and it is not at all nice I assure you. Major Crump says he notices it comes at the beginning of the rains and different chemicals etc., in the drinking water. The mango season also, and one is very apt to eat over- ripe fruit and so send one running the whole day. That we feel so slack and sleepy cannot be due to sluggish lives, at any rate. We have lots of exercise in the way of tennis. We have cleared out the wretched Butler and now have one by the name of Gabriel! They always choose something biblical, the awful humbugs. Gabriel hasn't disgraced his name so far at any rate and life is certainly very much more peaceful and the bungalow cleaner. The Syce does his work decently now he is not ordered about by Daniel and instead of going at the end of last month he asked to stay on. The Wroughtons from the next bungalow often come in after dinner. They had the most exciting experience the other night. Walking along one of the 'rides' just at dusk they saw something black moving along ahead and discovered it to be three black bears. On seeing one to be a baby they took to their heels and flew till laughing made them give it up! I had no idea bears came so near civilisation but apparently to see a panther or a leopard is not out of the way. Last Monday we had tennis with Colonel and Mrs. Loch at the club and hurried home as three men were coming to dinner. Harry Van Someren, Freddie's cousin among them. The old cook really spread himself well that night and things went off quite merrily, though I can't say I love giving dinners. When Freddie once more leaves me alone I shan't think to give dinners but have those I must entertain to tiffin. They are always quite keen to be off early to their forty winks after that meal. On Tuesday Aida and I drove up to Candacraig (B.B.T.C. Chummery) for tea and to watch Freddie and Harry Van Someren play in a men's pair. Aida left on Wednesday and travelled down to Pakokku with a Mr. Bostock, Aida's husband's assistant. I'm afraid she will find it fearfully hot down there, and shouldn't be at all surprised if she returns to me before July. Her baby is due at beginning of August. I shall be on tenterhooks all the time before, in case it's in a hurry to come into the world. Wednesday afternoon Freddie and I asked his boss Mr. Roberts and spouse to play tennis at Candacraig and that evening the Wroughtons and the Tews came to dinner. Yesterday Hunt brought his pal Hill in for tiffin. Hunt is awfully blighted because he is to leave Sabenago in June to give place to Hill who is supposed to be a better man and will take over that district when Freddie leaves in 1923. Hunt has had a jolly good chance but through slackness has lost it. Hill is a very much nicer boy, so like our 'Tweetie', same build, same coloured crimpy hair. He has very much more in him in every way and will be more of a companion for Freddie. Last night Freddie and I were out at the Loch's for dinner. They are such nice people, so cheery. Freddie came out on the same boat with Mrs. Loch.

Saturday May 13th 1922

I've had Freddie in bed all day with either a go of flu or fever but whatever it is it leaves him feeling an awful worm and terribly sorry for himself. I do hate this fever as it is so lowering and depressing. He has no temperature in spite of being in a cold sweat the whole time. He got up for tea and is now mooching about the bungalow. A drive would not hurt him. So, much against his will, we are having out the *'tum tum'* and will drive round the circular road, a great place for a joyride. It runs past our gate, on around by the Botanical Gardens, on to a lovely big lake with lovely wooded hills away off in the distance, and then round passed the club and golf course and back to our bungalow, making a nice drive of about three miles. We are the last bungalow on this side, the General's is about two hundred yards further up, and then nothing except a wild sort of Jungle for a couple of miles. The weather has been so heavy today, thunderstorms coming and going and nothing seems to clear the atmosphere. We had very good tennis at the club yesterday but had to chuck all other games until Freddie is fit again. We go to another dance at Government House on Monday, also tennis there next Thursday: I expect that will be pretty rotten. Garden party tennis always is. Well, we have been out for a hard drive and very nice too - as far as the Botanical Gardens and a walk right through. It is so pretty, a Lady Cuffe started it years ago and since her husbnd retired presented the whole place to the government for the use of the public. There was great excitement on our part when we spotted a little shrub with the Kings Acre Nurseries label on it. It made me feel quite homesick. Freddie's remark being: *'Hem! That's where your blooming long net came from, isn't it?'* I like Maymyo much more than I did at first; knowing more people I suppose. My Jungle days will begin again about October I expect. We shall have to turn out of this bungalow in any case and go to the rotten one next door but it will really mean only storing our boxes.

Thank you so much for yours of April 18th enclosing a list of uncle George's legacies. The dear old thing! How very very generous he has been. Why ever I am to have £300 I can't think. Even that makes him no dearer. Every time I think of uncle George I realise the awful blank he leaves. Freddie and I shall feel it still more when we come home and there is no Nunnington to go to. One thought about the £300 is that I could have it now and so pass it on to you. How I wish I could give you something like that. We have just about enough but no more at present. This keeping up a double establishment takes all the pay but we hope for brighter days when Freddie has his acting managership next year. I hope next week to send an order for the papers and an extra three shillings for Emma Turner. She very kindly sent me out a couple of new refills for my torch which I find indispensable out here. I do hope Aunt Mary is fixed up with the new servant. It's too bad she should have all this worry when life should be a comfortable thing for her. When Freddie was at Sabenago he sent me a whole lot of photos we took in the Jungle and they have not been receive this end yet. We have asked at the post office and may get them in time. I do hope so as I want you to have some snaps. Our little garden is a sight just now with masses of tall red lilies. I often long to be home to see the Spring flowers. Are they as advanced as last year? This will reach you just about my birthday, so don't forget to drink my health in peppermint beer. Last year I was at Dilwyn. Oh dear! I would love to be home with Freddie and amongst you all. Did I tell you Aida Barton's uncle is Mr. Ewing, uncle to the man Jack is with. In 1915 Aida was staying at Braemar with the Ewings. The uncle lives at Bexhill and has just come back home from visiting his nephew in South Africa. I wonder if George came across him. The Wroughtons leave for Rangoon on Tuesday. I shall miss Mrs. Wroughton so awfully. She often pops through the garden hedge and I do the same in our bungalow when we want to chat. Mr. Wroughton will be head of the B.B.T.C. one day. He is acting now for Mr. Johnston who is on leave. Mrs. Wroughton paints very well and is a great admirer of Helen's lampshades and Edith's pictures of Champery. I miss Aida so much. She always used to sit in one corner of the veranda sewing and it was so nice always having someone there when I wanted to talk. It will be dreadful when Freddie departs for Sabenago at the end of this month but sufficient is the day for the joy of it, at any rate. Goodbye for one more week dear. I'm so looking forward to your next letter which I suppose will be from Malvern. You are so faithful with your letters, you dear old thing, and I should miss them terribly. Even happiness out here would not be complete without the weekly home touch you give me. Bless you. Toodleoo,

Glenside, Maymyo, Friday May 20th 1922

Mail day seems to come round in a flash these days and days themselves even go quicker, so here I am not started my letter and it has to go tomorrow. However, I must do my best to give an account of myself. Thank you so much for yours of April 25th. It took less than a month. The mail service is certainly becoming much better. I am sorry the weather has affected your legs so badly. It is disappointing having to suffer so much pain after having the course. But one never knows what it may do for you as time goes on. By the time you receive this I hope the weather allowed you to sit out on Aunt Minnie's little back patch and enjoy the lovely view. I bet you have many an hour knitting and chatting to one another. What a relief it will be to have a change from the likes of Miss Draper. In spite of such drawbacks I hope you will return to Tupsley for the next winter as the Miss Macs look after you so well and I know they love having you. You probably make them quite frisky in spite of being about the oldest hen! I am glad you got over to see Aunt Mary, but can imagine what a sad visit it must have been. Yes, that old chair in the morning room would look horribly empty. I can just see dear old uncle George's bald pate. I had a letter from solicitors to the effect I was to have the £300 on the death of the widow. I must get Aunt Mary to give me one of the large photos. It is very good of them both. Freddie and I have such an awful soft spot for

Nunnington, and had rubber and Freddie's other money affairs gone right, he always had in his mind he would like to have bought Nunnington and farmed a small part of it. Freddie would do so awfully well in a job like that and it would suit him very much better than his present one. However it's a blessing to have a job at all these days and the Bombay Burma is certainly looked on as one of the best shows in the East. What a family party at Dilwyn. I bet Ethel is beginning to feel restive out in Ceylon and longing to be out of the rains which will break any time now. Every day we expect the first deluge which will put a stop to our daily tennis. I believe the rains up here are not very serious and golf goes along in spite of it. When tennis is no go I mean to try golf. I shall be keen when there is no tennis as a counter attraction. I really am having a top-hole time now and like Maymyo more and more now that I feel happier about the servants, and knocking down the Bazaar bills etc., life is not so difficult. The servants are much more peaceful without the turbulent Daniel. Rather funny thing, the other day Freddie and I were at tea and tennis at the Field Clark's where Daniel has managed to get a billet. He quite lost his head and, on pouring out his hand shook so that he could scarcely aim straight at the glass, and then on being told to leave the whisky he took that off leaving a row of empty soda bottles. Mrs. 'F.C' swore and said she couldn't make out what had happened to Daniel. I enlightened her but as we refused to give Daniel a chit she did not know that he had been with us! Freddie has been very much better since I made him have a day in bed. He went to see Major Crump (the B.B.T.C. doctor) on Wednesday who has given him a fever medicine and says Freddie simply must not return to the Jungle yet. We all know that with all their drastic economising, and losing one subordinate assistant, and a new man to take the place of Hunt, Freddie can't well be away from his district. However I hope he will be here anyway until about June 11th. Last Sunday we drove to the entrance to the botanical gardens and then walked the one and a half miles to Kontha where live a Mr. and Mrs.Louis Baker. He was once in the Corporation, got fed up and leased an area of good land and is now clearing it, and hopes to make things pay as a farm. Everyone is very sceptical as a European has never done the likes before and whatever he sells is sure to be at a loss with expensive labour to be paid for, whereas in all other places Burmans work their own projects, to say nothing of having very much cheaper labour. However Mr. Baker puts all his trust in his pigs! I hope he succeeds. Kontha is a delightful spot in rather a valley with the creek running away before the bungalow and way off is a range of hills in the distance. I suggested starting Hereford cattle as grazing is so good but meat though inferior to home is very much cheaper. In a country where the greater part of the population eats no meat a large or good herd of cattle is not wanted as there seems to be plenty. The other day I sent our Durwan[28] for some bacon and when he discovered what was ordered he refused to bring the parcel as it is against his caste to touch pig! I don't think I told you Freddie has bought me a second-hand 'Perfection Stove' only with two burners and a good-sized oven. Cooks are no use at making cakes out here and I can now muddle away and make my own. The stove fits into my store room where I have all I want around me. Aunt Mary has a Perfection Stove only with three burners. I shall find it very useful when I return to Sabenago where Jungle cooks are quite impossible. Last Monday morning Mrs. Wroughton and I motored down to the Bazaar where we bargained with all the sharks for different cloths. Mrs. Wroughton's mother and sister live in the British East Africa and seem to farm. Clothing out there is ruinous so she buys stuff in the Bazaar here and gets a durzie[29] to run it up for next to nothing. On Monday we had good tennis at the club and dined with the Wroughtons who afterwards motored us to the Government House dance, which was awfully jolly. Not such a crowd as at the last. Jolly good refreshments and I made a pig of myself with the strawberries with the result that I woke up next morning with a terrible tongue. However, I never usually

---

[28] Interpreter or caretaker.
[29] Servant.

have such tongues here and feel as woozy in the head as I used to in Ceylon. My innards behave so well here. In fact I feel awfully fit in spite of the rather strenuous life. I'm still thin *but that doesn't matter. I hope to increase Freddie's weight by giving him a morning egg flip.* The Wroughtons returned to Rangoon on Wednesday. Elseburg, the next bungalow is now empty, so the road is rather lonely. The Wroughton came in to say goodbye and Freddie and I then raided their bungalow (Corp. property) and found a very useful kitchen table, a broom, and some plants! Mrs. Wroughton is awfully nice and we became quite pals. She wants me to go down to Rangoon to stop with her when Freddie is out in the Jungle but the fare is rather expensive so must wait a bit. I had tennis every day last week at the club or private courts. We went out to an awful dud dinner at the Clarks' in the Staffordshire Regiment on Thursday where we played footling games. Freddie and I could scarcely smother yawns. We have come to the conclusion we haven't been married long enough to be keen on going out in the evenings. Burmans are bringing in lovely orchids from the Jungle now and often call here for us to buy. They look very pretty hanging in the veranda. Flowers in our garden are just about done but about every third day the Mali produces an enormous bucket full for me to do the vases with. I suppose he raids other gardens at the break of dawn. There is an extraordinary fly about now which stings like *old billy*. Rather like a horse fly and has a black and white body. The other day one little blighter got me on one hand and ankle. The swelling is not down yet and they feel just as though they have been sprained. After the lamps are lit, flying beetles and insects of all sorts make it rather impossible to do anything. Goodbye mother dear for one more week. Here the year is slipping by. In another eighteen months we shall be home. I wonder what spot that will be. It is a lovely time to look forward to anyway. Lots of love dear and to Aunty Minn, bless her. My love of course to Helen and you.

Glenside, Maymyo, Friday May 27th 1922

By last mail I received your first letter written from Aunt Minn's and so glad you managed the journey alright and are feeling so cosy and happy with your frisky sister to look after you. A change from Tupsley, where you have been amongst illness for so long, will do a lot of good. I know from previous experience how well one is looked after at *Birchwood* both Aunt Minnnie and Helen were so sweet when I was bereft of my *"pore 'usband."* I was so glad to read Jeff's long letter. How he loves talking over past days. I don't wonder, Jeff[30] was certainly a handful to you and a hero to us kids. I remember so well the day he sold a pair of father's best boots and the Bobby in the town brought the boots and the beggar woman up to Edenhurst! I will send the letter on to Jack. I think Nora's friend in Swebo must be a Mrs. Jackson. She was up here the other day with her husband and came to lunch. Before her marriage she nursed and lived near Minehead. I believe that is where Nora[31] came from. I wish I'd known when she was here. I want Mrs. Jackson to come up to Sabenago for a few days next cold weather. Her husband is in the B.B.T.C. and his district is no distance from us. Do please carry on sending my letters to Ealing. You talk of my having more time for writing but things here are even worse than the Jungle. The days fly. I fear my pals at home will leave me in the lurch. However, you and *The Hereford Times* are ever faithful! When thoroughly digested I always put it as the cover to the washstand in my bathroom and on the table in the storeroom so that I still see names of home places before me! We daily expect the rains to break but so far nothing except a few slight showers making Maymyo fresher and greener than ever. Freddie is much better and feels more inclined to do things. I wish he could stay up another month which would set him on his legs for the coming hard work during the rains. I still feed him on egg-flips and the doctor's medicine seems to have shed

---

[30] Walter Jeffries Britten, Mully's brother.
[31] Nora, the wife of John Jeffries Britten (Mully's brother Jack) living in South Africa.

him of the miserable fever. We have just finished tiffin and Freddie is already in the arms of Morpheus (don't know how to spell it) but anyway I think it's time I found him there.

Sunday May 29th 1922

Here's Sunday. The mail goes today so must get a move on. Freddie went again to see the doctor last Monday who says he is better but must stay up longer. Whether that will be possible after June 11 remains to be seen. The same day I had a long visit to the dentist who finished fixing in the crown to one of my lower teeth. Always seem to be in trouble at the dentist. This man is very good and has a large practice in Rangoon and comes up here for the hot weather. He has a never ending stream of patients, men who come to Maymyo for leave from the Jungle once a year. Two B.B.T.C. men came to tiffin both staying at Aintree, the chummery almost next door. It is quite a new house and very sparsely furnished and no curtains so far. The men have asked if I will fix them up with everything, or as far as the fifty rupees allowed by the company will go. I have patterns from Cawnpore and think curtains of a buff coloured cloth will look as nice as anything. Some men have such queer tastes, one chose pale sky blue! So I told him he had better wait till he had a boudoir to fix up. Monday evening we had a great time going to a cinema of all things. We were told the film *Sorrows of Satan* with Gladys Cooper and Owen Nares acting was good, so risked a possible Jungle of Burmans, with their everlasting cheroots, and Mrs. Lely came to take pot luck with us, and we all drove down after dinner and were very pleasantly surprised. Very fine hall. Atmosphere all it should be, and a very good film. If we go again I shall certainly take a joss stick to keep off the mosquitoes which fairly kept me alive that night. On Friday morning Freddie and I made an effort and got up early and walked over to the bathing pool where we had promised to meet Mrs. Hay and have a dip. (Not Freddie. He is afraid of fever) However, we were all disappointed as the pool was empty in order for it to have a clean and incidentally searched for several rings lost by fair bathers. On our way back we met a Burman going along with some roots of lovely orchids which after much bargaining Freddie bought and all thirteen plants of different kinds are now hanging in our veranda. When finished flowering they are to be sent to Ethel's pal Mr. Viellars in Ceylon who is a keen collector. The Cleavers (B.B.T.C.) gave a very cheery tea and good tennis afterwards up at Candacraig. That court really belongs to the men in the other chummery, and any corporation man can have it for private parties. A Mrs. Jackson Jones and Mrs. Stewart came here for tiffin on Wednesday. We find that is a useful meal to give folk as they are generally so anxious for their forty winks that they leave almost directly. On Thursday it was a terrible chore at Government House. Much to our disgust it rained. Tennis was impossible, so Freddie went up for tea. Our clocks must have been terribly slow for we arrived just as everyone was getting up after tea. Knowing gloves have to be worn to the dances I took them in case. When I arrived I left my coat in the cloakroom and I waited hoping that another girl, who arrived just behind would appear so that I could see if she wore hers but the annoying creature did not come in but stood talking to Freddie with the ADC Captain Drake Brockman waiting outside. I peeped through the curtain and got a glassy stare from a Burman servant in return. Then Freddie bleated out to me to buck up so I had to go. The wretched woman had got gloves and it was then too late. Besides I only had sort of half tennis kit and the wench was dressed in best bib and tucker. We trailed into the enormous room behind captain DB who bawled out our names again and Lady Craddock, the poor old thing, came waggling her head nearly off, with white silk gloves on! And then I noticed every woman in the room sported white kid gloves, even to eat their tea with! Silly asses! However it was I who felt the 'ass' and my beefy arms and hands immediately felt even larger and worse than they are naturally. Lady Craddock pinned me down and I did my best not to stamp on my 'aitches' etc! I was relieved when the gramophone started and they all danced. I was determined for the folk to see I had gloves and donned them after tea! That night we had a very cheery dinner at the Sherman's (he is head of the police) which made up for my worrying afternoon. I tried my oven for the first time on Friday to make some sweets as I had a couple coming to dinner that night. It goes beautifully and the truffles came out well. I had my first game of brag after dinner. People out here don't play a great deal. Old and young seem to go in for tennis golf and dancing. Yesterday we really had our first heavy downpour in the afternoon. I was having my usual forty winks when a regular thunderbolt made me sit up. The rain on our corrugated roof makes it difficult to hear anyone speak. Tennis was quite impossible and so Freddie and I took a long walk right across the links. Except for the occasional clump of bamboo trees one might think oneself in Surrey or some low-lying county thickly wooded.

Last evening I felt energetic enough to turn out for the usual Saturday evening dance at the club and Mrs. Freeman dined here first and then came with us. Not many there and quite a nice dance. The great thing dancers seem to fancy after dancing is black beer and potato chips. Mr. and Mrs. Cleaver came to tiffin today.

On Sunday Freddie and I went out and came home early as he felt so rotten. This beastly fever seems to roll him over so suddenly and he had been so very much better than last week. Fever is such a depressing thing and nothing seems to rouse Freddie. However, he seems better now after a bath and a dose of quinine. You remember me telling you about a Miss Pringle I liked so much on the boat coming out? She is still in Assam but says she can come to me about August which will do beautifully. Aida Barton comes some time the end of June and will be with me a month and then, if I had Daisy Pringle, the months I shall have to spend without Freddie won't be so bad. This morning we drove down to the Bazaar and looked around the stalls. I am sending you a small Shan bag to keep your work in or pack up your sandwiches when you walk the Malvern Hills (Wish you could dear!). I forgot to ask if I sent you a ring made from wicker from an elephant's tail. Do tell me and I will send one if not already done. Do tell Helen I never have anyone here without they admire her lampshades. They do look so pretty. Ask her if she will do one for candle-shades (The fruit design we like) and let us know her charges. Nothing like earning an honest penny. Her Swiss watercolours have just arrived from being framed. They and the etchings look topping and are a great source of interest to everyone who comes to the bungalow. I do wish you could see our little home, let alone come to stay in it. The one thing I have against this life is never being able to see my own folk. However time will soon go. Lots and lots of love mother dear and to my saucy Aunt and her still saucier daughter.

Glenside, Maymyo, Friday June 2nd 1922
Yours of May 9th received last Wednesday, so letters seem to be coming quicker than ever. I'm so glad the weather is at last warmer and you are able to sit out of doors. I can just picture you and Aunt Minnie sitting in the corner of the garden enjoying the lovely view etc. I also heard from Mary and Connie,[32] the former enclosing a letter addressed to me at Princess Risborough from Kenneth Elliott!! Do you remember the boy who lived with his parents in O'pery? He wrote from Palestine where he is on the air force staff, wants to know where I am etc., after eight years!! I feel he was married early in the war but says nothing about his wife! Isn't clear. This letter was written in November so he will put me down as dead not having had an answer. Kenneth was such a very old admirer wasn't he? But only I think because he wasn't so shy and didn't stutter so much with me! Oh dear, I have no peace from scratching

---

[32] Constance Alethea, nee Jeffries, the wife of Mully's brother George Britten.

these days. Our bungalow is infested with fleas. But one has to expect such visitors and white ants at the commencement of the rains. The little blighters don't seem to like Frddie. If I stand a minute before my dining table and look down I find dozens popping only white stockings. I have a terror of white ants which can do so much damage. I pour down Jenoil[33] into any suspicious looking holes. This week has been full of very heavy storms, mostly at night, when there is not much peace for sleep with the rattle of thunder and rain on our tin roof. Only once has tennis been stopped though. Hard courts dry so quickly. Last Tuesday a Mr. Hay called for us in his car (or rather Ford) to take us to the bathing tank Freddie did not risk the dip because of his fever but I thoroughly enjoyed my first dip. The tank is about twenty yards square with a running stream going right through. Water chutes, springboards etc., give us plenty of things to do. Driving back up our very steep bit of drive, in changing gear, the car suddenly stuck and on looking down we found the mudguard right down on the wheel and then discovered the back axle had broken right in two. Luckily the car was only hired and Mr. Hay came in for no damages. For three days our drive was blocked by this old crock, propped up with bricks etc., while the fresh axle was forthcoming. Tuesday was the tennis party of Mrs. Booth Graveley, who is noted for her teas. Golly! It was more like having tea at a restaurant by the number of cakes and sandwiches savouries etc. After introducing one of the other guests Mrs. 'B.G.' then went on to introduce us to the cakes etc., and told us to get on with things. I hated it all as things were overdone including her straffing the servants before us all. Personally I prefer buns and peace rather than a spread such as that served up with grouse. However we thoroughly enjoyed the good tennis. Freddie and I had tiffin at 'Aintree' on Wednesday with the three B.B.T.C. men staying there, to decide about the curtains for the house which I have been asked to fix up. One can't please everyone's taste and no doubt I shall offend someone's artistic sense. It is King George's birthday today so we had a great banging for the salute early this morning, when there was a great parade. I'm afraid we did not go but drove later to see Mrs. Lely off to Rangoon. She came out on my boat and has been up here all the hot weather. We have been out to tennis every day this week. I finished up this evening with a hole in the centre of my racket in which the balls would have stuck! My young Bar Tai is still going very well and tends to all my wants including bringing in my false teeth to use one morning when I forgot to put them in! And I believe he would have done so had the King been here!

Sunday June 4th 1922

We have just come in from a very jolly bathing picnic with the Lochs. Colonel Loch and I were the only two bathers bar his small son and then we all ate and ate an enormous tea very much helped by a good old home plummy cake I made this morning. It turned out quite bon. The cook's cakes are always too stolid and rich not to say expensive. They demand about half a pound of butter, four to six eggs, and lots of sugar for quite a small cake. Besides I love meddling round making my own. For anyone at home having to do their own cooking I recommend one of these Perfection Stoves every time and they are most economical. Especially to us as the Corporation provides three tins of kerosene oil per month to every married man, so we have no expense that way. When the tins are empty they are converted into cooking utensils of every description and baking tins. A short time ago the Corporation provided firewood but some silly blighter began having twenty-two loads in a few days. In these days of economy Rangoon office made that an excuse to cut everyone's supply. The Lochs have asked me to go and stay with them when Freddie departs next week. I'd love to but must wait to see when Miss Ritchie is coming to stay with me. She's a grand sort who came out on my boat and has been in Rangoon all the hot weather looking after her sister's

---

[33] A non-toxic wood preservative patented by Jennison Wright Ltd.

kids and said she'd love to see a little more glamour before going home in August, so will keep me company. Aida Barton returns at the end of June and Daisy Pringle visits from Assam in August-September. They are next to come to me so I am well fixed up and shan't be alone at all. Freddie hopes to come to Maymyo in August otherwise he can't leave his district before October. If there was only one other white woman in Sabenago I'd go up there and be hanged to the rains but Freddie couldn't leave me alone while he goes on tour. The rains have brought all the roses on beautifully again and the drawing-room has a mass of lovely big pink blooms. We can get no decent strawberries now though but have had them since before Christmas. Mangoes are nice just now. Dates are particularly nice and come from Mandalay and around about. Mrs. Freeman (B.B.T.C.) brought us a huge basket the other day and Freddie and I have enjoyed our little selves. Yesterday a large bundle of asparagus was given us. I am stuffed so far up to the neck after tucking my large share into me. I do wish you were here to share some of these good things. Last evening we were dining at the Coopers. Mrs. C. has her mother staying with her and though she is not such a dear motherly old thing like you she is very nice. Just as we were off I noticed her going round the drawing-room putting things tidy and collecting ashtrays and I couldn't help remarking how like my mother. Just the sort of thing you'd do! I usually think Freddie is much better and has had no return of fever for some time. He still gets his morning egg-flip and I wish I could carry on with them for him in the Jungle.

What a knut George is becoming I enjoyed reading his speech and lecture in *The Hereford Times* so much. I heard from Ethel the other day, full of good times as usual, nothing about being ill, so I hope she is now quite fit. Sammy is very good and sends his love. Still no letter from Edith but Mary is letting me know how her particular world is treating her. Old Freddie is in the throes of some book but has managed to rouse himself to tell me to be sure and give you his love and to Minnie and Helen. I wish the latter could see how nice her pictures and lampshades look. It would encourage her to do some more. I heard from Stella Middleditch who was laid up in Derby Infirmary after a bad smash up on her motorcycle and sidecar and she feared she would be lame the whole summer. Your Shan bag is being sent by this mail. Lots of love mother dear and I do so hope the warmer weather will give you more peace with the rheumatics. I get none out here.

Glenside, Maymyo Sunday, June 17th 1922

No mail so far from home which I believe is due to the *'Egypt'* sinking. So the mails from Marseilles would come by a later boat. What an awful accident that was. I have heard of no one one knows on board. I am at last sending you some snaps dear. Am sorry there is not one of the outside of the bungalow. Freddie ran out of plates at the last and had not one to spare but will take more when he comes again. Don't you think the interiors are good? I have numbered them as the room comes opposite the door leading from the veranda. The ornaments on the sideboard thing in number two is ivory made from some bits of Freddie's collection of tusks. The smaller etchings are Helen's the bigger ones are what Freddie bought at Harrogate. Below the copper tray are Arthur's plaque and your brass tray and the Buddha given me below that. All the others are taken at Goeteik Bridge. You will be tickled and the silhouette of me in the tunnel. Freddie thought it would give a good effect with me standing there but the arm looks queer and underfed. That is where we had our tea owing to the rain, with trains running by! It is perfectly dreadful without Freddie and I think the partings get worse the more we have to put up with. I drove him down to the station last Monday and he went by the 2-30pm train to Mandalay. I heard from him there and on the boat going up the river. Said it is fearfully hot and he lives in shambambes the whole day long. I do hope Sabenago will be cooler or the amount of Jungle work Freddie has to do I'm so afraid will knock him up. Maymyo seems to be getting really cold at times. We still have heavy rains but only off and on and so far any tennis or golf arranged has not been prevented. Hard courts so quickly dry. I now have chota at 6am and a big breakfast, tiffin sort of meal at 10:30am, an arrangement I like much better as I get a longer day. Most mornings I get out and have a round of golf or a walk from 7-30am and then do the housekeeping after 10-30am. The servants clear off to their quarters about 11-30am. I am free of them until three o'clock. Soon after I have tea and out to tennis or whatever is going on. I always lie down from about 1pm to 2-30pm. One needs it after going out early. I'm awfully keen on golf and want to practise and know more about the game by the time Freddie comes back. Life alone is certainly very much more peaceful with this Butler than the other one. I get awfully fed up with having to always tell them what to do. Once a thing is done or cleaned it is not done again without telling the wretched servant. On Wednesday I had three wenches to breakfast one a Mrs. Macdonnell who went home in my boat from Ceylon. She had no idea Freddie and I were married or had any intention of being so from what she saw and knew the last time we met! Quite right too! Miss Ritchie arrived up from Rangoon last Thursday. She managed the journey with no boy to make a bed except on the train but had the company of a nurse some of the way, who helped her. She is a nice old thing (well I suppose she's well on in the 40s). Nice and respectable! She came out to stay with her married sister in Rangoon and goes home in September. She proposes going up the Irrawaddy to Bhamo after leaving here and will pass Sabenago. How I long to go with her. I'm afraid she will find it very hot. I had a great afternoon making cakes yesterday. My little stove is a great success. It is certainly very much more economical than the cooker for making cakes or buying them. The Bartons arrive on Thursday so Miss Ritchie will have to share my room if she stays on. Plague is very bad in Maymyo just at present so I don't allow my small Bar Tai to go down to the bazaar. We are well out of town so I don't think the servants need be affected. I'm having a bathing picnic this afternoon and have just been packing up the food. Goodbye mother dear my very best love and to all wherever you are just at present.

P.S. I have got my small Cocker Spaniel pup now. He is too sweet for words and inspects all his various puddles all over the bungalow.

Glenside, Maymyo Sunday June 25th 1922

Lordy! How the weeks do buzz by to be sure. Mail day always here and yet I don't mind how often they come now Freddie is away, as the quicker the next few months go the better pleased I am. Yours of May 31st received, also Aunt Minnie's for which please thank her very much. I am sorry she thought my last effort to her was on the saucy side!! Tell her it shan't occur again. I'm sure she will be disappointed. As Aunt Minnie gives so much she surely must expect some in return! I am so sorry your rheumatism seems no better. It always distresses me so when I hear of all you suffer and no cure seems to do any good. I suppose such things have to be and so long as you don't actually suffer pain when sitting we must be thankful for that. But I know how you feel having to be dependent on others. But you're always so merry and bright and comfy to get on with that you must never fear people mind doing things for you. You will always be young and frisky in your mind which is a great thing. Aunt Minnie's garden sounds so pretty with a glorious view as they have you couldn't wish for a nicer spot to sit than in the corner I know so well. What a gay old bird gambling on the Derby! I wish you had. A wretched Indian wormed his way into the veranda one morning when Freddie was here and insisted in telling us our fortunes. He told me I was to receive a large sum of money about June the 21st. I find since the blighter told nearly everyone the same thing knowing the Derby race to be coming off about them. How I wish a large sum of money would come our way. It would make a lot of difference to many things I'd like to do, but with the happiness I have got I can't expect much else! Tell Helen if she wants to add to her earnings for London visit to paint me four candle shades and I shall send her the where-with-all. By the way Freddie is writing to his Ealing Bank to send two pounds to Rosslyn for the papers and postage. Dear I do wish I could send you more but we both have to go so slow at present with a double establishment to keep up. We live above our pay but of course a certain amount is kept back for the Provident fund. A good thing too or I am sure we should have naught for our old age. Next year promises much better times when we go to Mawlaik.

Plague is very bad in Maymyo and I've had a lot of trouble insisting on all the servants being inoculated. They almost die of sheer fright before they go near a hospital but yesterday the last batch went and today my small Bar Tai is feeling very sorry for himself. At the worst they only have low fever with a headache and I let them off for a day after, so there is no excuse. Many of the shops in the Bazaar are now closed and the occupants have fled to the Jungle. A Mrs. Moran was in a small shop here which they found later to have plague and on taking off her stockings discovered a flea, which is the thing that carries infection, so she had to be inoculated at once. I suppose she is all right now I've seen her out playing golf. Our bungalow still has fleas from dogs but they are quite a pure sort. Miss Ritchie departs today. Se has found a kindred spirit in a Miss Craw who was at the same school in Edinburgh. These two went off to Goeteik Bridge for one night and are now off to Bhamo, motoring to Mandalay, then up by camp boat past Sabenago where Freddie will cross the river to see them. Gosh, the irony of the whole thing, why shouldn't I be with them? If it weren't for Aida Barton being here I'd feel most tempted to go up and catch Freddie on the hop. However I must be patient and with a huge bit of luck he will be up here in August. Mr. Barton brought his wife up here on Thursday and had to dash away today but will probably be up again before the event comes off early in August. So with Miss Ritchie here I have had a house full. Miss Ritchie is rather a fuss bag and dashes about all over the place when arrangements are being made or carried out. Freddie writes that it is cooler now in Sabenago. I feel I could so easily have gone with him to spend this month but perhaps it is better not. These separations make me boil sometimes. I have been playing quite a lot of golf in the early hours lately and was at tennis at Government House last Thursday and again for dinner the following day. Both shows were not so bad as I expected. A Colonel Bateman cut my little pup's tail one day last week. Quite a nobby little stump left. 'Pal' is such a dear but the mats etc., have suffered during his infancy. I am off to tennis at Candacraig this evening. I often go for lonesome walks with the other dog 'Twinker'. The Jungle all round is full of rides and walks and delightful walking now as it is much cooler. Flowers still thrive and you bet my rooms are full up with them. Well dear my two visitors are just about to depart so will wind up. Goodbye Mother darling. I do so wish you were more get-at-able so that you could come and stay with me. I am sure you'd love my little home. Best love to Aunt Minnie and Helen.

Glenside, Maymyo, Sunday July 2nd 1922

I have just come in from having breakfast (10-30am) at a Mrs. Union's and feel very stodgy and sleepy. I must get a start on my letter as it must be posted this evening. I went to the Kirk this morning so the morning has been chopped up. Aida Barton and I are both sitting in the veranda, a lovely cool breeze and peace all round. At midday everyone and everything seems to sleep in this country. I do hope it does not rain as I have some very good tennis up at Candacraig. Miss Ritchie departed last Sunday on her trip with Miss Craw up the Irrawaddy to Bhamo. I heard from Freddie yesterday to say he had gone across to the boat at Male. When he saw two skirted ladies his heart nearly jumped as for a wild moment he thought I had come up for a surprise visit. I am quite sure I would have done so were it not for the

Bartons being here. Freddie says it is much cooler. Mr. Hill, his hero assistant in the place of Hunt, had arrived and was a very different fellow to his predecessor. I am so glad they get on well as Freddie was so awfully lonely and Hill will be more of a companion to him. Freddie says it will be quite impossible for him to leave his Jungle work for a short trip up here in August as we had hoped for and that the only hope of seeing one another again before November was for me to go up for a couple of weeks at the end of August, which I shall certainly do, and have written to put Miss Pringle off. I am trying to arrange for the Bartons to come and take over here while I am away and think they would like to, as Aida will have had her infant by then. I don't think we shall have to put up with these long separations next year. I find it bad enough but poor Freddie can't console himself in any way. He finds the time out of office so irksome and is too restless to settle to anything. Thank goodness I have plenty of hobbies and find too much, if anything, to fill up my days, and I must say I get a lot in. Including a good time after my heart's desire for I get all the golf, tennis, and driving I could wish for and a very charming little guest to come home to and give an account of all my doings. It is dreadful to come to an empty house so the dog and his pup are always eagerly awaiting my return and give me a good welcome, chiefly I think on account of the jaggery (sort of sugar toddy made into balls to give the pony). I give them one every time I come in from a drive. We've decided on the name for the pup and suggest *'Spiker'* as a delicate compliment to his mother 'Spy' and father *'Twinker'*. Last Tuesday I had a lovely all day picnic with a Mrs. Twiss, her husband is in the regiment here. I drove up to her bungalow about 8-30am and then with a Mali to carry fodder set out to climb One Tree Hill, so-called for its prominence among the surrounding hills, with a flat top and one high tree standing clear of all others. We followed the path through dense Jungle at the side of a small creek overflowing from the reservoir which we reached after about an hour's walk. We had lunch by the creek and then I slept for a solid hour, moved on a little for tea and then walked home. There is a Mrs. Nugent James who lives quite near me and is mad on Bridge. She asked me in for pot luck and she had a ladies four after dinner which I enjoyed. Next day 11 o'clock she asked if I would come in for a game. At that hour if you please! However I think I made it clear I never seem to have the time for that so I suppose I shall be left in peace. Thursday I had a bathing picnic including three kids. They were so sweet and didn't mind the cold water a bit. Golf and tennis and one dinner filled up my programme last week. Dances are still on at the club but they are not worth going to without Freddie. No, the only thing I left at Nunnington was a packing case with a few odds and ends I really don't want. I shall not mind if they are included in a jumble sale batch. How sad it is to think I shall never stay in that dear old place again. I wonder if Aunt Mary means to stay on at the grey house?

As you mention that you have stopped the other papers when you cancelled my weekly Daily Mail I do hope you are still having yours? Freddie is sending you a cheque to cover the costs that there have been, so how much do I owe you altogether? I'm so sorry uncle Fred[34] does not seem fit. Perhaps he worries still about Dottie. Poor little Dick. I do hope the kid will go to strangers. How lucky of Miss Harker to win money in a sweepstake. A B.B.T.C. man Mr. Beamish won 110,000 rupees. That I should say will hasten his retirement. Hope so anyway as he is a manager and one less means of leg up for those of less service. Freddie takes over from Mr. Beamish at Mawlaik next year. I do hope my mail arrived. I believe on looking back I addressed one to Tupsley by mistake. Several people I know lost parcels in the 'Egypt'. The silk knitted jumper Brooksbank made and sent ages ago has not yet turned up but it can't have been on the 'Egypt' as all those who have lost anything have had an official note. I have had another winding up of my servants! You will think I get no

---

[34] The Rev. Frederick Mellor, Vicar of Dilwyn.

peace but this time t is more my fault. I came to the conclusion we had much too big a staff for so small a houehold. Freddie has to have extra men for himself in the Jungle so I have sacked the Durwan, a man who is supposed to guard the house and do messages. He sleeps in the house and fairly snores the roof off. So he won't be missed there and he and the Mali can take chits. I shall make young Bar Tai sleep in if I want anything. Then our old cook was getting much more than he was worth, so after interviewing several fresh ones he agreed to remain on at the wage I want to give. He does us very well really and it is a help to have one who speaks English. The weather is lovely at home. I always bask in all *The Tatler* and *Bystander* have to say and shall know all about the Prince's return soon. Lady Craddock the other day said she supposed it would be even a grander affair then Princess Mary's wedding. Well dear I must away and have a short shut eye. Very best love and to all who might read this rather dull epistle.

Glenside Maymyo Sunday July 9th 1922

Many thanks dear for yours of June 13th. That was the day after Freddie departed back into the Jungle and I was feeling very sore, and now only four weeks gone in what seems years, and still more so with the number of weeks that have to pass somehow before I see him again.

Still no rain in Sabenago. Freddie is stuck and unable to go on tour. There is nothing doing until the creeks fill up. He is still alone. Hill, his new assistant, arrived with dreadful prickly heat looking an awful sight so Freddie sent him down to Mandalay to see a doctor. I am so sorry one letter arrived late. I can't think how the mail was missed this end as I keep a record of all the letters I write and yours went off alright on Saturday, May 13th. I hope it won't occur again for if your disappointment at receiving no mail is anything like mine I'm sorry for you! You sound very happy and cosy with Aunt Min and I am so glad you are able to stay on with her. You never mention the Johnson girl. Is she still in Malvern and as great a pal of Helen's as ever? I heard from Auntie Bea this mail. They also are struggling along with two very young inexperienced maids. I have not heard from Ceylon for ages. Dolly apparently is remaining on until next spring I wonder what they will do without Liz at the vicarage. I must send her a wedding present. Don't forget to write to little Dorothy for her birthday August 7th. I happened to have a ten shilling note, so sent that, as sending parcels is always an uncertain job these days. I can scarcely believe it is a year since you and I were at the cottage. Another two years to go and we will all be together somewhere else. Freddie and I often talk over plans for when we go home but like everyone else we don't know where to settle. I'd love to be near the sea and yet that means it is so far away from all our friends and relations in Herefordshire and I do so look forward to seeing them again. It does distress me to hear of your rheumatism still being so bad but I suppose we must be thankful you have no pain while sitting. This weather, I get it in my hands but nothing very bad. Yes I'd love some snaps when Eddie takes some. I hope to send you some more soon, ones we took in the Jungle ages ago. Last week the weather has been so heavy with thunder hanging around. It makes me feel so slack but today it is quite fresh with the breeze and often drizzly rain, typically monsoon, but as I have said before, rains do not affect Maymyo very much. The flowers are glorious: roses, carnations, dahlias, sunflowers, in fact any sort of English flower one can think of. We do not spend much money on our garden as we shall be here so short a time. The Corporation has just finished building two beautiful houses at the back of this one for managers, all furnished with teak panelling with large gardens and tennis courts. Cost anything between 3000 and 4000 rupees. They do the rich very well in the house line. We seem to be the only ones who have furniture thrown in. I don't altogether hanker after one of these large houses when 'Freddie gets to be a full manager. They cost the devil to keep up and with a large place one is supposed to entertain accordingly. When we return we want to bring home furniture made of teak in our own Mills in Rangoon and fitted together in England. It is topping wood and lasts forever. Last Thursday I dined out and had a cheery evening at the Dunks who live near here, a party of eight, and we all played Bridge afterwards. Apropos of Armstrong's case being in Herefordshire: I discovered a Mrs. Grant who was there to have come from that part and played in the county team at the same time as Daisy and Ivy Carver and Joyce Howden. She was there and I remembered her directly she mentioned her name. She is a very good sort and we are playing golf together this week. I had a hen dinner party here on Friday; just four to play Bridge afterwards. In the middle of the dinner I noticed crowds of little black specks floating on the table and then the drawing-room lamp was discovered to be flaring inside! The cretonne etc., seems none the worse and I hope none of the hens went home with smutty seats to their dresses! Since threatening to sack the old cook he has pulled up his socks and really turns out quite good meals. He is remaining on at a lower wage. Freddie says his new Jungle cook, who has hitherto only cooked for Burmans, turns out the most weird concoctions. Freddie is very naughty when alone and doesn't care a wrap for food and I am always so afraid he will get run down from not having enough nourishing stuff. Mrs. Grant has just left after a surprise visit on horseback. She sat and talked as we had breakfast and we discussed old hockey days. Aida and I were up at the Lochs yesterday for tea and then I played cricket (and the fool) with their small boy and the family afterwards. It is extraordinary what we can do in spite of being thirty!! Today is a solemn tea fight at Mrs. Williams. She and her husband Colonel Williams were on my boat going home from Ceylon. I had several games of golf last week including two foursomes. At this time of year the dreadful spear grass sheds itself as one walks through it and sticks on and through stockings and skirts. It is dreadful and every tiny bit of it has to be picked out. The oil stove is still a great success and I often have great baking of sweets and cakes. Government House has departed down to Rangoon but will be up in August for the last time. The present Lieutenant Governor retires in the spring and after that there will be a Governor General and Ministers as the Burman is now to be blessed with a vote. Every one seems to think life won't be so pleasant in this country in consequence, and those about to retire are thankful their years in the East are coming to an end. Many who have been out here for years, or have returned after a lapse, notice the differences in the manners of the natives; more independent and thoroughly spoilt. My *'dawgs'* are flourishing. The pup occupies a lot of my time in its training, to say nothing of the flea hunts and brushings every day. It would grieve Freddie to the quick were he to see the state of my drawing-room carpets but when the pup is older the carpets can be washed and all will be well. Well dearest must write other letters now and I think this is about all the news I have. Life now is a round of home duties with a large mixture of games etc., all of which would be very much nicer were Freddie here. It is a waste of his life being tucked away from civilisation like this. Lots and lots of love mother dear.

Maymyo Sunday July 16th 1922

Your nice one long letter of June 20th received on Wednesday, also the photograph which is very good. Jolly well taken too. But you are naughty to leave your sticks aside!! I know you can't do without them, poor dear, and they are now a very good friend to you. But it distressed me somehow to see them! Am glad Aunt Min' was not successful in hiding her very shapely leg behind your chair. She has a skittish skirt on and no mistake. The garden looks so pretty and I can often picture you sitting up in the little corner with a lovely view over Worcester etc. Yes and I'm sure Jan will buck you all up. His cheery laugh is as good as any cockerels. You don't say how his ship raising stunt is getting on. Helen could get no end of orders for her lamp shades if she wanted them. A Mrs. Dunk out here admired mine so much she wrote from home asking if I thought Helen would do her some, so I'm sending Helen's address. Yes, do keep Helen up to the mark about my candle shades — the only ones I have are what Vi MacAdam gave me as a wedding present. They are getting very shabby. I use them every night with your candlesticks and the table always looks so pretty with a black bowl and the Doulton Kingfisher I had from Aunt Mary standing in the middle of roses floating. I shall be most interested to hear all Daisy Yates' news. Freddie and I often wonder whether our hopes will materialise and we will go to Champery one-day. I enjoyed reading Edith's letter so much. I get so little news of her. She does have rotten luck poor thing but, as of old, I am quite sure she squeezes very much more out of life than the majority of people. I do wish she would not shut me out just because her luck is low. I have written but have received nothing since I left home. I'm sure my sisters were luckier than I in their days in the East as far as receiving letters go. While Freddie is away so much I long for mail days and of course enjoy letters when he is here too, but in these endless weeks of being without him I would give anything to have my own people near. The Mrs. Jackson I told you about from Shewbo is staying up here now and I asked her about Nora but does not know her so I was on to a wrong track. Mrs. Jackson wants me to go and stay with her so I shall probably unearth the friend sometime. Mrs. Jackson lives up the Irrawaddy and if I get a chance of going up to see Freddie before the cold weather I may stay with her on my way back here. All next year's plans are altered as we go to Monywa instead of Mawlaik. Only heard of this alteration yesterday and don't know Freddie's verdict on it. Monywa I believe is quite a nice spot on the Chindwin river which runs into the Irrawaddy below Mandalay. We are not so tucked away as at Mawlaik and Maymyo is very easily reached if I have to come up here for the hot weather. If Monywa is not so hot I shan't leave unless I can't stick it. One thing is we shall only have one establishment to keep up and unless Freddie is touring he will always be with me and the expense of living is about half compared to Maymyo. I do hope he will be pleased, the poor dear gets terribly depressed about his work and prospects at times but I'm sure it is only caused by so much Jungle work, which makes him feel squeezed dry of all energy. This last week it has rained most days and quite cold and then lovely. I've just had to get a jersey as I felt quite goosey fleshy sitting here in the veranda writing. Both Aida and I are now hard at our English mail. We are nibbling at biscuits and I have lapped up my egg flip which I have every morning. Though I feel fit I am getting so thin! According to the weighing machine at Government House the other day I have lost a stone since I came out. I shall go to the other extreme one of these days I expect!! Not like Paula Dolly who was so terrified of becoming too fat and even I feel more satisfied with my legs and ankles these days. Last Monday I had to go out to a bun struggle at Mrs. Lees and play Bridge afterwards. Had fearful bad luck the whole time and did not win a game let alone play one. However I enjoyed all the good things to eat — no sooner finished tea and coffee and cakes came along and sweets and chocs the whole time! Have been doing a bit of a dull duty this last week by having various people to tea and on Wednesday I was at the Loch's for dinner again and a very cheery evening at General and Lady Fane's on Friday. General Fane is a rum old stick and behaves like a kid. After a fat dinner I sat next to the General. We played silly games including 'Dumb Grambo'and another girl and I were on the side of the General and two other men. Our one word was catastrophe — we did some wonderful caterwauling, the General and I spitting and fighting one another like two good old toms and then for ass I rode on the General's back as though I was having a donkey ride at the seaside. We had no sooner crawled up the room and the General leaned up and sent me sprawling off with my legs high in the air. It was most respectably done and an explanation had to be given that was not part of the show. And then we did 'de trop' when he and I sat out and pretended to be annoyed at another couple coming along and then 'fee' when we paid out money at a cinema entrance. I love silly games for a change and it was after 2am when we got away. I seem to play golf mostly now, the weather being so dull and uncertain, tennis is not so appetising. The doctor came to see Aida yesterday and gave a very good verdict since there is no need for alarm until about August 10th I don't know if Mr. Barton means to come up from Pakokku. It is very difficult to leave the Jungle work at this time. I'm enclosing a cheque for two pounds for the papers. You must tell me if it is more. In any case I hope to send along another little dollop before long. I'm so interested in the correspondence in The Hereford Times about the bishop going to preach in a nonconformist church. Mr. Hanin has stirred up a regular locust's nest and has made quite an ass of himself. I think the bishop is right every time and long may he carry on with his good work! The puppy is gradually being trained. I have made him a collar. He is very annoyed at being tied up in the veranda with '*Twinker*.' Father and son are the best of pals now. I have a bathing picnic with the Lochs this afternoon if only it will keep dry. Well dear *'I opes as 'ow this will find you as well as it leaves me at present - in the pink!'* I must get ready to go out to breakfast to Miss Craw's who lives quite near here. Very best love Mother dear.

Maymyo Sunday July 23rd 1922

I see by your letter of June 27th received yesterday you had not received my mail. I was told that the home mail boat had broken down and would be late, so I hope mine turned up eventually. Yours this week was late but all the more welcome with Ethel's letter enclosed. What a busy life she has with her family. Though I can't boast of that, my days fly past and I never get half the sewing done that I plan and want to do. I was interested to hear about Dora Whatney's wedding. I suppose she is done for by now. I wrote her ages ago but received no reply. I do hope Tiny will get over to see you sometime in her car. I wrote her giving your address hoping she would. She would so love to see Aunt Min as well. I have not got your old recipe book out here. It is either in my bureau or in the chest at Rosslyn. Fancy Jeff wanting it. I remember writing up that book for you years and years ago. How very good of Stookey to send you a fiver but I expect all thanks are due to our Mary! You don't know how I long to do the same, mother dear, but until we can live within our income we have to go so slow. Next year things will be much better as Monywa is about half the expense of Maymyo and there is always our fare and expense at home to be remembered for 1924. I am longing for this year to be gone so that I can say next year we go home. However happy, or however much one enjoys oneself in one place, if it is not one's own country it is somehow not the same. With Freddie away so much I don't feel as though I have started on home life yet. When he is here everything is such a hectic rush with a nasty feeling in the back of one's mind knowing we shall be separated again before long. Freddie gets awfully fed up with the Jungle life now but as it means our bread-and-butter we must swallow all the nasty with the nice and after all to have a job nowadays is the chief thing. So many men I know out here have had the chuck from the army under the new cuts and go home with no prospects. They say it will be the same with government officials under the new government next year when many of the heads will be Burmans and the white men gradually ousted. What a lot of interesting 'tits' Daisy Yates told you. You did not say if she mentioned Daisy's grave. I wonder if it is cared for at all now. Why can't you have a fortune left you? I'm sure you deserve it just as much as old ma Harvey. I am doing exactly the same as this time last week, writing you on the veranda and Aida stitching away in the corner. (Sounds as though I put her there for being naughty.) She is now busy making up the basket for the baby's extras, lining it with silk and muslin. Last night I got an awful scare and really thought 'Bill Jim' was about to make an appearance into the world! I heard Aida calling. I shot out of my bed to find the poor girl having an awful time in her room with a rat which clambered up the table by her bed. What use our Mali would be if we had a burglar, because we went into where he sleeps to fetch a candle and he did not stir! However there is the safe feeling of having someone in the house in case anything is wanted. Later: We have just come home from a bathing picnic. I provided tea and spent most of the morning making cake. One a plain sponge the old cook did so nicely and was in honour of a small boy of one and I had a red candle burning on top, much to the delight of all the others. We were ten grownups and eight children so it was some scrum. The tea disappeared very quickly and I have brought home only two buns! It has been topping and a good day for bathing. We have whole days of lovely sunshine sometimes when one makes the most of airing one's clothes. Things so quickly get mildew and pillows and bedding get to smell frowsty, so a sunny day is welcomed. As usual my week has been filled with tennis and golf and on Wednesday evening three ladies came to dinner and we played Bridge afterwards. I can't tackle the men folk while Freddie is away, besides they're too expensive with their drinks, and another thing men are really quite few and far between now as most are off at their various works in low country. I like Maymyo and the people here more and more, and being able to play games I have a very cheery time. One has to take a notebook around with one to jot down engagements. It is quite impossible to remember what is fixed on different days and often make awful muddles and get thoroughly tied up. All this week I have something on each day. I have given up playing golf in the early morning as I don't want to do too much. Besides house jobs take up quite a time. I'm busy altering my grey going away dress which will be useful when the cold weather comes. Last time I tinkered with that dress I was in our little patch of garden at the cottage. Do you remember? You were reading to me and a Mrs. Leake came to tea much to our annoyance! I still live in hopes of going up to Freddie at the end of August as there is no chance of him coming here unless his health gives way which is the last thing we want. Last letter he was very fed up! On looking into things at Weboung he finds his late assistant (Eurasian) has made a fearful muddle with his accounts and can't account for no end of rice. I forget if I asked you whether Aunt Min knows of any people by the name of Partridge in or around Ledbury and whether a Mr. Partridge was ever out in Burma. I must have my tub and will finish anon. I feel very much better thank you. To dabble in the bath is certainly very nice and pouring water over one with a bowl. The ménage is so peaceful now and my small boy is quite happy having his food with other Burmans in a compound quite near. Up to now cook who is a Madrassi did for him. There were always complaints about the curry which was either too hot or not hot enough. I have put Miss Pringle off until September owing to the possibility of my going up to Freddie so when Aida goes to the home early in August I shall be alone. I don't think I shall mind with 'Twinker' sleeping in my bathroom. I always get plenty of warning when anyone is near. Our road is very quiet with the General and his household away. There are plenty of cars buzzing by when he is at home. Next mail will be the one for your birthday I think. I am sending you an ivory plaque to wear dangling over your 'buzwum' threaded on a piece of black moiré ribbon. I do hope you will like it. Postage is so expensive so it is no use getting anything large to send home and one can't nose in the bazaar for things these days owing to the plague which is still virulent. And now my dear I must write to Aunt Mary. I was so pleased to get a letter from her last mail.

Glenside, Maymyo, Saturday August 5th 1922

A whole chapter of accidents to do with the last mail letter from me. Dear, I am so sorry that I was busy writing at my usual time last Sunday afternoon when Mrs. Juxon Jones arrived to say the mail had left that morning. A breach on the line between Mandalay and Rangoon and mails had to go a day earlier to catch the boat. I was so fed up because it was your birthday letter. So I tried all this week to send your little present and sent a man down to the post office to register it this morning and blowed if it is not the Mahomakidaus (feast day) and the post office shut up. The English mail goes out tomorrow (Sunday) when again it is impossible to send parcels, so my letter of July 30th won't arrive until a week after this one. You would know I was alright anyway as I addressed a letter to Mary care of you and which was posted earlier in the week. The same reason applies to the lateness of your letter of July 11th enclosing one from Aunt Mary for which many thanks. It is so sad to think of poor Dotty sending back her presents. I do wish she would follow in my footsteps and make a very nice man's life nicer! It is nice having a man to commit to until the end of one's days. The Ceylonites ought to be shaken up in a bag to see if letter writing would come easier to them. I'm afraid I have not had the pleasure of meeting Mr. Booth tell Helen. Any relation to our friend in the Salvation Army? No Hunt's people come from Shrewsbury. His father is of independent means and has a very nice place outside the town. After telling you of my hopes of going up to Sabenago next week, for about three weeks between Freddie's tours, all my hopes have been dashed to the ground since receiving Freddie's letter last evening. Gosh! This is a ....life, as far as wanting to be with Freddie goes! Everything was arranged and then Mr. Agar (temporary Forest manager in Freddie's forest) looked Freddie up on one of his tours and Freddie happened to remark I was going up to him next week. Agar immediately asked if Freddie had received Rangoon's official permission. Did you ever hear of such rot in all your life? Of course we know they are against wives being at Jungle HQ during the rains. That is the busiest time of year and men are supposed to be on tour but in our case Freddie was only to be in HQ a short time to do monthly accounts. However, the subject was well discussed. Freddie's conclusion was that we had better not risk any unpleasantness so here I am, stuck. Oh damn! There is just a glimmer of hope that Freddie will come up here for a few days during this month. Nice as that will be it won't be nearly so nice as my going up to Sabenago. Here there are always a certain number of duty calls. Freddie and I can't abide going out to dinner when we have so short a time together. Of course a breather in a cool spot will do Freddie a bit of good, and yet it does not always suit their innards coming from a hot steamy climate to one very much cooler, as it is here. Although the room was booked for Aida to go into the home today I persuaded her to remain on here. There seems to be no need for alarm yet and she may as well remain out of hospital environment as long as possible. I know what nurse conversation is like; shop all the time and being the only one in that home she would probably feed with the staff. Everything is in readiness including a nice basket of odds and bobs which I helped to make. In fact I am full of knowledge and titbits for when my turn comes along!! I am thankful to have Aida, as a house to myself would be such a waste. I have not done an awful lot this last week as the weather has been so unsettled. Fearful storms and then brilliant hot sun so one never knows where one is and as I am not yet quite free of rheumatism I am not keen to get a soaking. I often drive down to the bazaar before breakfast at 10-30am but don't go into the native shops now as the plague is still bad. Thursday I had a very nice day to say nothing of it being exceedingly amusing and strenuous. A Mrs. Twiss and three officers out of the Staffordshire Regiment, who Mrs.Twiss has known for years, all went off for a day picnic to Ani Sekan, the first station down the Mandalay line. Mr. Vale, who is supposed to know the way to the falls there, was put on to act as guide. Very soon after leaving the station at 10am we started along a Jungle path and after about half an hour's walk and much nagging at our guide he had to admit it was the wrong path. So we had trudged up the steep sticky path, over creeks and almost over a dead cow on the side and back to our original starting point. Captain Turner was all for sitting down to eat. (I don't wonder as his load consisted of six bottles of beer and two of ginger beer to say nothing of fodder). However, we voted on tripping on to reach the falls. Mr. Vale was sent out to scout on his own to return in about half an hour very hot and cross and puzzled. So we then tried another path and trudged on and on. Mr. Vale in the meantime had shot off on his own, certain of the way but by this time we had lost all faith in him. We coo-eed and called but no answer, so we put him down as food for a bear or something and went on. About half an hour later who should be coming towards us but Mr. Vale. How he came there is still a mystery and so on we went on our Jungle path, knowing all the time it to be the wrong one. At last our tummies failed us and we sat in a very muddy spot and felt decidedly better after a very fat lunch. A Burman having come along we managed to make out we were heading for Mandalay and were only about six miles from the falls! So up we had to trudge again, the invincible Mr. Vale giving us no peace for a snooze after the feed. Within the next hour, to our great joy the spot was found and well worth even losing ourselves for. From which one could see for miles and miles with the Jungle on either side widening out to the view of the plains in the distance. After a rest we went down a very steep zig zag path to the falls which dropped from a height of over 1000 feet. It was lovely. While the others bathed in the deep pools at the bottom. I lit a fire and had tea by the time the other four were ready. While waiting for the 5-30 train we stuffed away six pineapples eating with our fingers and making a nasty mess generally. It will be a long day before Mr. Vale hears the end of our outing! Well dear I must now start my letter to Freddie before going out to tennis this afternoon. Lots of love and to Aunt Min and Helen.

Maymyo Saturday August 12th 1922

Mails are normal now as the line between Mandalay and Rangoon is connected up so yours of July 4th arrived last Wednesday, August 9th, quicker than usual. I was so thankful to have home letters at that particular time as it was my first meal alone and the mail arrived in the middle of my solitary dinner. Aida went along to the home that afternoon but is still going strong and I take her either for a walk or a drive every day. The home is very nice, and it takes two patients. Branches were started by Lady Minto in the chief places of Burma and staffed by private nurses. The snap of you all sitting in the garden is very good. Helen's swanky check shirt takes my eye. Ma Johnson seems to look well upholstered! I love snaps and I'm glad you liked mine. When Freddie comes in this time I will get him to take more. I am sad that enterprising sort of people have taken Nunnington. I shall be interested to see it some day with all its alterations but I shall hate to see strangers in such a dear old home as it has been to me. I will try and find out about Booth. I expect he is in Rangoon. It would certainly be a hopeless thing for the girl to attempt working out here unless as a governess and there are very few of these because the children all go home quite young. Whoever this girl is she is very silly to risk coming out here to an uncertain young man. You will certainly find crutches with springs very much more comfortable. I remember the men at hospital always said so. Oh dear, it does seem so sad that you have to take to them but so long as they help that will be the great thing, but you must not be too venturesome and come a cropper. I expect I shall reach your stage of rheumatism a long time before your age. I get it very badly in my knees and right hand, which I can scarcely move first thing in the morning. Why did our ancestors drink so much port etc? Yes, I'm sure I received your birthday letter for you have missed no mail which is a splendid record and very much appreciated. I'm afraid I am rather amiss in acknowledging them at times. Well this time next week I shall not be writing in bed as I am now. I'm not ill only a bit achy in my old body so came to bed early to write and am quite cosy under the mosquito net with the pup snoring happily in his box and 'Twinker' keeping guard under by bathroom table leading off my bedroom. The Mali (gardener) sleeps in the dining room, and am thankful he does not snore like the late Durwan. I don't know what use the man would be if I was attacked because he sleeps so soundly and never stirs, in spite of all my shouting, when I come in late and want him to lock up. However he probably acts as a preventive by the fact a man sleeps in the house. Anyway, as I was saying, this time next week my poor dear husband will be here to protect and keep me in order, bless him. It will be topping to see him again after more than two months! Really we always seem to be just beginning to know one another and off he goes. It is such a dangerous thing to do because it seems to get nicer each time and the parting a worse wrench. However, even the Corporation can't prevent us living our old age together. I'm afraid Freddie won't be at all fit when he comes and is part of the reason for him leaving the Jungle. Fever seems to get him so easily now and affects his tummy. I hope a couple of weeks of feeding up will improve matters. I warned him that I shall take no refusals of my egg-flips and milk puddings and such like dull but nourishing things. At least the latter is. I take egg-flip myself every day to try and get fat. It always reminds me of Ceylon when Ethel used to make me one each day after I had fever. We are still having a good deal of rain, chiefly fine drizzles, but which manages to clear off by evening and each day this week I have played either tennis or golf. Last Sunday Aida and I went to tea at the Rories. He is the head of the Forest department. They took us for a run in the car afterwards and then finished up by going to church. The old girl nearly deafened me with her singing. Quite a small congregation and she fairly bellowed forth to make up for the missing members. On Monday and Tuesday I dined out as usual and had very cheery evenings in spite of my preliminary grousing at having to turn out in the evening at the Stomboes on Monday. We were twelve and played 'vingt et un' and other card games. At the former I won a box of chocolates.

Tuesday night I was at the Roberts. He is 'Burra Sahib' in the Corporation up here. He is such a dear and so jolly with plenty of back-chat so we get on well together. Mrs. Dunk, also Bombay Burma, was the only other so we were just a bridge four. I actually won that night for I generally have very bad cards. Wednesday I played tennis at the regimental lines. Aida left for the home that afternoon. She really could have remained here but felt fidgety in case anything happened in the night and perhaps it is just as well. I miss her awfully. Thursday I was called for in the car by a Mr. Phillips to play tennis at his place, and he arrived when I was still sound asleep in bed. It is very seldom I sleep in the afternoon but I was caught fair and square that afternoon. However, it did not take me long to dress and found him quite happy nosing around our drawing-room when I finally appeared. Last two days I have played golf. One books up for days ahead and it is really necessary to carry a little book around with one as it is so difficult to remember what one is up to about a week in front. Well dear, I don't think there is any more to yap about. It seems extraordinary to think of the thousands of miles this effort is to travel before you read it. Bless you dear and keep your dear old self fit. Lots of love.

Mully in a sampan on the Irrawaddy

Mully in 'The Tum Tum' with 'Spiker' and the Syce

'Glenside' Maymyo

The Diningroom at 'Glenside'

The livingroom at 'Glenside'

The Mantlepiece at 'Glenside'

The Club at Maymo

'Candacraig'

Under canvas in the Jungle

Mully sewing in the shade

Hunt's quarters on tour

Mully standing outside a 'Tay'

Making friends

Inspection: 'Say Ah!'

Off to work

At work

Hard work

Sheer strength

Crossing the river

Back to dry land

Elephants enjoy bathing

The elephants disappeared under the water making it look as though the Oosies were standing on it

Going on tour

A mighty teak trunk

Freddie and friend

Touring in Burma 1923 style

Roads were often difficult

A good map was important

The means of transport was sometimes primitive

In some districts timber had to be moved by rail

Logs had to wait until the rivers rose to float them down to Rangoon

A paddle steamer on the Irrawaddy

A passenger ferry

Possibly the 'Chinwarra' on which Mully travelled up the Chindwin

Logs and a sailing barge

The leg rowers

In some places tractors were used instead of elephants

Staff transport

The staff

Palm bungalow

Moving teak by rail

A ride on a bullock cart

Burmese celebrations

Bath night

Mully, Alice and Rodney

Glenside, Maymyo Saturday August 19th 1922

Great news this week! I have actually a husband with me. Such a change, but what a topping thing. It is just lovely to have Freddie again after two months of being separated. I drove down to meet him on Thursday presumably to arrive at 5-30pm. The Lieutenant Governor and his Suite arrived by special train that afternoon, which made Freddie's train nearly an hour late. However, there were others meeting their spouses and so I went for a short drive with one of them. Freddie looked much better than I thought he would but went down with a mild go of fever last night. It is miserable how it attacks and leaves him feeling so low and rotten. He is better again this morning and is now down at the office. I'm afraid Freddie will not be here much more than a week which will scarcely do him any good. However, we are making the most of our short time together. It will be quiet as I never feel much inclined to go out when we see so little of one another. Next excitement is that Aida had her baby yesterday afternoon at 3-30pm, a little girl, so her wishes for 'Bill Jim' have not matured this time but am quite sure she will have many before many years have rolled by. She is made to have babies and is awfully fit and strong and the nurse said she has never known anyone to have such an easy time. I saw Aida on Thursday evening as fit as can be and had a chit from her the following morning about 8-50am. At noon I was at the home and the nurse said she did not think things would be long, and she was right. I have not seen Aida yet but hope to tomorrow. Her husband has been wired for and will come dashing up at once. He was very keen for us to put him up but seeing so little of Freddie we want our little house to ourselves. I'm afraid we always shall be rather unsociable out East. Everything would be so different if we could have our own people to stay. Mr. Barton writes that he will be touring all September and part of October and asked me to take Aida again with the addition to the Barton family. It would be a tight squash here but so long as Aida doesn't mind all is well. I don't know what they would have done without Glenside to come to and of course their arrangements and ours have fitted in so well. I must put Miss Pringle off, which is rather a blow, but the Ma and child must have the first claim. Freddie brought your letter of July 25th from the office, for which very many thanks dear, also the enclosures. Aunt Helen's letters always are so interesting. She doesn't seem to think Ethel and Dorothea's wear and tear on poor old Sammy is very good for him. I know when I was there he was simply splendid in going out and I'm sure he much preferred to stay at home. Edith is naughty to have bobbed her hair. She had so much that there was no real need. I must say I often long to do likewise to mine which comes out a good deal. I shall soon only have a bowl the size of real one! However there is a husband in the case here and he won't hear of my bobbing my few remaining whiskers. I wrote to Edith on July 3rd to ask her to do a little shopping for me but have heard naught in return so I suppose she can't do it. You never mention Miss Parker these days. Is she still at Rosslyn? I wonder if she would like lace or embroideries sent her. People often get boxes sent up from a convent in India and pass them round here. Aida got no end of things, and so cheap. I would love to send a whole lot home but just at present Freddie and I have to go very slowly. The move down to Monywa next year will squeeze us. Then the passage money in 1924 has to be considered. Poor Jack! It does seem rotten luck being left out in South Africa to struggle along alone. I know I wouldn't leave Freddie; for nothing short of illness anyway. Am afraid Nora will be disappointed at the prospects of a job in England. A secretarial job in South Africa would have been better but I suppose the kiddie would prevent that. Your little titbit at the end of your letter re my appreciating Freddie more after so many and such long separations tickled us as we read your letter together! No doubt you're right. You are dear but my appreciation would be very much more if it were possible to spend more time together! Freddie already seems better. It is extraordinary what a little wifely attention will do! I feed him on milk puddings and egg-flip which is impossible in the Jungle as no fresh milk is ever obtainable. Freddie is quite pleased with the prospect of going to Monywa. The district Mahamyaung is totally different to any other. The whole of the work is done by tractors and with no elephants and their various diseases to fuss about will give Freddie a fresh interest. Another thing is that all touring will be done in cars and Freddie will obtain his wish to know all about cars. Mr. Roberts the 'Burra Sahib' is doing a tour of inspection through Sabenago in January which, I expect, will put the lid on my touring that month, as with four men things would be rather awkward. I shall go up in November and in January probably go to stay with friends. We have had several good old soaking days and directly a spot of sunshine comes, out goes every bit of clothing, cushions etc. The sequins on my black evening frock are done . Shoes are always going mildewed. In fact the bally stuff gives a lot of extra trouble! Freddie thinks I have trained the pup jolly well. I want him to take him back to the Jungle as there is a better chance of a good training there. I shall miss him awfully as he and '*Twinker*' are so amusing together. Well dear I must away. Lots of love and to Aunt Min.

Glenside, Maymyo, Sunday August 26th 1922

The days fairly buzz by with Freddie here to recoup every minute of my time but I fear that by this time next week he will be gone. This next separation of two months and possibly longer won't be quite so bad as we have Jungle touring before us. My months in the Jungle have been rather cut up. I'm afraid Mr. Roberts the Forest Inspector and top dog is doing a month's tour in January and it would be impossible for me to go there with three men and an awful lot of inspection work. I shall probably go down the river to Pakokku to Aida Barton for that time. Your letter of August 1st received last week enclosing Mary's all about Dorothy. It does distress me to hear about the kiddie. I can't believe she has changed so much. The six-weeks she spent with us at Withington no one could have wished for a nicer child. Ann Bowden is a good judge of children and she was very struck what an unselfish and intelligent kid she was. I can't help thinking Dorothy misses all the chance of her charms showing from not being with her own people. Don't you remember how pathetic she used to be in longing for a real mummy and real Aunties. Gosh I wish I could have the upbringing of the kid and I bet she'd be happier in every way. Under the circumstances I think school is the only thing. Of course Holmes who was her old governess and who has started a place at Bexhill for children whose parents are abroad, would be the place, but I doubt if Crofton would allow it out of pure cussedness! He could easily afford the £200 per annum which includes everything even clothes. Dorothy will always have to be led by affection. No doubt the Browns are simply splendid, but their own children naturally come first and even last year Dorothy I'm sure used to feel that. All the wrong traits will come out in her if she is not very carefully brought up. Today it is actually sunny. Freddie is in the veranda printing photos we took in the Jungle and which I will send you anon. Freddie has put plates in the slides to take the larger photo of the bungalow, our *''tum tum''* and '*dawgs*' and by degrees you will see and get a good idea of our life and few possessions. After getting up late we drove around to Mrs. Stomboe for breakfast at 10-30am. She reminds me very much of Aunt Mary with her devotion to the garden and china. She fondles the latter just as dear old Mary used to. I try to look intelligent and Mrs. Stomboe chatters away about the different beautiful glazes. This afternoon we play tennis at Candacraig and dine out at the Lochs. Having nights out in succession our bazaar bill has been nice and low. I am becoming quite an '*Ikey Moses*' these days and always so pleased when the bills go down a bit. I had no tennis at all last week but it was fine enough to play golf or go for a walk after tea. Freddie looks very much better. It is the change and food which bucks him up more than anything. Golly! This is a different life with him to trot around with. Mr. Barton is still here and often fills in his time here when

Aida is busy with the baby. Both are very fit. I was allowed to see Aida on Friday. The baby is absurdly small despite weighing seven pounds. You remember I told you I had postponed Pringles visit as they wanted me to take Aida and the baby until October. My letter did not reach Pringle in time and to my horror I received a letter from her in Rangoon, where she was breaking the journey and staying a few days with the Lolips. I couldn't have her before Freddie goes and the only spare room is taken up as a nursery. We shall be a tight squash but Pringle will have to fit in Freddie's dressing room and lump the baby's squealing. So she will come up on the 13th which will give Aida just a few days to settle in. After dining out last night we went on to the club dance with the party. It was quite good fun. First dance I have been to since Freddie was last here. Long letter from Ethel enclosing the crowds from home last week. She and he appear to have the same cheery time as of old. Today I'm wearing a cream jumper unit. It is so nice and I find it so useful. Brooksbank made me one which evidently has got lost in the post. It was sent ages ago but has not appeared.

Well mother dear I must away for an afternoon snooze before going to sleep as soundly as though I've drunk too much! But I mean before I play tennis. Best of love dear.

Glenside, Maymyo, Saturday September 2nd 1922

I'm not feeling particularly grand today as yesterday I was inoculated against plague. It is still very bad in Maymyo and spreading out this way. All servants have been done a long time ago of course. It is only just lately civilians have been advised to be done. Major Crump our doctor had his lugaley, wife, and eight kids die in their compound. So the Crumps have had to turn out of their house to have the whole place fumigated. The disease can only be carried by fleas, chiefly on rats. Numbers of dead rats have been found in houses and on being dissected found to be plague rats. Plague hasn't been so bad in Maymyo for many years. The natives seem to snuff out like flies. Major Crump sent me a report that Freddie ought to have longer leave and that he should not be allowed to have so much Jungle work. Freddie can't possibly remain away from his work longer so has decided to go down on Wednesday. That gives him three days more and we are thankful for small mercies these times. All doctors have said the same thing about the Corporation men; that they have too much Jungle work which wears them out physically and mentally. Thank goodness Mahamyaung next year will be for Freddie a totally different life, and give his brain a rest from the constant petty worries he has at present. In Mahamyaung the work is all done by tractors and train lines and it is essential to have a man there with a knowledge of engineering, which Freddie has. We walked round to see Aida Barton this evening. She is now up and dressed and this time next week will be back here with me. The baby so far is doing awfully well. I hope she won't wilt when she leaves the home! Mr. Barton left yesterday. Freddie is coming so will switch off for the present.

Sunday 3rd September 1922

Freddie came in to say he had met a Mr. Holmes at the club who was on the boat going home in 1920. Mr. Holmes is coming here to breakfast this morning so we shall talk over old Gloucestershire days. He and Ethel were great pals. I feel in an awful stew at the thought of the breakfast because the piece of beef I had sorted has got too passé for consumption and fairly knocked me down when I smelt it just now. The silly old fool of a cook said it was all right but I'm not risking anything. I had it for Freddie really and I have probably kept it too long. I shall do the next piece myself and see what luck. I thought it would give Freddie such a nice change from the everlasting chicken he has in the Jungle. Last Tuesday we went up to the regimental lines for tea and tennis with a Mrs. Dixon whose husband is in the Staffordshire Regiment. Mrs. Dixon I knew in Ceylon when she was a Miss

Clark and staying with her sister quite near Carolina. The day I went there with Ethel one of the kiddies fell off the swing and broke her arm and funnily enough the next time I met Mrs. Dixon it was to find her husband with a broken arm! So we wondered if one of us would break more the day we were there. We dined out four times last week which was rather an effort. One evening was especially jolly with a Captain and Mrs. Twiss up at the lines and they took us on to a very good concert got up by the Tommies. The audience was made up of chiefly Tommies and the cheeriness of it all took me back to Netley. We all went back to the mess afterwards for refreshments.

Sunday Evening September 3rd 1922

It is such a horrid wet evening that Freddie and I have a fire which makes the room so cosy in spite of rather thick smoke. We had to use such a lot of blow on the fire because the wood is so wet. After tea reddie and I drove round to see Aida. She is looking very blooming and very pleased with life at having a waist once more! Her wretched Ayah is laid up with a bad tooth which she refuses to have removed. Can't think why the Bartons keep the woman as she is a thoroughly bad lot and I wouldn't like to trust her in any way. It is now decided for Pringle to come up to Maymyo on the eighth but for the first week she is to go to the Lochs, friends of ours. Major and Mrs. Loch are going away and want a girl to keep her sister company. Pringle is delighted to fill the request and I should be able to see her every day. I feel until Aida is settled down I don't want any extra in the house. It is wonderful how everything has paned out because in spite of Freddie being away most of the time I have only spent a few days alone. The dates of the comings and goings of husband and friends have always fitted in beautifully. It is just lovely to think the days for another Jungle tour will soon be here. I am sending you a snap of the outside of our bungalow. You will see what a nice lot of trees shade us and how we are perched up. Not much of Liza can be seen, but quite enough. Anyway it helps to show off the background! On the right of the drawing room is our bedroom with our two bathrooms round the corner and leading to the kitchen and backquarters which cannot be seen. Spare room is to the left of the veranda with the good overhanging roof. Rain does not force one to shut the windows during the awful storms we get. The corrugated roof is red so does not look so bad. Your letter of August 8th came last mail. You do seem to be having wretched weather at home. The rain in Maymyo is abnormal and Freddie hears that the creeks in his district are still dry and all work is held up. Mr. Holmes who came to breakfast today held forth on the 1924 Exhibition at home, representing all countries in the British Empire. He has had a great deal to do with the Burma part of it. Freddie and I shall hope to see Burma at Wembley. How awfully good of Miss Mackenzie to arrange for you to have a downstairs bedroom. That will be so much easier for you and just as sunny as the bedroom you had before. It is nice to know you were with Aunt Min. all this time and the possible corrupting influence she may have had on you will tone down when you are again near the.........at Tupsley! I am enclosing Miss Holmes' letter which gives a very different account of Dorothy to what Mrs. Brown told Mary. That child is perfectly all right if taken the right way. I do hope Crofton consents to allowing Miss Holmes to have her permanently. Well dear I'm off to bed. Something upset my innards today and I want to cuddle a hot water bottle. Best of love mother dear.

Maymyo, Sunday September 10th 1922

I was so pleased to get your extra long letter of August 15th this last mail and it was especially appreciated as I had it to read during my first lonely meal. Freddie left in the afternoon on Wednesday and your letter arrived during dinner the same day. I had also a long letter from Aunt Bea and actually one from Edith for which I felt very bucked. She does have a rotten time and it's just as well she has more than the usual allowance of cheeriness to help her through. How very nice to get in touch with Jeff again. Mrs. Kelly seems a very good sort and you must have loved pumping her with questions. Billy seems to follow in father's footsteps. I wonder if he is such a hero in his sisters' eyes as Jeff was in mine!! Jeff was always so delightfully naughty and we were only too glad to follow him blindly. Why I asked about the Partridges of Tenbury is because Freddie has a subordinate by that name. All subs in the Corporation are half-Burmese, sons of white men who in the past married Burmese women and this man said he had come in for some money left by his father who owned land or something near Tenbury and he had relations around that part and Birmingham. It must be a different family. Must carry on with this letter later. Am just driving down to the station to see Mrs. Roberts off en route for home. She is our Burra Memsahib, so think it tactful to do the polite thing. Later. That's done! Quite a lot of people there. It's a great thing to do out here and reminds me of Champery days when we used to see off those we liked. Last

Tuesday was the first of the Government House shows and I was thankful to have Freddie to help me get through it. A sort of afternoon dance from 6-15pm to 7-45pm. So none of us had too much of the other's company! Nearly every one rather dreads the Government House struggles as there is a certain amount of stiffness. Sir Reginald and Lady Craddock are a cheery couple. He retires at the end of this year when Sir Harcourt Butler is made the first Governor. He was once a Lieutenant Governor in Burma and a great favourite. On Wednesday I drove Freddie down to catch the 2-40pm train for Mandalay. He stayed that night on board and reached Sabenago about six the following evening. Freddie was and looked much better for the fortnight in Maymyo and I don't think this next two months of separation will be so wearisome to him. With luck Freddie will come up from the end of October and I shall return to Sabenago with him. If he cannot leave his district I can easily pack up here and go up alone. We shall leave our staff in the bungalow until February when we go down to Monywa. The afternoon of seeing Freddie off I went to tea at a Mrs. Clogues who had lent her house for an at home exhibition of frocks made by Molly Peters who is the sister of Mrs. Loch. You have often heard her mentioned. Molly is awfully clever and the frocks were smart. To my horror after tea Mrs. Loch asked me to act as mannequin and dress up in garments ranging from tennis frocks to evening gowns. It was a fearful ordeal. I felt it at first. The thought of thirty odd women gazing at me was too much. However I obliged them and tripped about and of course the frocks sold like wildfire. Also several orders were given. It was quite good sport after I had become used to the ordeal and I couldn't forget myself and remember not to stick out by hindquarters and generally fool around. Mrs. Loch saved me from a lonely evening on Thursday by insisting on my dining with them. They are topping and have been awfully good to me. Thursday I met Daisy Pringle by the morning train and drove her straight up to the Loch's where she is being housed. The Lochs go away on their tour on Tuesday until the 24th, when the sister, in her turn, also has to be out as there is no room. I feel I have put them to an awful lot of trouble but it really isn't my fault and the Lochs don't mind a scrap and it was their idea originally. Aida Barton and the infant arrived back yesterday and so far the change does not seem to suit the kid as she won't sleep and cries a lot. However, things will settle down I suppose. She is a dear little girl and filling out very well. Prams etc., about the bungalow makes Glenside look really important and as I don't sport one myself glad to have someone who does! The weather is still very stormy but I have had some good tennis and golf this last week. During October week there is a tennis tournament! And I am playing with Mrs. Jackson Jones in the ladies but have not yet fixed up for the mixed. This continuous wet weather today plays an awful game with one's clothes. They soon smell stuffy and silk splits terribly. I am hard at it making new tennis frocks. One gets through such a lot. I am doing my best to make the evening frocks last as when I go to

Monywa I shan't want so many. I must say I have an awfully good time but it always seems a waste when Freddie isn't here to share it. When one goes out one always has to have a book for engagements as tennis and golf games are booked up a fortnight ahead sometimes! Going out to evening shows leaves me quite cold but the games I love. Plague still seems pretty bad in Maymyo and when shopping I never go into the shops but sit in the *'tum tum'* and make them come out to me. I do miss the pup so much but at the same time the bungalow is better for his absence and I am having the chair covers washed on the strength of it. He will be a splendid companion to Freddie in the Jungle. I'm sorry you're having such a rotten summer at home. The prophecy of last year that we were to have seven years drought has gone wrong somewhat. I will send you the photos next week. They are very good especially of the *'tum tum'*. Two Freddie took of me in the veranda I shall not include because they look so dreadful. I told him not to put me too near the camera - it was fatal!

Well Mother dear this must do for this week. The baby is bleating away and Aida trying to get her off by shaking the pram. Lucky Aida came back here yesterday, as a Mrs. Moody, who wasn't expecting her baby until October, suddenly had to dash to the home and in three hours her small daughter arrived and the room Aida vacated was the only one. Maymyo is full of those doing their duty by increasing the population. My very best love dear and to Aunt Mini.

BOOK 2
Glenside, Maymyo, Sunday September 24th 1922

I received yours of August 29th this last mail, with its many enclosures, for which many thanks. I have been dreading a letter telling me you received no letter from me and you must have thought it horrid just at your birthday. I always send your home letters to Freddie as he so enjoys reading them when tucked away in the Jungle. His people don't often write. They have such a busy life and the old lady has a large family abroad to write to, as you have. It is such a lovely morning, a real nip in the air, and I am now quite glad of a couple of blankets at night. I wish Freddie could say the same. He says it is still very hot and muggy in the Jungle. September is always looked on as the worst month. Yesterday I had a tin box full of lovely lavender from cousin Emma. She promised it me from her garden last year but I never thought she would remember. It is so sweet of her and will do well to try and drown the everlasting musty smell one can never get rid of in ones clothes. I have been having a fearful time with the servants this week when I thought blue murder would go on in the compound. As usual the women folk were at the bottom of all the trouble. The Ayah is a thoroughly bad lot and we warned the Bartons of the fact ages ago but they took no notice. The Ayah has been a constant worry quarrelling and all came to a head last Tuesday when the Waterman and his wife, both Gurkhas, came home a little tipsy, the latter set on the Ayah and the small Bar Tai. I came home from tennis at about 7pm to hear an unholy din going on. Aida was barricaded in her room for safety with the baby! In the dining room the Butler was trying to deal with the Waterman's wife, who was yelling the roof off and looked a nasty sight, with both ears bleeding, either Bar Tai or the Ayah had pulled a huge gold earring out of her ear and torn the lobe through!! Beads and other bits of jewellery were strewn all over the dining room. I suppose they heard the goings on! I chivvied the women off, and threatened to call in the police if there was any more noise. She then attacked the Ayah in the garden so I thought things weren't good enough and dashed off to a bungalow nearby to phone for the police. No answer from any of the three calls, so I rang up Mr.Dirk (head of the Bombay Burma Trading Corporation office up here). He promised to send someone to our rescue. I waited at least half an hour, the din was worse. The Mali and Syce were then fighting the Waterman to protect the Ayah who was 'as a red rag to a bull' whenever the wife saw her. So again I sallied forth and bagged the car of a Mrs. James, who lives near here, and went down to the club to fetch someone. We are so absolutely isolated up here and no one near. The Assistant Police Superintendent, Mr Smith, was there but he didn't seem to care how much bloodshed was going on but promised to send up a sergeant. In the meantime, a Mr. Grant volunteered to come up and stay at the bungalow, which he did until 10-30pm, when all was fairly peaceful. He had no sooner gone when Mr. Duncan Smith arrived plus a couple of bobbies, one of whom slept in the veranda all night. Bar Tai was scared out of his life. When I arrived home, he could not be found anywhere and then was discovered locked in my bathroom scared to come out. His coat was in shreds so he must have had a good old tussle. Anyway I sacked the Waterman next day. I was very loath to because he was a splendid worker. I told Aida it would be impossible to keep the Ayah on. She is a perfect nuisance and I know would upset all the servants if she remained here. We are not yet fixed up with a new one but I hope to be soon. Everything was so peaceful before, but I have no doubt at all it will be so again. I haven't heard from Freddie this last week. He is touring and during the rains there is always difficulty sending back the mail. Mr. Roberts was here just now and said he wouldn't be touring through Sabenago this time, which will please Freddie enormously. These big trips going round means a lot of extra work and responsibility and I hope it will mean I can be out in the Jungle the whole of the three months, in about six weeks time. I hope Freddie will be in to take me up there.

Invitations are coming out for the bun-struggle during The Week which commences on October 4th with a big dance at Government House. The General and Lady Fane give a Garden Party on the 14th and it is rather an ordeal. The necessary glad rags for such things always stump me. I have seen quite a lot of Daisy Pringle this last week and she comes here *on Thursday. Early one morning she arrived plastered in mud in her riding gear. Her pony* had slipped and chucked her and afterwards bolted for home leaving the poor thing stranded and some way from home. Luckily Captain Keiling who had lent the pony was at home and came and found her here and took her back to the Lochs'. I have given tennis parties at Candacraig several afternoons last week. It is the only way of returning the many times I am asked out. Now there are no B.B.T.C. men, the place is empty but always a Butler left in charge. I have a duty tea party on this afternoon and have been making cakes for the fray. I do find my stove so useful. I have had a shelter rigged up under one of the trees in front of the bungalow for the pram to be under. It was quite hopeless having the baby on our small veranda, she woke at the slightest sound, but now sleeps the whole day. We dread Major Crump coming any day now to vaccinate her. I expect Aida will be with me until October 20th. We have spent most of our grass widowhood together. This makes it very nice for me. Shirley is a darling baby and doing very well. Well Mother dear, I must try and write some more mail letters. I always feel so lazy after I have finished yours. Best of love and to Rosslynites if you are now back at Tupsley.

P.S. Herewith a snap of our barouche plus my precious pup '*Spiker*' who seems to think Freddie, who took the photo, only worthy of his back view.

Maymyo Sunday October 8th 1922

Quite a fat mail last week including four nice long ones of September 13th. I always forward on all my letters to Freddie, which he much enjoys and is often rather tickled at your wise remarks; for example: That there is perhaps a compensation in these separations in the fact that you cannot possibly tire of one another, seeing so little of each other. He thinks you are a bad old thing to contemplate such a prospect. I also heard from Stella, who was much better but still has to use sticks. She is so good in sending papers and Cousin Emma who sent me a box of most lovely lavender and a book on embroidery last week. All these things are so appreciated. These days are very busy ones with all the festivities and the club is now packed with strange birds from all parts, up for the week. I don't know why it should be called a week because the gaieties go on longer than that. I have played two rounds of my mixed doubles at tennis and am still in the tournament. The next round will be in the semi-finals when I expect we will get up against some 'stingers' and get knocked out. I have to play ladies doubles at 7.30am tomorrow morning, which is rather an effort. I hope it will keep fine for the big Government House party tomorrow. This will be the last show there before the Governor and Lady Craddock retire. The poor old things look as though they will fall to bits if they have to go on with this strenuous life forever. Last Wednesday was a big dance at Government House to open events. Daisy and I had dinner at the Cleavers' first. (He is in the B.B.T.C.) and then our party of eight went up to Government House where there was a huge scrum, but I enjoyed everything awfully. All was decorated with lanterns and the different uniforms made everything look so bright, including the funny old Burmese servants outside, with long grey beards, turbans and red uniform. Captain Broadwood on going away before a huge crowd dashed up to one of them and said 'Where's my car Bearer?' Tickled everyone enormously. What a daft game that is. I couldn't understand the jokes in Punch about it for ages. We have just come home from a big bathing picnic. Daisy went in but I'm getting wise in my old age and gave that a miss. I'm still getting rheumatism but not so badly thank goodness. Aida's Ayah left today. She was an evil woman and I'm glad to see her go. Aida has only a temporary one but very nice. Ayahs are very difficult to get up here especially when they know they have to go to a bit out of the way place like Pakokku. Poor Aida has been so upset this last week because a letter came to say that her father was dangerously ill and had to have an operation very suddenly. However a cable came today to say he is better. Freddie writes that he may be in at the end of this month if the rains are not late. I can return to Sabenago with him. Of course I daren't think of such a wonderful possibility and the fact that we shall have about four months uninterrupted bliss. Fair leaving me dithery. Course you know dear we are very fond of one another!! Queer aint it? And these separations are difficult and make me long to give way to a good old grouse, but we both know that would do no good! Daisy is very keen to do a trip up the river to Bhamo and to treat me. I'd love it of course and I believe the river above Sabenago is very lovely, so as plans are now I shall go with Daisy on about the 25th after Aida's Ayah has left. And on the way down the river Freddie will join me of course and come up to Maymyo with me and Daisy can go down to Rangoon from Mandalay. Daisy is returning to Assam until March and then home. She is an awfully nice girl and I love having her here. We all get on 'as snug as a bug in a rug', and everyone wonders how we fit in this bungalow. I have borrowed a pony for Daisy and she goes out for early morning rides. I have had offers of ponies for myself but find I have plenty to do during the day without riding; I shall have all I want when I return to Sabenago. Freddie has decided not to keep my grey pony. He's on the lookout for someone to buy him. On Thursday a Mrs. Twiss dined here and we three went on to the theatricals at the club where 'Nothing but the Truth' was acted. It was simply splendid, all people we know, and it went with much gusto. Last night after playing tennis Daisy remained on and had dinner with the Twiss' and then a party of us went to the club dance which was great fun; a lot of people there. On Tuesday next it is a fancy dress dance. I am having a dinner for eight here before going on. Where we shall all fit in I don't know and I am bagging a dining table from the bungalow next door and shall wear my same old Dutch costume. I wonder if Helen means to paint my candle shades, if not I must order some from home, mine are so shabby. This morning I was busy making a cake to send to Freddie. He will be in Sabenago for a few days and cake makes a change of diet for him. Well fair thee well mother dear-my very best love and to all at Rosslyn. Please remember me to the Miss Mackenzies and thank them for all their loving kindness to my dear old Alice.

Glenside, Maymyo, Saturday October 14th 1922

Many thanks for yours of September the 20th, written just before you left Malvern. You will be sorry to leave Aunt Min but will have lots of pals at Tupsley and with plenty of comings and goings in the house you will be kept amused. I'm sure the Turners will be as faithful as ever in coming along to give all the titbits. Do give them my love. My letters seem as though they are irregular. I am so sorry dear you are disappointed at receiving no mail some weeks. Unless someone always sees the daily papers one cannot say when the boat leaves Rangoon. Just by chance we hear it is a day earlier this week- so here goes for my letter on Saturday instead of Sunday. We have had a most hectic week and are really quite glad the festivities are over. We three girls have just come back from a very cheery garden party at the General's where all the world and his wife sported their best clothes. There were games of all sorts to play; obstacle golf, treasure hunt, and good tennis to watch. Luckily it has been a perfect afternoon, not a spot of rain, which was such a change from the daily storms we have been having. Last Monday was even a bigger bun struggle at Government House, when we had the normal amusements and finished up with a dance. I always enjoy these shows though the tussle before getting one's 'glad rags' in order is somewhat of an effort. It is such a joy to find Daisy is just like me and always having to make or alter something before going out! Aida has such a wonderful trousseau that she has to simply take up some luscious garment et voila! She is dressed a perfect lady. The General's party is the first Aida has been to. With the baby always to come back to at 6pm she is rather tied. At 7.30 am last Monday I played the first round in the ladies doubles. We had a jolly good game and won. Our opponents were a strong couple and we ought to go through now. Madge and I got knocked out in our mixed semi-finals. I am not nearly steady enough for tournaments. I like to have a good old bang and be done with it. On Tuesday night we had a great time here giving a dinner for ten. My biggest effort, and it was such a success. The servants out here always love a special occasion and come well up to scratch. Bagged a table from the empty bungalow next door, which held 10 easily, all except Aida; fearful scrum. Daisy and I weren't home before 3am so weren't too merry and bright the next morning but we went along to the church at 10 am to help a Mrs. Copper to decorate for a wedding in the afternoon. We could not be bothered to go to the show in the afternoon as we felt too much the day after the night before. Freddie's assistant, Hill, is up here for a few days. He came in one morning and you bet I pumped him dry all about Freddie and what they have been up to. Daisy is very keen to go up the Irrawaddy to Bhamo before she leaves for Assam where she has to be back on November 25th. So we have fixed to do the trip next Thursday. Mrs. Crump has offered to motor us to Mandalay, about 30 miles, to catch the night boat. It will be simply lovely to get away for a few days and Aida doesn't mind being left alone. The lovely part is that Freddie comes in on the boat on the 24th and we shall travel up to Maymyo together as Freddie will get on our boat at Male on its return journey. Freddie will be only able to stay here for about five days as Mr. Agar is doing a tour for which he must be back. This wretched tour means I cannot go up to Sabenago before September. I shall be here alone for a month. I shan't mind that but I do object to being done out of an extra month in the Jungle. However, when I do get there it will take a lot of stirring to oust me. I long to get away for a few days. At times I get heartily sick of housekeeping and scrapping with servants and no Freddie to keep them in their place. I shall miss Daisy awfully as she is so cheery. Last night we dined at the club with friends and dancing afterwards. This morning I was up a 6.30am for a round of golf at 7.30am so I am feeling rather sleepy. Freddie's letter must also be finished so I must stop now dear. Next mail I shall be on the move but I shall get a letter off from somewhere. Goodbye mother dear my very best love. See you soon.

Glenside, Maymyo Sunday October, 28th 1922

I got back from my topping river trip last Tuesday with Freddie at Glenside but fear his days are very short as he will leave again for Sabenago on Wednesday next and not with me with him, as I had hoped, drat it! Mr. Agar is foolish enough to want to do a tour until the first week in December and he is not the sort to want a woman going along with the party. He is quite nice but not a social bird and can only talk shop. Poor Freddie will be bored stiff with him and shop is very bad for him as prospects for the future are not very cheery and to chew the subject does no good. My last letter was written before we reached Kattia where our boat tied up for the night; quite a small village but it is the only spot on the river that the railway touches. Daisy and I walked through the smelly old village with its street full of smellier people talking with tongues tied as usual. All of the temples were lit up as it was after sundown and several men and women prostrate before their hideous, but to them wonderful, Buddhas, shouting out prayers. The evenings on the boat were rather painful as the other passengers were mad on musical evenings, of the very worst kind, so Daisy and I always decamped to the top deck and sat and talked there until an early bed. Poor Miss MacDougall was ill the whole way up with fever and could not even enjoy the lovely scenery very much. We left Kattia early on Saturday morning where the scenery became even prettier than before as we went through a defile for many miles where the steep hills, thickly wooded, come right down to the waters edge. At 3pm we arrived at Bhamo but did not go ashore until after tea.

Bhamo is the further most point steamers go and is quite a busy trading spot for goods of allsorts coming over from China. The small town is full of men and women from all parts. Chinese men bringing in ponies laden with packs which are shipped on different boats and in return take what the boats have brought up from Rangoon and Mandalay; chiefly cotton goods. Since republican days in China one does not see so many pigtails being worn as I believe fashion proved the men to be more or less slaves. We saw several women in their quaint dress of broad black trousers, tiny tiny little feet hobbling along on equally tiny shoes with very high heels. Daisy and I first of all walked along to the Kohus shop, which is supposed to be the celebrated place for jade, amber and embroidery. I was rather disappointed that I didn't see much and certainly not worth the price they asked, and like so many other places, they have been spoilt by trippers. We then walked away past the club where I spotted a girl I knew so I went up to talk to her for a bit. Back to the boat for dinner and the usual music and rowdy songs. As the boat did not leave before eleven Daisy and I went ashore and explored the queer old Chinese Joss House, supposed to have been in existence for about 2000 years. It was very dirty and fusty and we did the correct thing by going. The first thing that confronted us was a pile of coffins which were being made there; enormous things with the panels being about six inches thick, the rest was full of hideous Buddhas and distorted figures. The old man who showed us round tried to persuade us to offer up and burn Joss Sticks to Buddah but I didn't think he wanted any more by the number of sticks surrounding him burning and giving off a rather sickly incense smell. On our return through the defile at Bhamo an officer had a gun hoping to pot at something on the bank but nothing doing so another officer went on to the top deck and dropped glass bottles down for him to hit. We again tied up at Kattia by which time I was becoming fidgety to get on to Male where we picked up Freddie and the small *'dawg'* about 2.15pm the next day. Monday we stopped the night at Kang Maung where Freddie, Daisy and I had a nice long walk. Tuesday morning we started off again very early and as there was plenty of time the Captain stopped at Ming Goon about 10 miles from Mandalay, rather a noted sightseeing place with its biggest bell in the world. It is very ancient and at one time the Burmese tried to remove it elsewhere, but the bell sank in the river where it remained for years. At Ming Goon there is also the beginning of what was to be the biggest pagoda in the world but an earthquake cracked the foundations which were a quarter of a mile square so no more was done. One Buddha reposes inside on the part that was built. All the nations dashed up the umpteen steps leaving their shoes at the bottom and said a prayer or two and then chivvied back to the boat. Back to Mandalay at about eleven where Captain and Mrs. Keiling met Daisy and whisked her off to stay a couple of nights before she left for Rangoon and then back to Assam. I shall miss her most awfully, as she was so jolly. A Mr.Burbridge met us at the landing place, and took Freddie, Miss MacDougall, and myself up to his house for breakfast and my word we didn't half enjoy it after the food on the boat, which was so unappetizing. We caught the 7.30am train up arriving at Maymyo about 6pm. We were very surprised to see Mr.Barton at the station and who travelled on up with us. He had to sleep at the B.B.T.C. chummery near here, and came for all meals. On Thursday we had a treat show here with a christening in the morning. Freddie and I decorated the font, which looked so nice with the white flowers and maidenhair. Just before 4pm we all went down in a car, the baby being very peaceful. Only five others were asked and I acted as proxy to Shirley and I held her all the time and in my agitation bleated out all the responses in quite the wrong order. However Aida and her husband were standing by me and did their bit. After the show we all came back here for tea and ate all the top layer of Aida's wedding cake, kept for the special occasion. Everyone ate and drank most heartily and we got on well with our new padre. The days since we came home have been very busy with men folk coming in for dinner and breakfast and Aida and her husband in the house. The whole family left yesterday motoring for Mandalay and by now they will have reached Pakokku. I shall miss Aida and the baby most awfully. They have been part of this household for so long now. Freddie and I had some tennis yesterday but neither of us felt exactly tip top. Freddie always has low fever when he comes up here at first and I have started a rotten cold in my head. Polo Week starts tomorrow so there are still quite a lot of people in Maymyo. The weather is lovely now and real nip in the air at night. I feel so glad to think you are back again with the Miss Mackenzies. You sound so cosy. You are very vague about the lace Connie would like. If she will let me know the quantity width etc., I will order some from India. Uncle Jim seems to be becoming more and more queer and I do think he is the limit. Bea wrote to me very indignant about the way he is going on. A pity Jim doesn't return to Canada to plague them for a time. We went to the bazaar yesterday. It does one good to find out prices occasionally as the cook wouldn't turn a hair charging double for anything from the bazaar. I'm fed up as my nice Butler has left, perhaps only temporarily, as he is not fit At present we have a queer little bird with fearful flat feet.

I remember the Spiddings at Hatton very well and so will Ethel. I believe he is rather a pal of hers. Hatton is quite near Watawalla and is where I spent a happy month in a Nursing home. Freddie is bleating for me to go and lie down so must tootle off. Lots of love mother dear from us both.

Glenside Maymyo, Sunday November 5th 1922

Yours of October the 11th with Aunt Min's letter enclosed; both received last week for which many thanks. I'm so glad everything is made so easy for you at Tupsley, but it is sad to think you can't walk to church as of old. It is a nice warm house and I do hope dear your pains will become less. Anyway it is a great joy to me to know you have so many friends around you. You are such a comfy visitor to have and no wonder they all love having you. I often long for you out here where so much of my life is spent without Freddie. It seems such a waste that you can't take his place. I fear Maymyo would not improve your rheumatics though mine are much better since I came back from the river trip where I had none at all. Probably the Jungle and then Monywa heat next year will take it all out of me. Nice as Maymyo is it doesn't suit everyone and I think this altitude, nearly three thousand feet is trying after a time. I get to feel most awfully slack and it is an effort to get started at anything. What a kid John is for catching infectious diseases. Poor Mary doesn't sound overjoyed at her new mansion. I'm like her I never want to be saddled with a large house. Thank goodness Freddie has small ideas in housing too. We long for a house of our own. It was very sad to let Freddie go again on Thursday and I'm just counting the days till I can join him at Sabenago. He won't come down for me as Rangoon office start fussing if men leave their Jungle work too often. But my packing won't mean much as we shall do it together in February before we go to Monywa. So with luck young Bar Tai and I will sally forth on our travels on December the 10th. In the mean time I am here quite alone and with a strange Butler who is an awful little worm but quite harmless. When Mr. Cleaver goes out touring I am going to stay with Mrs. C. They have an awfully nice house quite near here and two topping kids also a car so that ménage will be much nicer than just having my *'dawg'*. All last week I had such a rotten cold and still feel buzzy in my head and as usual Freddie had to go through his low dose of fever. I dined out twice last week preparatory to going again to see 'Nothing but the Truth' at the club. Last Monday we had the most dreadful storm in the morning. Even in Ceylon I never saw such rain and wind; trees toppling over all over the place and a lake at one side of our bungalow. The polo ground has been under water practically every day and the players are thoroughly fed up after coming long distances to play. Aida writes that they all managed the journey down to Pakokku very well. I do miss Aida and the baby so much and wish I had one to take Shirley's place! Maymyo is beginning to look quite wintry. The trees are bare but I miss the autumn tints, which we don't get, like at home. I have had fires in the evening several times as there is a decided nip in the air now. We have put up the *'tum tum'* for sale, as we shan't want it in Monywa. Most people have cars now but Mr. Street promises to take it back, when he returns in September, if we can't sell it. Good bye for this week Mother dear.

Croxton, Maymyo, Sunday November 12th 1922

Many thanks for yours and Jack's enclosed, Dear old Johnny[35] always writes such a nice letter and never grouses at his bad luck and he does seem to have had a hard time. I wish it wasn't such an impossible job for him to get home. I expect it will be years before he will have the cash for passages. It is a relief to know that Freddie anyway will have his passage paid. One only will come to over 2000 rupees which is a big hole when one's keep at the other end has to be thought of. Neither of us is blessed with a home in which to dump ourselves to start off on our arrival, before finding a house of sorts. But no doubt something will turn up for us. We shall soon be able to say we go home next year and that will be topping. I am getting through a nice bit of sewing making old garments into new etc. Aunt Bea marvelled at me having so much sewing always to do, but one has no idea how quickly things rot out here and I always save by having no Dhobey. Dhobey's are so disappointing in this country and I always thought out East one's clothes were washed and made most beautifully nice for nothing but that very much belongs to the old days. Yesterday I meant to go to the open-air service (Armistice Day) but it was impossible to go out on account of the rain and wind so I don't know what happened. Red poppies were to be sold too but I don't suppose the poor things made much. I think the memorial Hereford decided on is awfully nice by the pictures in The Hereford Times. St. Peters Square is a good spot for it. I wonder when you will get into town to see it for yourself; doesn't the perfect lady who owns a car ever take you for a run? I went to early service this morning and drove on to Glenside. Poor old *'Twinker'* has sneaked down from Mr. Agar's to welcome me and he has dogged me all the time I was doing odd jobs in the bungalow. I could not bring a dog here with children in the house. They are such sweet kids and, I tell you, to come back to find others in the house makes all the difference. To live alone in England is not nearly so bad because one always has a servant of sorts about but when dinner and tiffin are finished in this country the whole lot clear off. Maymyo is almost deserted now as nearly everyone has gone down to Rangoon, but personally I prefer it with more room to move on the links and courts. Freddie had started a tour last time I heard and said it is beautifully cool and fine in Sabenago now and had it not been for Mr. Agar I could have been with him quite well. However, the days are slipping by quite quickly and by the time this reaches you I will be once more in the dear old Jungle. Freddie has had a new thatched hut made in the compound. I enclose a few snaps, taken last cold weather in the Jungle, which have been waiting ages to send you.

Well dear farewell for this week. I'm just off to have a lie down. To do that is quite the correct thing to do in the afternoons I assure you. But I often think of the days at home when Daisy and I used to do the same, and directly we heard you coming upstairs, up we'd jump and start tidying a drawer or something, and how Ethel always said if she and Dotty did a lazy thing Aunt Helen would invariably start rolling or cutting the grass below their window which made them get up. Lots of love mother dear.

---

[35] Lt. John Britten, M.C., Mully's brother.

Croxton, Maymyo Sunday November 26th 1922

Only one more letter to be written from Maymyo as I start on my travels to Sabenago tomorrow week. I hope my letters then won't be very boring as I will probably repeat my experiences of last year, and yet to me they will all be fresh, and I am looking forward to the Jungle again as much as I did a year ago today. Then I was on the briny after dear old Uncle George and Cousin Emma had seen me off. I had then just finished a whirl of packing as I have now and am quite certain I shall be doing likewise a year hence. Not until we have our little cottage at home and Freddie has earned his old age pension do we expect peace an the settled life we both yearn for! However, lots of it now is very nice and even the separations slips by somehow and at present we have naught to grouse about with at least two and a half months of one another's company unadulterated in any way. The change of climate will probably do me good. I don't think this height suits me and I seem to thrive more in the heat. Today is awfully cold and I feel all goose fleshy, such a wind and yet bright and sunny if only one could find a sheltered spot. Fancy young Nolan having the sauce to try for the Council. Tiny Carver seems to have quite overcome her *nervousness* if she is driving people to the poll. Tell her she owes me a letter the bad girl. *The Hereford Times* always rolls up. Thanks very much but will you ask someone to ask the newspaper rates now for I nearly always have to pay a little on excess at this end. When you pay Smiths again be sure to let us know. I'm sending to them for a couple of diaries and for the bill to be sent to you and please forward. I thought they would know we were respectable folk and trust us. I have been so busy this last week writing Christmas letters and sending small parcels, chiefly Shan bags, which I hope, will be liked. We can't afford much this year. My Christmas mail to you will be next week. I was playing tennis yesterday with a Mrs. Dixon who I met in Ceylon. She is married to a man in the South Staffordshire Regiment here. We had topping games. I have played golf mostly lately. I had a round with Mr. Dunks, the secretary, on Friday, who has reduced my handicap by 4, at which I am very bucked. I have picked up a set of clubs from Mr. Dunks office, odd ones left or lost by people and which he says have not being claimed, so I may as well give them a home. Jolly nice because clubs are so expensive out here. I have your grey woolly scarf on and it is such a comfort and has been most useful all the time. What do you manage to work at now? Mrs. Cleaver is a great knitter and does all her kids' clothes. Oranges are plentiful now and Mrs. Cleaver has an excellent cook who has made some topping marmalade for me to take to the Jungle but also he is salting a ham which Freddie will love as a change to his chicken diet.

There is a great scheme, started out here by an Englishman, called the 'Southern Shan State Produce Company' and pigs are among the many things to be produced; about 8000 a week are wanted in Rangoon alone. Chinamen, of course, eat pork. Tea, fruit and vegetables are also to be in the enterprise. I hope it goes as well as it has up to now. So many army men who have been axed have been taken on, and the B.B.T.C. men who got fed up with the amount of Jungle work are in it. If Freddie and I think of breeding pigs it will be at home and not out here thank you. Freddie by his letters is getting thoroughly fed up with Mr. Agar on this tour. He is such a hopeless gasbag with one long grouse, which is rather a poor sort of companion to have in the Jungle. Freddie longs to let off steam himself sometimes but he only allows a very little. Well dear this is another rather short letter I'm afraid but nothing much doing these days. Lots of love dear.

Sabenago Tuesday December 12th 1922

I do feel so sad today the little black cocker pup Freddie brought with him from Maymyo died yesterday. She was such a perfect little beast and directly I arrived here seemed to attach herself to me, and '*Spiker*' the other dog to Freddie. Sunday we thought she didn't seem very fit so gave her a dose of castor oil which she fairly lapped up. During the day she seemed rather sad but always was of a quieter disposition than the others. In the evening she was keen to go out with us when Freddie picked up his gun, and for a pup was an excellent follower. All yesterday she wouldn't leave me and seemed to become weaker and died in the evening. We gave her brandy to try to revive her. We were both so upset. It is too absurd how attached one can become to a mere pup. Major Perry who gave her to us would be very upset as he prides himself on his dogs which are known to be jolly good. Our family is now reduced to '*Spiker*' and the small pup I brought up last week. Both perfect little devils and tear about all over the place. '*Inkoo*' was such an affectionate little beast and I do miss her so much. We were in the throes of packing our kit for our first tour tomorrow. (I seldom write to you without mentioning some sort of packing). We shall be out for about fifteen days before coming in for a couple, to replenish our stores and kit. It turned so cold and raw yesterday and we had rain the whole day, which is rather unusual at this time of year, and I expect travelling tomorrow will be decidedly dirty work. Of course there are no fireplaces in the bungalow so we turn in very early in order to keep warm. The hut Freddie has built this year is simply topping. The same site, only a different shaped hut, a round one with a roof coming up to a point made of grass. A little bathroom is attached for my special benefit which is very draughty at present and with the light on inside at night. I'm sure the local folk get a good knowledge of how an English lass bathes. I'm thankful we do not sleep in the bungalow which is overrun by rats, and even where we are, we can hear them gnawing and scampering about. I am glad I brought out woolly combinations. I put them on for the first time today and feel so comfy. Last year I left one black round topped trunk here with my Jungle kit and a few odds and ends, overalls and woolly jumpers etc., and when Freddie looked into the box a short time ago found the whole of the inside thick with mildew and all my things alive with white ants. They had eaten their way through the bottom and not a thing was left untouched and riddled with holes! My beloved pyjamas I had made at Gloucester were impossible to wear again. White ants do for things in a very short time. Freddie and I went across to Male after tea on Friday to claim money sent from Mandalay by the Mail Boat. This boat only ties up for special things like that and does not stop like a cargo boat for trading purposes. We dashed over and had a chat with the Captain who introduced me to a Mrs. Tilley who was doing the Bhamo trip. She had just come from Ceylon and knows Ethel well, also Dorothea whom she met when 'D' was governess to her sister Mrs. MacMullian's kids. I had not time to talk long as the boat tooted and was off. Saturday evening Freddie and I went through the village to see the cook's wife and Freddie's boy's small son who are ill. You can't imagine the filthy state of the huts. The Burman is a thriftless race and wages are spent chiefly on gambling and they never trouble to till the land to get more money. When anyone is ill all the neighbours look on and sit outside on their haunches smoking and spitting! The small boy, in spite of being unconscious most of the day with fever, was being stuffed with rice and his tummy looked as though he had swallowed a football. I can't imagine how they manage when it rains. I can't think, as the roof had scarcely any covering. The Karens caste of the Burman is very clean and the girls are awfully pretty and generally beautifully dressed. The garden promises well and we already have had beans and salad out of it. Owing to economy men have had to go so we have not the Malis we'd like. The ham I brought up is still going strong; only in the sense of still being in existence. Freddie loves it and we both enjoy it at our meals. He only seems to eat a decent meal when I'm here. I wrote to Edith by the Christmas Mail and addressed it to the Manor House. I now think it is The Grange. I wish you'd let me know, especially as I enclosed a hankie. I also sent a small parcel to Mary but wonder if I put the full address of her new house. Well dear I must away and sort out a few clothes for the Jungle. It's too cold yet for only a string of beads! I have had no mail yet but hope it will arrive before we start tomorrow. Lots of love mother dear and I do so hope you are able to get to Rosslyn and enjoy your Christmas.

Camp, Saturday December 16th 1922

Your letter of November the 15th was my one letter last week, I don't often hear from any member of the family. I do wish Edith wouldn't disappear into her shell so effectively. Our spot will be Monywa next year. Pronounced Moan-u-ar. It is not a very large place, but is the trading centre for the whole Chindwin River, which you will see flows into the Irrawaddy some distance below Mandalay. Monywa is at the mouth and all the boats start there. Where Freddie's work will be is about a day and a half's trip by boat. I believe the Chindwin is an awfully pretty river and I hope to do the trip up before we leave these parts. I take a huge interest in the lively council meetings in The Hereford Times. Young Nolan will begin to wish himself out of it all. I too can't think why the people voted for him unless to tickle things up a bit for fun, which apparently is forthcoming. I should not think the new Padre is likely to want the Church House. The present Vicarage is such a nice little place and everything one could possibly want in a garden and I hope for your sake no changes will take place. I always like to think of you with the Miss Mackenzies where I used to find you looking cosy last year. I'm so sorry to hear about Aunt Mary she always dreaded the thought of an operation and am so longing for further news. Well here we are away in the thick of the Jungle once more and at the same camp as last year. Yesterday was the second anniversary of our wedding and Freddie couldn't get away from bellowing at the top of his voice 'Ding Dong Ding Dong this is our wedding day.' Some song from the days of his youth and when he little thought he could apply it to himself. All we could produce as an extra to celebrate the occasion was a tin of mushrooms which certainly made a very nice change to our usual chicken diet. However all is well today and we are risking some tinned fish tonight. One's fodder is very difficult on tour, even chicken seems difficult to procure from the villages and game is so scarce compared to last year. A dove is the only bird Freddie has had a shot at so far. Although the paddy is cut and lying in the fields the jungle fowl do not show themselves. We shall have a bean feast after bagging a duck from the village and I may as well add that we paid for it and did not really bag it in the dead of night. We got away from Sabenago at about 2-30pm last Wednesday after receiving our mail. We have found travelling elephants slow. Two are with small butchars,36[36] which are a perfect nuisance, for when these elephants are small they can't leave their mothers and being untrained they are so mischievous and come for anyone nearby. They are quite equal to sneaking up behind one and giving a smack on ones bum. Freddie and I did not start for some time after the elephants as it is nicer, not only to escape their dust, but also to arrive at our destination with our kit unpacked. Our ponies already look better under the care of our Syce who I brought from Maymyo. He is quite new to the Jungle life but seems to like it alright. We spent the first night at quite a nice"Tay" at Onbeighn but golly wasn't it cold. Perhaps the first night out we felt the cold more, because we do not feel it nearly so much now. The horses were stabled under the "Tay" and what with the cold and smell from the animals the night was not all it might have been! The view from the bungalow was very lovely, looking directly on to the range of the Shivendow; which goes up to a very pointed peak in the middle, and when the sun sets the whole range is a bright pink coming down to mauve on the wooded part. All the travelling so far has been through very lovely country, bridal paths winding up and down the hills through thick Jungle.

---

[36] Baby elephants.

Yesterday at Kauckeys I was able to see some very interesting work when Freddie went to take over about a hundred and fifty logs. Each is measured at the pone (or depot) where logs are kept, before being put in the creek. The man who has dragged or carted the logs to the pone is paid according to the cubic capacity of each log. This particular pone was well above a creek and each log was dragged by an elephant to the top of the To-Char, or small precipice. Then the log was unchained and lifted by the elephant and hurled down the Tochar to the creek below, where more elephants were waiting to drag it into position further down the creek. The logs remain close to one another all facing downstream until the next rains when the first good rise will carry them further on to where they are made into rafts and floated down the Irrawaddy. Today we have remained the whole day in camp which has been a nice rest and a chance to wash a few things and give our kit a good sunning. I stayed in camp while Freddie went off to inspect some work this morning. Work will soon have to close down in this area as there is no fodder for the elephants and they are already looking horribly ill and thin which naturally worries Freddie as the death of an elephant means some eight thousand rupees. I wore a jersey most of the day as it is so cold but such healthy sort of weather and I love the Jungle quite as much as my first experience last year! We both eat a colossal amount and Freddie is always exclaiming "Gosh this is good, you know I scarcely touch a thing when I am alone!" I can quite believe that as this must be a dreadfully lonely life. Freddie is beginning to get some of his old keenness on photography again and we have the camera with us and shall develop our negatives when at Sabenago again and shall soon be sending along some more photos. Goodbye for now Mother Dear.

P.S. Are you still sending my letters to the Bowdens? I think they'd like to see them and I'm afraid I do not write to them as often as I'd like but the time does go so terribly quickly.

Camp Monday January 8th 1923

We left Sabenago for camp on Saturday and as there has been no work to see, only marches, there is not much to say. We had to be up at the crack of dawn on Saturday in order to let the elephants set off, as the seven mile march to Twinge is chiefly along the sandbanks bordering the Irrawaddy, and with not much shade it soon gets hot for the beasts with their heavy loads containing our kit. Each day out means a lighter weight when the men eat their rice etc., and we reduce our fodder which all helps. Twinge was the first stopping place in my first tour last year with a nice bungalow perched on a bit of a hill from where one can see miles over the flatland across the river. Sheltering the bungalow is a huge people tree, the sacred tree of Burma, with very thick large leaves and it is the original rubber tree. Burmans nearly always plant a people tree near their precious pagodas. Twinge is a great place for cattle of sorts, mangy animals, and of very little use. They say there are six thousand in this village and all come trooping home in the evening making the air thick with dust. As the cattle are housed under their respective huts, consequently the village is filthy, and you'd never catch a Burman cleaning the place. The road from Twinge to Dourgbon, where we are now in camp is new to me. Quite pretty, all through dense Jungle, but already bamboo and other trees are drifting up as we are gradually getting to the hot weather. On our arrival here we found that the Thugyi or Head man of the village evidently thought the Zayat37[37] good enough for us to stay in and had cleared no camping area surrounding the Pongyi Kyang,[38] That is where the Burman priests live, and hold school for the lads of the village, and

---

[37] Pagoda.
[38] Monastery.

generally teach them all the evil tricks of the trade of being the biggest set of rogues in the country. This morning Freddie has ridden to inspect work about a mile off. I didn't go as a day off does me no harm and my mail must go in tonight. I received yours of December 5th last mail. I heard from Ethel who said Sammy had been ill with a high temperature for several days, and that she herself was weary nigh unto death looking after him. She is due to sail on the Leicestershire leaving March the 6th. A very cheery crowd of people I know over here will be on the same boat. I told Ethel ages ago to choose that boat if she wanted some nice fellow passengers. Mr. Roberts, (Freddie's Burra Sahib) will be one and is awfully cheery and quite Ethel's kind. Haven't you our old magnifying glass to enable you to see our snapshots better? I know they are small but it's such an expense with Freddie's large camera. It is a difficult job to take good photos in this country. There is no way of washing negatives or prints but this next lot really are good. But Freddie is such an expert I feel even these don't please him.

What a dreadful fire it must have been. They seem to have had bad luck in Herefordshire I wonder if any of Mr. Farmer's were among those burnt. He must be a regular Jonah. How nice to have Arthur's medals.[39] You must prize them and I hope we shall see them all framed one day. Perhaps when Freddie and I come home we can see about it. Hope Connie and George enjoyed the London trip. They never write, though she owes me two letters! I am writing a long letter to Jack this mail and sending a lot of enclosures. Goodbye mother dear keep cheery. I always love having your weekly letters and think you are splendid to write so often. Lots of love from us both.

Tonkine Camp Sunday January 14th 1923

Yours of December 15th and 20th both arrived since I last wrote. I can't think why the latter has come so quickly and I hope next Wednesday's up-boat will not fail to bring me another one. How much quicker letters come now. Thank you so much dear for always remembering to send me *The Hereford Times* it is much more appreciated out here than at home! A penny-halfpenny for postage is alright. Mince pies certainly were not included in our Christmas fare! The cook turns out pastry at times but with only a little camp fire it is wonderful what he does produce. Kerosene oil cans serve for everything for cooking and heating water. I do hope your cold is quite gone I can understand how low it must leave you but it is always a comfort to know that you are in good hands. It is a pity you could not manage to get to Rosslyn for Christmas, but with twelve in the house you should have quite a cheery one at Church House; though you must have wanted some of your family with you as much as we all wanted you. Dear, do tell me if there are any undies or anything you want made, I would so love to do something and with a pattern sent from you it would be quite easy. I have just finished making some lace pillowcases for Mrs. Lock who is daily expecting another infant. Her husband is in the army and has just been ordered to Simla where he writes they have had six weeks of snow and skating. I did not know Sammy was going at the same time as Ethel. I'm very glad for he seems to need a change badly. I wonder where they will settle. Poor old Dottie, it is sad for her going home. I doubt her remaining at Dilwyn though she will probably want to if Aunt Helen does not keep fit. You will see we are still having our camping life and if the temperature did not get steadily higher I'd love to go on for months. Today we really felt the heat and I fear it is goodbye to the cold weather. This year I shall

---

[39] Lieutenant Arthur Britten, Mully's brother, was awarded the Military Cross for conspicuous gallantry in action in France; vide Supplement 1016 of London Gazette dated 27th January 1917. He was killed subsequently on 14th April, 1918, whilst serving with the 8th Bn. of the Gloster Regiment. He is commemorated on the Tyne Cot Memorial, Zonebeke, Belgium, for officers and men who died in the Ypres Salient and have no known graves.

know what's what in heat, Monywa is a little hell I believe, but I don't believe it is time for me to frizzle yet. My last letter was from Donunabow on the edge of the paddy fields. The second day there Freddie rode off to inspect some work and I enjoyed a day's rest in camp. In the afternoon Freddie made me have some shots at doves with his gun. My first shot was at a couple making love to each other on a branch and blowed if they didn't both come tumbling down. My luck seemed to be in so I went on and finished with 5 doves with 6 shots! Doves are awfully good to eat and we did enjoy the pie next day. I have shot several since so it is nice to be able to add to our larder. The next day's march ran to about six instead of three miles . No one knew the road and we tried track after track in the Jungle which always turned out to be a blind alley. We at last came across a bullock cart and the man sent us off and eventually we got to the creek which we followed up until we came to the usual paddy fields outside the village. Mr Hill joined us there having come in the day before. Our camping ground was cleared on top of a very high bank with a sheer drop to the very twisty creek below. It was rather a hot spot and if Hill had not been there Freddie would have chivvied off to another spot. After our usual little snooze in the afternoon Freddie and I went off to the paddy fields with the gun and came back with quite a nice bag of doves and one Jungle fowl. Hill came along to have dinner with us that evening which we always have within comfy distance of the fire. Hill has his separate camp, finding his own fodder. He is more talkative now but I'm sure he prefers his own company and one of his beloved books. Hill is a very different man to Freddie's assistant last year. He (Hill) passed his Burmese exam with credit within three months for which he was presented with five hundred rupees by the Corporation. Wednesday was a very long march but most interesting; following up a creek through to an area Freddie and Hill had never been before which is to be opened up next rains. Except in patches the creek is quite dry and we had to find our way along its the stony sandy bed. By the marks on the trees on the banks there are very good rises so the logs will fairly nip down once the rains start. On either side tall kine grass grows and we could see fresh pad marks of wild elephants, tiger, and many smaller species of game. In one small pool one of the Burmans spotted crowds of small fish and in spite of breaking all forest laws the men all set to and scooped out the fish onto the surrounding sand, where they hopped about in hundreds. We went on but later the men arrived with a good 3lbs of these small fish which are excellent fried, rather like sprats. During our travels we came across a Kedda in the Jungle, which was used last year for catching wild elephants. A Kedda is a structure built of very strong poles in the shape of a "V". The two points go some way out into the Jungle and the elephants are gradually herded in by thousands of coolies and driven up the drive and so to the narrower part where there is a huge tall gate about a hundred yards from the point of the "V". Directly the elephants get past the gate a coolie on top lets down the gate. Et Voila! About forty or fifty elephants are captured, sometimes even more. About twenty-four hours later Oosies riding tame elephants go in and one on either side of the wild elephant they slip a rope down with a slip knot and catch the animal round two legs. This elephant is then laid out and put in a "Crush", a wooded device where he remains until starved into submission. This only takes about three days and one Oosie remains with him day and night until the elephant is accustomed to him and allows the Oosie to feed him. On our way past the same spot today Freddie and Hill took several photos of the Kedda, which you will have soon. It was about six miles to the first spot for good water where a place had been cleared on the bank of the creek and where we pitched our camp. Good fodder and water are the first considerations in fixing a camping spot, for the elephant requires so much. The next morning I spent in camp alone while Freddie and Hill went off to inspect the country higher up where work is to be opened up. They returned late, full of their adventures down some wonderful cavern away down in the bowels of the earth! On the strength of this excitement Freddie decided to spend another day in Bawdwn camp and to take me up the three and a half miles to see everything. Next morning we all started off like a Sunday school treat. The men had heard of the wonders of the cavern and taking it to be a place of the gods, came trooping along in their best "bibs and tuckers" to offer candles to the many little figures of Buddha that travellers from all parts have brought here. Men had gone before to open up the track and we arrived at the top of the hill to find them preparing great long torches from split bamboo branches. When these were ready they were thrown down this huge hole and we then descended fifty feet down a rickety bamboo ladder to the depths below. First of all I must tell you about one funny old josser we spotted putting a little lighted candle stick on a rock at the top. This he told us was an offering to the gods for our safety. So I felt quite safe to go! By this time the cavern was echoing with the boom, boom, boom, of a Burmese gong one of the boys was knocking. We then started off on our tour of inspection, men all round lighting the way with torches. The smoke nearly did for us in some of the smaller caves. At the only spot where water was dripping we found men with bits of bamboo which they filled with this so called holy water, and this was carried carefully back to their village with a full belief that a sip will bring them back from death's door! This underground cave is quite a hundred yards in length and leading off are numerous smaller caves with endless niches or hollows in the walls where one sees the everlasting Buddha. Our men dashed about planting their little candles before these images and gradually the place looked like some cathedral with the lights showing up the arches and pillars. The furthermost end of the cave is alive with bats which whirled all round us. The bats manure is a great source of income to the Burman and every now and then he collects it and ships it down to Mandalay where they are able to extract saltpetre from it! Freddie took a photo of a very fine stone column formed from centuries of dripping water and fossilised with a work of millions of tiny shells. We had a group of about eight Burmans holding torches and then Freddie gave an exposure of fifteen minutes. I wonder if we shall get anything as it was jolly difficult to take. I teased Hill that he is exactly like you on a picnic for he never goes anywhere without a book or paper, and after a short time with us in the cave he went up on top to read the Daily Mail until we appeared. We all arrived back at camp none the worse for our adventures and I am lucky to have seen what might be a show place at home where all the trippers would arrive from afar in their charabancs or tin-lizzies and pay their sixpences at the gate and go away feeling they had had their full money's worth. I'm afraid we gave this place rather a tripper's look with orange peel. We never do a march without oranges to eat at the end. This morning we came back to Sonkive and are now camped down by the creek which is very much nicer. Everything is so peaceful after Bawdwn camp where elephants were trumpeting and roaring so often on account of wild herds which come down quite near the camp, and the Oosies had to turn out with torches to frighten the wild ones away, and comfort their own by bringing them nearer the camp. Well dear I must away to bed. We have just had a very good five course dinner and while I finish this I have put Freddie on to improve his education by reading *The Hereford Times*. We have taken photos of Burmans with one reading *The Daily Mail* and think of sending a copy to that Journal's office. Perhaps *The Hereford Times* would like one to show their worldwide fame. Freddie has said "Poof", chucked the paper down and gone to warm his back by the fire, and so being a well brought up wife I go now and keep his one side warm. Good bye mother dear lots of love from us both.

Sabenago Monday January 22nd 1923

I got your letter of December 27th when Freddie and I arrived in from tour last Saturday the 20th. We did the double march from Chaukgyi of eleven miles to Sabenago to save an extra night out at Bhubeighu. The boys never mind a long march with their nose towards home. Freddie and I are alright of course as we rode the ponies more than half the distance as they too seem to smell home and went along like *'gooduns'* finishing up with a canter. I like riding so much better than last year when I was in a blue funk nearly the whole time. I couldn't accustom myself to the narrow precipitous and rocky paths we travel along. I love the old white pony now and don't feel I am about to take a header each time he trots. We left Mr. Hill at Chaukgyi to go on elsewhere before coming into Sabenago at the end of this week. I like Hill very much but must say things are nicer and easier without him! After Soukuie where I wrote my last letter we went on to Ofenifaoo Boom through the village surrounded with paddy fields, where we stayed last year. We stayed about a mile and a half out where a very nice Tay is built on top of a high bank overlooking the creek. At this point a huge Boom has been built to prevent logs floating further down where there are many weirs to divert the water in small channels to the acres and acres of paddy fields. Last year owing to a big rise and a large number of logs coming down, the boom broke, with the result about 500 logs went through causing a fearful lot of damage below, all of which had to be paid for by the Corporation of course. Elephants work about the boom and drag on the logs directly the water subsides. Next morning we had only four and a half miles to go to Suinhein our next camp. After a short walk we joined the very good road the Forest Department has made, and we were in Suinhein before I realised I had walked all the way! This is our second trip to this place this year, but it is now very deserted for the work is finished and all the elephants are out at rest camps. We had a long time to wait for our elephants with the kit so we sat on a log in the sun and ate our oranges which we always take with us. Hill fairly blossomed forth in conversation on this particular occasion, and we had a long discussion on our ideas on the next world and our prospects in the same! Hill's chief fear is to die at all, and also lest his heaven does not include those he'd like! Anyway, many and diverse ideas kept us going until our respective camps were ready. Hill had a tent a little way off and Freddie and I stayed in the Tay. About dinner time we heard a fearful roaring and trumpeting from our travellers and the Oosies had to turn out en masse with huge burning torches and stripped bamboos and brought the elephants in and up to another feeding ground as wild elephants were about. This put us on the lookout but nothing was heard until Freddie and I had just got into bed and Freddie was fumbling away under the blankets putting in photo plates. And then we heard a rustling and presently a cracking of dead bamboos. "Good lord it's an elephant!" says my husband but too calm for Liza he dashed out to peer out in the dark. By this time the whole camp was in an uproar, boys yelling and beating tins and lighting flares to frighten the beast or beasts away. Poor old Hill came along pretty quick, I can tell you, shouldering his gun and or first remark was in reference to our morning talk! He, Hill, apparently had heard movement near his tent and later tracks of an elephant were found. Freddie let off a volley with his un and now we look back on events, the whole thing was most amusing. There was Freddie in his queer Sahmbambees looking very sheepish at the back and I in my dressing gown. Hill the only respectably dressed of the party. The boys made up our camp fire and all crowded round. Oosies again went off again with flares up to where they had left our elephants. Golly! I do think they are a plucky lot because a wild tusker is no joke. About a quarter of an hour later the sound of the "Kylocks" coming nearer and presently all our elephants except one were ridden in; a very fine spectacle with the Oosies still with their big flares. These elephants were tethered near the camp and again the poor wretched Oosies had to go off in search of the one missing which had broken her chain and gone further afield, She was found alright and marks proved the naughty lass had gone off with a wild tusker, but with the wonderful control each Oosie has over his particular elephant, they will always come when called. We then went back to our little beds but not for long as all this excitement brought us very near dawn. Nothing more was heard but it was certainly very, very thrilling at the time. At Chaukgyi, our next stopping place we felt quite safe as we stayed in the village. Freddie took a very amusing photo of a lot of children sitting on a plank over a stream, a lovely sight. The little nippers, about two feet high carrying a fat little brother or sister about one foot high. The latter always with a hat on of some description and nothing else except perhaps a string of silver coins around the neck. We stayed at Chaukgyi for three days. Freddie and Hill going off each day to inspect work and I filled in my mornings sewing. I feel awfully sad my touring in this district is finished. Mahamyaung will all be so different but I'm glad to see more of Burma. We have started to pack here and the kit will be able to go on the boat here straight to Monywa. The next and rather ticklish job will be in the packing at Glenside. We have decided to take up our Jungle cook and make shift at the bungalow instead of going to the club which would be much more expensive and some way to walk to Glenside each day. We shall miss the *'Tum-tum'* which I think I told you Mr. Street has bought back. Since coming into Sabenago we have spent most evenings doing photography with very good results. I enclose a few, dear, of some we took some time ago. Pass them on to Mary or whoever you think will be interested. I'm sorry you could not manage to get to Rosslyn for Christmas but glad you had so happy a time at the Mackenzie's. It tickled me the way you said the two Ledger sisters had another Christmas dinner at the vicarage as well as the midday one with you! Poor dear how you must have wanted to join them. What a lovely little lot of presents you had. Christmas is observed so much more at home. Edith wrote that she is sending me two hats of her own make but no sign of them yet. I hope they are not lost through not being registered! Well mother dear the mail goes this morning and I must get one or two more letters written first.

Lots and lots of love dear and from Freddie, although he does not write (like most men) he does love reading your letters.

Sabenago Tuesday January 30th 1923

How quickly the week goes! Mail day always seems to be here and from now and onwards the days will go even more quickly, until I can sit down in my own house and be peaceful once more. The first load of Freddie's kit to Monywa has just come off the bullock cart shipped in the Sampan to wait on the other side for the mail boat this afternoon. Some thirty odd packages, which is small compared to when we leave Glenside. The Corporation pays all expenses so we don't really mind. Your letter of January 3rd with its many enclosures arrived last week. Thanks so much. I love receiving oddments and am interested in everything. I will send on those of interest to Jack. Like the Bowden family, letters seem to travel far and wide and we often receive letters from home four months old from Norah Bowden in Canada and Alan in East Africa. So glad you like the silk. You will now be able to show as much leg as you like with such a choice garment underneath. The silk is hand woven and probably from Annaporah, a great silk centre just outside Mandalay. What a blood thirsty lot of people seem to be in Herefordshire. Some murderer or other is always giving interest to their neighbours and I suppose we ought to sympathise with the man for shooting his mother-in-law as they always seem to be held as such fearsome people. I am quite sure Freddie is content with his! You must find out all particulars about the patent knee supporter you mentioned. It is sure not to be very expensive and the great thing is if it can be of help to you. Last night while Mr. Hill was talking over his school days at Shrewsbury, I suddenly thought of Gussie Davies being Matron there, so asked him whether he remembered her. With a broad grin on his face he said he did! Old Gussie seems to have the reputation of being very fierce! On the strength of Gussie being my second cousin - she is isn't she? We find Hill and I are connected by marriage! Hill's brother married a Miss Harris whose mother was a Miss Freer who lives at Stourbridge where Hill comes from. This Mrs. Harris and Gussie Davies are sisters apparently, so that's that. Freddie and I are having a fearful time hunting ticks! Fleas were the fashion last year and now we breed ticks! They seem to prefer the taste of Freddie more and although I get plenty running about me, they don't seem to care for a meal. One evening last week, an elephant came in from one of the camps for medicines etc., so I nipped up and had a ride in the "Kah"[40] or basket on the top, Freddie took a photo, which I will enclose, though the light prevented giving a good result. I think the photo gives a good example of a pimple on an elephant, do you? Mr. Hill got in from camp last Wednesday and will stay until we depart next week. He and Freddie are busy in the office all morning settling up. Hill has two dogs with him and we have '*Spiker*' so there is some noise going on at times. They have huge games together rushing madly all round the bungalow. The joy of Jungle bungalows is that they are not supposed to be clean and tidy, and it is so peaceful not to have to boost round the servants to clean corners or behind furniture etc! And it quite pleases my eye to see mud on the floor with as few mats as we have in our sleeping hut instead of polished boards. Last Wednesday Freddie and I dashed across to Male in the sampan to go on the cargo boat. A man is always posted to the side of the river and beats a gong when the boat is in sight and then we have to tear down the half mile across sand and mud to the boat and get over the half mile of water as soon as we can. I was glad we crossed that day as a Miss Beck who I knew in Maymyo was on board doing the trip to Bhamo. We went across again on Friday as Freddie had to claim 12,000 Rupees sent up from Mandalay. The boat was horribly late as she had stuck on sandbanks about four times on the way up. The river is getting very low now and the channels seem choked with sand more than last year. It is already warming up and we get 87° on the veranda, which is a month earlier than last year for the same temperature. You remember Daisy Pringle who stayed with me in Maymyo. She writes me of her engagement to a planter in Assam. I'm awfully glad as she is such a good sort. She goes home in March and he may get leave to get married in England. Daisy's father is managing director of the Estate so I should think the man will get leave alright. He is an Australian and never been to England yet. In this country the Burmans always feed their Buddhist priests. I had not seen it before yesterday morning when I heard a gong being beaten and upon looking out saw a priest in his flowing yellow robes with a large black bowl into which women from the compound were putting rice, fish or any other titbit to fill the tummies of the biggest scoundrels in the country. They do this all over the country, and prayers for the donors of food are supposed to be given by the priest. I must be off now dear, I'm afraid not much of interest in this letter Lots of love mother dear from us both.

[**Editor's Note:** There is a gap in the recorded letters between 30 January 1923 and 17 March 1923 due to Mully's illness the nature of which is not known].

Croxton, Maymyo, Sunday March 17th 1923

Here I am back once more with the Cleavers; sooner than expected as an urgent maternity case came into the home last Wednesday and the only other room was booked for a case due to come in any hour. The only thing we could do was to send an SOS to Mrs. Cleaver and of course got the answer she would send; that I was welcome any time! So I was fetched in the car that evening. Mr. Cleaver is in from the Jungle and as I have his dressing gown he has to have a tent in the garden. With two kiddies and an English nanny the house is full. I don't know what I should have done had I not been able to come here as everyone is full up with people for the hot weather. If this case had not been a month early in the home I should have stayed there as I feel so guilty dumping myself. The Mrs. Noyce at the house was fearfully ill and nearly died; baby only three and a half pounds. I was so sorry to leave all the sisters they were so topping to me. Major Crump came yesterday and says I look much better, and I feel it too. My walks don't take me far as yet, so, as motoring does not hurt so much as it did, I often go out with nanny and kids after tea. Everything is fixed for me to go

---

[40] Basket seat on an elephant.

to Kalaw with the Grants next month and leave Maymyo on the 31st, motor down to Mandalay and on to Sharzee, where we have to stay one night. Major Crump does not want me to motor the 60 miles up to Kalaw as he says it is a very twisty and bumpy road, so the Grants will do that and I'll go up by train. Colonel Grant has two months leave and will be with us and they intend having the car all the time which will be topping. I believe the country round about Kalaw is lovely, It is a thousand feet higher than Maymyo, all among pine trees. Colonel Grant is on the staff and the old General gets very annoyed when they go away for the season to escape the entertaining etc., which would have to be their lot in Maymyo, but they don't see why they should waste money on a life they don't care about. I have had one long letter from Freddie since he reached his destination. He had been dashing about on a motorcycle thing, converted so as to run on lines and holds about five people going about sixty miles an hour. Sounds some going compared to elephants doesn't it? He says it is not a bit hot and the temperature does not go above 98° which sounds hopeful. Taking over from another man everything always seems in a muddle so at present Freddie sees no prospect of my going up before the next cold weather. But one never knows and I shan't be very far off in Monywa where I shall go at the end of June. Mr. Milton (from whom Freddie takes over) is a bachelor and fearfully extravagant. Freddie says he has a standing order for twenty chickens per week. His messing costs ten rupees a day, which is absurd of course in the Jungle, so Freddie will have a job cutting down expenses all round. A new boy he took on at Monywa decamped with an advance of fifteen rupees, also a case of whiskey and other drinks! That's mild compared to what one has to put up with in this country sometimes. You remember I told you Mrs. Cleaver had all her jewellery taken just after I left here in December. Not a trace of it has been found but they have not given up hope. So sorry Edith thought better of sending me the hats. I'd have been glad to have them and willingly have paid the postage. No, the candle shades have not arrived yet but perhaps it is my fault as Emma wrote asking what colour I'd like and my reply was late. The cardboard ones last much better; silk splits so quickly out here. Dear I am so very glad you have decided to go with the Miss Macs. Ross is not so very far and after all friends around you in the house is most important. I should hate to think of you dependant on a typical landlady who would have no idea how to make you comfy. Freddie and I hope the Miss Macs will be able to house us on our arrival next year. We must see you as much as ever we can and his home is no use to anyone in the way of accommodation. You will see dear Gussy again! I wonder if you would like to see Gladys Wright again. She lives in Ross but as her Papa keeps a tailors shop the two sets of society would clash.

This is a very dull letter mother dear but there is nothing doing these days as I stillhave to lie low. I'm on Gaston Syrup, trying to improve my appetite and get fat. It is absurd how skinny I have become. It won't be the Cleavers fault if I don't soon weigh ten stones at least. I'm fed on masses of cream and egg-flips etc. Lots of love dear and I'm most awfully glad you feel happy at the thought of the new arrangements. I am too, for I know how fond the Miss Macs are of you and that you will have every care.

Kalaw, Sunday April 14th 1923

I was so afraid no mail was coming from you this week but that of March 21st arrived this morning, two days after my other letters, one from Mary. Post is noted for its wild ways up here and I hope my letters to you are received regularly. Thank you so much for enclosing Edith's. I am always so pleased to read her news. For one thing she writes rather rarely and then she keeps in touch with so many folk about whom one hears of from no one else. I'm glad Edith is more pleased with life. It is a pity young Denis can't be fixed at something but I suppose jobs at Home are still scarce. No dear I am not going to hurry to play golf and tennis again much as I love them. I am too fed up at feeling rotten and tired so I mean to get really fit now. Major Crump says I may begin after three months but even on the strength of that I shan't until I can go on decent walks without feeling tired. I feel the wound still of course and want to clutch on my tummy when I sneeze or cough and think weight is being put on steadily. Mrs. Grant weighs well over eleven stones and is a very hefty lass and we often wish we could exchange some flesh. She feeds me up on egg-flips and porridge so it won't be lack of food if I remain skinny. I'm still on Gaston Syrup but the quinine it contains has made me horribly deaf and fuzzy in the head, so I will leave it off for a bit. I'm glad Aunt Mary has been to see you. I'm sure it is not that she has forgotten you but having no trap makes a difference. I hear from her occasionally and was glad she received the Sham bag at Christmas. Cousin Emma and young Dorothy are the only two now who have not acknowledged the parcels but I'm sure I do not expect the latter to write now Miss Holmes has left. Miss Holmes is now on her own in a little house at Bexhill and wants children to board and educate and she will also take paying guests. Bexhill is a nice spot and perhaps Freddie and I may go there when we are home. Poor Aunt Helen I'm sorry she is still so ill. Can't they have a good doctor? I do hope nothing will happen. How they must be looking forward to Ethel and Dottie coming home. I bet the latter won't remain at Dilwyn though I should think someone will be wanted. I think Aunt Bea is such a brick. They do so much for those kids. I wish Sammy and Ethel would retire. Aunt Helen is so bucked when she has her family around her. Uncle Fred would simply crumple up if anything happened to Aunt Helen. Life up here is jogging along in the same peaceful way. I believe the residents and some energetic visitors are now in the throes of a week of tournaments and dances etc. But nothing doing for us, thank you. Mrs. Grant and I have not been inside the club yet but mean to sometime. So many quite nice men marry these blackywhites which is such a pity. Kalaw swarms with them and it will never have the white population like Maymyo in consequence. But for scenery, Kalaw can take its hat off to any other place I have been to in Burma. We are right at the edge of the Jungle which is not dense like Maymyo, just hills with trees, and any possible spot cultivated with potatoes. In the narrow valleys are paddy fields, all terraced up, which are just being flooded ready for cultivation by diverting the stream through. The walks are lovely and I long for Freddie to be here and see everything. A nice place is wasted without him. Colonel Grant returned last Monday and he loves mooching around. Yesterday we went out in the car to some paddy fields and got three snipe, which were jolly good, and appreciated, to vary our menu. Food is rather a problem up here as there is no meat other than on big bazaar days every 5th day. Mrs. Grant gets up early and motors the servants down to scrap for meat and vegetables and return with the car fairly bulging also with duck and chickens which are fattened up for our consumption. The last couple of ducks did a bolt and have not been seen since. We have had several fearful thunderstorms and golly can it rain up here. However we are never prevented from going out at some part of the day and Mrs. Grant doesn't care a rap for using the car in all sorts of weather. I'm doing a lot of sewing and have passed the enthusiasm on to Mrs. Grant who is hard at making crawlers for her young copper headed daughter aged two. She finds my bundle of transfers and silks very useful; the latter are still kept in the green American cloth case you made me in Suisse. Do you remember? We all go in for the comfy side of life and after a tub at night appear in Kimonos for dinner and then are too sleepy to stay up very much longer. Young Bar Tai is having a very easy time here. Except for doing my room and helping to wait he has no work. He is becoming an awful little swank and I have often seen him in the bazaar dressed up to the nines bobbing along in the brightest of brown shoes which give him agony every step. Freddie does not see his way to leave the district and come up here yet. I long to grouse sometimes because we do have such long separations, and he will be so sweet to have to look after me now. Goodbye mother dear for this week I do hope you are comfy and happy in your new home

Chianglun Lodge, Kalaw, Wednesday April 17th 1923

I was so pleased to get yours of March 14th dear and to know you are not fussing over my welfare. I told Freddie not to send a cable because I always think they are so short and unsatisfactory and I took it for granted that you'd know me to be sensible enough not to go into complications but to get fit as soon as possible and here I am up in the most heavenly spot completing my cure. My last letter was scrappy I'm afraid and it had to be sent via Rosslyn as I had not got your address with me. I quite enjoyed the seven hour train journey up here as the scenery is so wonderful. I had the Grants two spaniels in the carriage with me which acted as a protection for me from two other female travellers also with dogs. Fearing a scrap they took themselves to another carriage so I was able to spread myself. At Thazi, the junction, I arranged for food which did not arrive until just as the train was off and then discovered it too horrid to eat, so the dogs came in for it and I kept the hard boiled eggs. Luckily a Mrs.Tollard I know was on the train and she provided me with bread and butter Mr. Tollard is on the railway and is entitled to a special coach so I went along and travelled part of the way with them and enjoyed the big electric fan. Mrs. Grant drove the car up to Kalaw in great style and Colonel Grant was waiting at the station to meet me. This is a most lovely bungalow about two miles from the station and Bazaar. Kalaw is so well planned and no houses under several thousand rupees are allowed to be built, so they are all superior in every way to the ones in Maymyo. The place reminds me of Church Stretham, only the hills are covered with trees, mostly pines, and the smell is lovely. A great many houses are owned and lived in by Eurasians and the club is rather impossible owing to most members being blackywhites and one is supposed to quickly adopt the accent and 'oh melee' after each sentence. However, that does not trouble us for we never go near the club and have not spoken to anyone outside our house so far, which we both enjoy. Sounds horrid, but at Maymyo one has an overdose of other people and their entertaining! And we can safely have peace here. Colonel Grant had to leave for Maymyo again, the day after we settled in, to go to some rifle meeting, but he hopes to start his two months leave next week and return here. Mrs.Grant drives the car everywhere and each morning we go down to the bazaar and after tea go along one of the many roads out of Kalaw, often taking a picnic tea. Coppy, the three year old copper headed daughter is dumped with her Ayah, or with some kindred spirits, to be called for later. We are in the Southern Shore States, the ground owned by the Sawbwa (Ruler) who lets tracks out to the Shores who cultivate it chiefly with potatoes, which do awfully well. The spuds are bought up by the Southern Shore State Produce Company, not long started, and run chiefly by axed officers. Pat Grant is a director. Another product is pigs. Thousands are wanted so they seem a pretty prolific breed to go in for with three litters a year, producing about fifteen babies per time. Some going isn't it! Patches of ground are railed off for certain numbers of pigs and they live chiefly on roots and scratchings. They are all the black sort and near the wild kind out here. The Shores are such queer and stumpy people, very industrious and hardy. They grow their spuds in groups with the ground mounded up. The last two days have become fearfully thundery. Storms give one a rotten head, otherwise I feel fairly alright. I went to see Major Crump two days before I left and he assessed a good verdict. He weighed me and I have gone up five pounds since I left hospital and so hopefully I will soon regain my ten stones. Poor Freddie is awfully fed up with life; stuck in the only district that does not work through the hot weather. He still cannot see any prospect of me going down yet as he cannot leave his district. It is so rotten for him he feels like swearing at it all, not at all like Freddie poor dear. I am jolly lucky to be in such a nice place with such topping people the only fly I ever have in my ointment is Freddie having to be away so much. Major Crump says heat won't upset me now so I will try and go down to Freddie next month. The Grants have this bungalow until the middle of June but I really can't leave Freddie all that time. Stella Middleditch is being married on April 23rd. We are sending her an ivory necklace. I heard from Aunt Mary last mail and she mentioned how sorry she was not to get in to see you but she has sold the horse and float and is so tied. She hopes to let her cottage for the spring. Mrs. Grant knows so many Herefordshire people and was interested in your *Hereford Times* this week. Her father Mr. Houghton was vicar at Dimock for years. She knows the Rileys, Greenprices etc., and her uncle is the present Lord Chancellor, not that that is of much interest. Mrs. Grant is a perfect dear and just one of us, dear. I enclose a cheque from Freddie to help in any small things, a pound for the papers and a fiver to bust. I wish it could be more but like everyone else we are near the touchline all the time and it would worry us both to get beyond our pay. However, we always hope for better things next time out. The best of love mother dear, and I'm longing to hear of your new abode.

Kalaw, Saturday April 21st 1923

Not very much news this week, I'm afraid the English mail is not in yet but hope for it tonight. The Regional Office is very prompt in forwarding it as a rule. The thunderstorms here have at last cleared off, I'm thankful to say. I was scared stiff of them at night with no one to protect me. Maymyo is having very rotten weather and spoiling the tournament and polo. I see in the paper Government House gave a dance for over three hundred. Golly there must have been a squash. The new Governor is evidently not going to entertain like the late one and this dance which included everyone has got to do for his short time in Maymyo. The government officials are not going to have such a cushy time under the new regime with several Burmans as ministers. These are very averse to moving up to Maymyo for the hot weather owing to the expense of nine thousand rupees for the moving alone. This won't be popular because the Europeans will have to keep a double establishment for wives and family to go to the hills in the hot weather. The houses in Kalaw are so much nicer than Maymyo which shows the Eurasians and Burmans are the ones with the money. Some houses here have decent long baths, with water laid on and their own electric light! Both fearfully swanky in this country I assure you. Freddie writes that he hopes to get away for a few days leave in the latter part of May. He intends going to Rangoon first to see Mr. Johnston to talk over affairs in the new district which seem to be in a hopeless muddle. We may hear where we are to go on our return from home leave next year. After Rangoon Freddie will come up here for a few days and take me down. I believe it is pretty hot down below until the rains break in June but that won't hurt me. If I am near I always feel I can keep Freddie's mind off his work more! We are still doing a bit of motoring. I think I told you the Grants drive and do everything for the car themselves, which about halves the cost of the car. Mrs.Grant is a jolly good driver and I never feel a bit nervous with her and not like these native drivers who go at such a pace and are absolute road hogs. I've just received your letter of March 27th. Thank you so much dear, I hope arrangements are possible for *The Hereford Times* to be sent you at Ross. By the way did Smith's charge your account for a couple of Letts Diaries? Don't pay if they have because I have never received them. I also had a very nice letter from Aunty Bea. She is so splendid at writing and wonders will never cease; a letter from Crofton! He wrote from London having gone up to see the specialist about his eyes for which he took special leave from India. Apparently severe poisoning set in from dust. At one time he lost his sight completely. The specialist holds out hope that all will be well in time but he advises Crofton to keep away from hot climates. Crofton will return to India in September for about six months and then take two years leave pending retirement. He had seen Dorothy whom he intends leaving with Mrs. Brown at Michaelmas. I wonder if these instructions you mentioned will be of any use; you must make every enquiry dear and let us know and I am sure Freddie will add a contribution. The poor dear would so love to make his fiver much bigger but until rubber smiles again we are none too well off, I'm sorry to say. We young ones can put up with it and never having known what much money means I really don't mind, but of course Freddie sees very much further into the future and has not so much of my rash ideas of live today for tomorrow we die! And of course Freddie's people are so hard up he naturally feels he wants to send them an occasional cheque. I don't have an allowance yet. Freddie has the old fashioned idea though personally I think an allowance is much better, but there again I shall wait until he is less worried over his bally old rubber shares. It is better of course, and some out here say that England has exhausted her supply of rubber and the price of shares will go up within the next few months but that remains to be seen.

Well dear this must end and I go to bed. We have just finished dinner and all sifting round the fire in our Kimonos, our usual dinner attire. You have no idea the interruptions this letter has had. Beastly beetles and pooches of all sorts buzzing around giving Mrs.Grant and me the jimjams. Lots of love mother dear and I do hope something will materialize re: these patient instruments. It would be so lovely if you were able to move about once more.

Kalaw, Saturday April 28th 1923

Yours of the 4th received last mail for which many thanks dear. I also heard from Emma Turner. Poor thing is still fussing about the candle shades and has sent to London for them now. Emma received my Christmas parcel but like Aunt Mary and Emma forgot to write to say so. I'm so sorry you've had such a nasty thing as shingles. I hope the motor trip to Ross did not make you worse in any way. Poor dear you must have looked a sorry sight with your face all done up in bandages. Does one catch shingles or is it from a chill. Young John seems to have a cold nearly every time he's mentioned. He is a big boy by the photo Mary sent of their mansion at Weston. Smiths are blighters to charge you for the diaries which have not turned up yet. I'll write them again they must credit your account for 6s.6d. Parcels must always be registered and more valuable ones insured. I'm glad you told Emma Turner to do that. I shall miss the odd bits of Hereford news you always give me. Freddie and I are already thinking and making plans for our leave next year. Did I tell you Freddie has received official news that our passages have been taken on the boat sailing February 28th next. Isn't it topping. That time will soon be gone. Freddie wants to spend the summer school holidays with his people wherever they go, otherwise we shall see nothing of them as their house is quite hopeless during term-time. Emma Turner wrote an awfully kind letter telling us to be sure and make use of them and that Fayre Oaks is open for us to make our headquarters with good attics for the kit. Of course that is a godsend to us and we shall probably go straight to Hereford and then on to wherever you happen to be. It will be so topping for us both to be sure of months together and no dreaded separation ahead. It is over two months since Freddie left me in Maymyo and I do get so depressed at times! And it will have to be another three before he can come up here for me. The poor dear is having an awful time in his new district; men going on strike, the extra assistant left on account of ill health and Rangoon does not seem inclined to replace him, which of course means much more work for Freddie. He had to turn himself into a bit of a surgeon too for there are so many accidents to do with the various lorry's etc. One day an old girl tumbled off a lorry and split her head open to the skull and poor Freddie had to go out and attend to the gory sight. Milton the man before Freddie couldn't stick any of that so left the men to attend to themselves. Freddie hasn't got to do it but it seems the only humane thing to do.

Last Monday we had a most lovely run in the car to HeHo. Twenty-four miles each way. We climbed up and up over land looking very like the Sussex Downs and then came suddenly to a spot where we overlooked an enormous plain and in the distance at the foot of the hills could be seen the small town of HeHo. The terminus of the line and the starting point for Tourggyi, a lovely spot in the hills nearly five thousand feet up. After a picnic lunch at the PWD[41] bungalow we motored back to some paddy fields where Colonel Grant got some very good snipe shooting. Most evenings we go out with him and the gun and come home with doves if nothing more exciting is to be found.

I'm in alone at present with a rotten ulcerated throat and what feels like a good old go of rheumatism. I'm never free from it so I should cuddle into bed early and see what a dose of aspirin will do. I am busy embroidering and making some nighties. I think there must be too much dressing in the material which rots in the sun out here. All mine I brought out are in ribbons. Goodbye mother dear I am longing to know what you think of your new abode lots of love.

Kalaw, Sunday May 6th 1923

I am just about as fed up and disappointed with this life as it is possible to be. The whole of this last week I have been in bed with the most awful ulcerated throat and so far there seems little improvement. I feel like giving in to a good old howl because I was so full of hope to be really fit and fat by the time Freddie came and I shall be as skinny as ever when I get up again. It is agony to get anything down and my tongue looks fit to plant potatoes in and needless to say I don't fancy much. I retired to bed last Saturday and on Tuesday Mrs. Grant got the wind up as I had a temperature of 102^0 so routed out a funny little doctor, a Sikh with a very black fuzzy beard, but he seems very good and his paint got rid of the ulcers on one side very quickly. He took a blood slide and after examination says all the trouble is due to the rheumatism. I have had it off and on ever since I came to Kalaw and some mornings I can't sew or write as my hands are so stiff and I also get it very badly across my shoulders. The Doctor advises a course of injections as he said I should go on having throats or swellings if I don't. I had a few injections after rheumatic fever in Ceylon and think it well worth trying again but have written to Major Crump in Maymyo to ask his opinion first. It really is bad luck isn't it? You don't know how good and careful I have been all along because to feel really fit is my greatest wish and I've wasted enough life by being crocked or feeling cheap. I shall have to start all over again to try and get fat and if Freddie comes this month I shall have to buck up. Probably the heat at Monywa will suit me better. Kalaw seems to have come in for an early monsoon as scarcely a day passes without a heavy storm. This bungalow was finished only just before we came in and I was wondering if the damp walls etc., have had any effect, but in any case there is no getting away from the fact that I am a cheap creature these days. Gosh! And to think what I used to be able to do without turning a hair. The Grants are most awfully good and do their best to cheer things up for me but naturally they are out a lot and the cocker pup is my chief and faithful companion. I was so glad to get yours of April 11th and to know all your belongings reached Ross safely. It would be a big help to you to have Connie and it was very good of her to go all the way with you. I received a letter from Smith's saying the Lett's diaries have been sent off. The fool probably never registered them. I shall say they must claim compensation and credit your account for the money. I suppose you are having your papers from Ross now. The Grants go off for a shooting trip tomorrow. I read and sleep most of the day as I haven't the energy or inclination to sew. How silly of me to say Gussy in my letter. I meant Patty Downes. She will be quite

---

[41] Public Works Department.

near you and I hope will get over to see you one day. Well mother dear needless to say there is no news to tell you and I am about ready to cuddle down in bed and I shall be better next time I write. Anyway it will be a week nearer to my seeing Freddie which is the next most important thing in life. Lots of love.

Kalaw, Saturday May 12th 1923

At last I am up and about once more and have just come in from my first ride in the car after a fortnight. I really did have a very cheap time and up to Wednesday last I felt my wretched throat was getting no better, and then during one of the paintings Mrs.Grant noticed a whole lot of puss coming away and the whole of that day it seemed to carry on. So there must have been a large abscess hidden behind one tonsil. Since then I have steadily got better and am not feeling at all bad now, in spite of ten days in bed. The little doctor says I shan't be really rid of the rheumatism until I have had a course of injections. I wrote to Major Crump who wrote that he does not advise them, but will go into the matter more next week when he and his wife come here to spend a few days with the Grants. In the mornings I am still a crock with rheumatism and am disappointed Major Crump does not approve of the injections but perhaps he wants me to get stronger first.

At last there seems something definite about Freddie coming up. He writes that he must go down to Rangoon to see Mr. Johnston the head of the firm, and will leave the district about May 21st and hopes to have finished with Rangoon and up here by the 28th. It will then be three months since we have seen one another, and I daren't build on this too much for fear of disappointment. It will do Freddie a lot of good to come up in the cool for a few days. It is so hot down below and the poor dear has had a fearful worrying time. One great thing which has bucked us up is that there is every possibility of Freddie having Madaya district when we return from leave. Madaya is a good spot and Freddie will take over from Mr. Cleaver and we shall have Croxton as our house, as the Cleavers are retiring. Croxton is awfully nice and to be in Maymyo will be topping. Freddie has only to motor out some way from Mandalay to get to his district at Madaya and if it comes to pass he will have much more home life and not this continual Jungle work. He deserves something good as he has had more dirty work to do than any other man in the Corporation, just because they find he is conscientious. There is no mail in yet; late on account of the fearful storms in the Bay. Burma has now been cut off from India for several days and one ship is lost altogether. The weather is very unsettled here and seems just like the breaking of the monsoon which is very early. Rain seems to have fallen all over Burma. We have not done without a fire on a single evening yet.

My young Lugaley[42], Bar Tai is having a very easy time here but he was very good while I was ill and waited on me so well. It is an awful joy to have one's own boy; other People's butlers are all very nice but they don't care so much for other Memsahibs, and don't see why they should have any attention. Your letter of April 18th has just arrived for which many thanks and for the enclosures. Emma Turner also wrote that she had sent the candle shades off from Harrods. I'm glad the Macs have got Netherwood in Hereford. But Mother Dear can't any arrangement to be made for you to go there. Surely something can? I would so love to know you were back again in Tupsley and when Freddie and I come home next year it will be so nice for us to stay there with you and so see all the Hereford people. Perhaps when the Miss Macs have sorted themselves out other plans can be made. To have two houses is rather a large job I should think. How sickening the weather sounds at home and disappointing you're not being able to get out but hope you have a nice warm summer to

---

[42] Boy servant.

make up for it. Who is the Mrs.Tailor who travelled with Ethel from Colombo? Ann said so many friends saw her off. I haven't heard from Ethel at all. I am glad Aunt Helen is better and able to go downstairs. I stay in bed half the morning and I go to bed all afternoon and again about 9:30pm so there is no excuse for me not to get fat is there? I take Ovaltine at night and find it helps to get me to sleep, a thing I have had great difficulty in doing. Well mother dear I must get ready for dinner now. Getting ready consists of putting on my kimono as we all parade like that in the evening! Best of love and I do hope your shingles will have quite gone when you write next.

Kalaw, Friday May 18 1923

Just by chance I saw in the paper this evening that the mail leaves Rangoon a day earlier this week, so this must go tomorrow morning. Thank you so much dear for yours of the April 25th. You are simply splendid the way you keep up with your letter writing and I should be awfully lost without your usual efforts. Mary doesn't honour me often and of course Edith might as well not exist for the letters I receive from her. I'm glad that the rash has quite cleared off now, also no fresh attack of rheumatism has come since going to Ross. I can see myself being trailed along in a chair at an earlier age than you old dear! My last week's letter told you my throat was alright but I spoke too soon. On Saturday night one side swelled up again and I had to stay in bed all Sunday. The doctor came and said he was going to take the matter into his own hands and insist on the injections, otherwise the throat and the awful rheumatism round my shoulders, back, and hands would never clear off. So on Monday I had the first dose and another today (double strength). My throat is certainly quite right now but I can't expect the rheumatic pains to clear off at once. The doctor thinks two injections ought to be enough but if the pain doesn't go I must have more. I told you Major Crump was doubtful of the serum doing any good, so I had decided not to have them. I don't know what Major Crump will say when I tell him I have gone my own way. He and his wife are motoring up here on Sunday for a few days. I hope Freddie will be here at the end of the week. I really feel I have come to the end of my patience in making the most of a bad job through these separations. Mine is such a silly sort of married life and oh, I do get so fed up being alone months on end. Somehow in Maymyo, with my own house to look after, life did not seem so bad but living weeks on end with others is pretty hopeless, in spite of the Grants being most awfully nice. They are a devoted couple and I feel horribly de trop at times. The one compensation I had during my fortnight in bed with a bad throat was that the Grants were at last having some peace from me being the third party! The heat down in Monywa won't hurt me and Freddie says in his district it is not at all bad. It will not be like other camps where we march to different camps each day. Freddie has one headquarters and motors out to all the different branches of work and he said that going along in the old tin lizzie it is never too hot, and of course I can do all that with him. I feel I can stick anything rather than be alone any longer. The weather up here is still awfully unsettled and thunderstorms roll up most days. I suppose we must expect rain now as the monsoon has broken. I have been out for several nice motor runs this last week. Don't think I don't care sufficiently about my weight etc. I assure you I am an absolute old fuss bag about myself as I'm so keen to get fit. How nice of Connie to go over to see you so soon. I suppose Will is a big boy now. What does he look like? Is he still as fair? I did not know Mrs.Harold James other baby died. Was it born dead? I have been making a few cheap washable frocks for the Jungle. A dress length of strong cloth in the bazaar comes to about two shillings, so that won't ruin us. I have got a move on with Mrs.Grant too, who never touched a needle before she came up here and has now made a whole lot of garments for her kid and a red dress for herself. My sewing machine is jolly useful and goes very well. The candle shades from Emma have not appeared yet but parcels generally come about a couple of mails later. Do you get enough books to read?

Wouldn't you like to join the library at Ross dear and we will pay the subscription? I do hope you will say if there is anything you want. I'd love to make you something but don't know what unless you say. So don't forget. The country is a beautifully green and the potato crop is coming up like smoke. They grow more potatoes than anything else up here. Well dear, I must write a line to Freddie now to catch him on his way down to Rangoon. Lots of love mother dear and I do hope you're happy at Ross.

Kalaw, Saturday May 26 1923

Many thanks for yours of the 2nd of May, the enclosures and the papers. It is very sweet of you to think of sending me the Mail which certainly gives one every possible detail of the wedding. I feel quite glad the Duke of York is married. Papers for weeks past had been full of preparations and now they have really done it. I wonder who the next one will be.

I wish I could say Freddie had arrived. I get so desperate and horribly depressed at times as three months of strangers and no one really belonging to me begins to pall but there is no use grousing. I must just hang on and hope next mail will be full of his arrival. Things at Mahamyaung and then the Rangoon trip has to be got through first. I'm feeling all right in myself now but feel full of rheumatism which is probably due to the heavy storms we have had for some time past. The rains are earlier this year, so it will not be too hot when I go down with Freddie. I shall welcome heat too and try to get the rheumatism baked out of me. I think you are wonderful to keep so sweet and cheery with all your troubles and pains. My aches etc., plus Freddie being away always makes me long to grouse and give vent to my feelings. I probably should if there were any relations near. The Crumps arrived in their car last Sunday having motored the 62 miles from Tharzi at the bottom of the hills. Major Crump is an awful dear and so is his wife. The former might appear grumpy to some for he is a man of few words but is really very cheery. The first day, Monday, Mrs. Grant and I were desperate as it poured the whole time and we were so afraid Major Crump would be bored. However, on Tuesday the weather was a bit brighter, so after breakfast we motored out to one of the pig farms where a Captain Fluke and a Mr. Spencer have about six hundred pigs going strong. We saw pigs of all sizes in all stages and, as he remarked, Mr. Spencer would show us an old sow having babies before we finished! Major Crump slopped around and though I don't think he was bored he certainly looked it! It is very sad that at the other farm where there are over seven hundred pigs some fever has broken out. Three sows were imported from Rangoon having been passed as fit and two died on the way up. They think the third infected the others there, who are now dying by the score. Awfully bad luck on the three men, ex-officers running the show. They think the whole lot of pigs will go in the end. Luckily the other farm is some miles away.

On Wednesday we started out on a perfectly lovely motor trip and finished up on the third day having done 200 miles. The Crumps had their big car in which was packed all our bedding and a few clothes. I went with the Grants whose car was piled up with fodder for all the days. The Grants don't go in for a chauffeur but the Crumps have one. We left here about 7:30am and got down to our first stopping place Yaungwey about 11-30am. I can't describe the run as the country is so beautiful with huge plains running for miles to the foot of mountains thousands of feet high. At Yaungwey the Grants had a bungalow lent to them and we were soon laying the table and getting down to a really good breakfast. Luckily it was big bazaar day so we prowled round and bought various odd things. In the afternoon we took a boat up the five mile canal to see the enormous lake running for a hundred of miles with most lovely mountains right down to the water's edge. This country and its people are most primitive. For boats they have a tree trunk hollowed out and instead of paddling or polling the native does what they call big rowing. The man stands at either end and balances on one leg and with his other round the paddle and hand on top, dips into the water and gives, a good shove and so we go along. It is marvellous how the balance is kept. The canal ran through paddy fields with the paddy just coming up. All is lovely fresh and green. At the end we had tea in the boat and after a good look round returned the same way home. The lake has numbers of enormous floating islands on which huts are built and people live. The islands are pegged down and if they want to change residence the whole island is poled along! Some way out is a bungalow in the middle of the lake where people can go and stay. We made an easy start the next morning and once more did another lovely run to Hlarmsung. We first of all went to Tournggyi, a spot higher than Kalaw, with a most wonderful view. A lot of Europeans live there but Tournggyi is very cut off as the railway does not run up there yet. From Tournggyi the twenty five miles to Hlarmsung took longer on account of the bad road but we got to the PWD bungalow and again set about getting breakfast directly we arrived. The PWD has jolly fine bungalows about every 30 miles along each main road and a Durwan is in charge but one has to shift for oneself. Lots of love Mother Dear.

Kalaw, June 1st 1923

Here I am at last with a husband. It is so topping, and all the last three months of trying to be patient gone. I hope to goodness we shall not have so long a separation for a long time. Freddie arrived last evening. He looks so fit, thinner than when I saw him last, but as he has had no fever in the new district he looks a better colour. Our days are very short up here now as Freddie has to be back at his work. So we leave here on the fifth. The Crumps left by car yesterday morning. It suited everyone beautifully, as it would have been a fearful crowd here otherwise. This week has been a very full one as we started off on another tour of three days on Monday. We motored out about seven miles to a spot where we left the car and transferred to bullock carts for a tidy fourteen miles to a place called Poila, where we stayed the night, and then on again the eight miles to Pindia, such a pretty village on the edge of the huge lake. You've no idea of the bumping we had in the cart. We walked until it was too hot and then lay down on the paddy straw on the bottom of the cart. There were four carts one for each married couple, and I was able to spread alone, and then the servants with food and some of the kit in the other. There were no metal roads, of course, and the tracks had been worn deep with heavy storms, so it was nothing to be bumped down a dip of a couple of feet on the one side and on the other right up high. We had several very heavy storms, which made the clay soil fearfully slippery, and the poor bullocks could scarcely get along and kept slipping down unable to get up without the yoke being taken off their shoulders. This meant the occupants of the cart having to jump out in all the pouring rain and do their best to shelter under brollies. At Poila the first stop, we got in just as it was dark after trekking fifteen miles. The rest house had a table in and nothing else. We brought in beds, so these were put up and used as chairs as well. After tea, we felt able to tackle anything and helped the boys unpack and then washed in our scanty allowance of half a bucket of water per person, and had dinner, by which time we were yawning our heads off and soon went to bed. Up at 6 am and once more started with the trail of carts for Pindia eight miles on. We left our kit behind and returned to Poila that evening. At Pindia, some festival was on and everyone was at the theatre. Such a show too. They go on all day and night with three performances and the most fearsome row going on from the band at the back of the stage. Major and Mrs. Crump and I went up intending to look only for a short time, but directly we showed ourselves there was a stir in the crowd and a Burman came bowing and scraping towards us and waved us through the crowd to seats in the Royal box of the Sawbwa, (the chief of that particular State). The Sawbwa is the little tin god. We were all for turning and running away because we couldn't speak the language and felt such fools squatting there. Especially as we had a sea of blackfaces with their glowing eyes glued on us. The audience was much more interested in us than the girl on the stage wriggling and waving her fan about not able to do much owing to the tight skirt pinned around her. After a bit, two most fearsome men got up and started to bellow or sing I suppose they'd call it, some sort of song. By this time the smell and stuffiness was becoming too much for us and so we got up and shook the very weak hand of Sawbwa's daughter and departed. I was awfully glad to have seen it all. On Wednesday we started our homeward journey and on arrival found a wire from Freddie telling us of his arrival the next evening so you bet my trip was complete.

Sunday June 3rd 1923

I had no time to finish this before. Yesterday we were motoring from 7am to 8pm. We went again to Yaungloey and on to the lake, being rowed by the leg rowers, to a bungalow inthe middle of the huge lake, where we had lunch. Freddie loved it all so much. In fact, we all did, as the day was lovely in every way, especially for me, who had at last a husband to keep me company also to save me rattling about in the car. We are just going to walk down to the station to post this or the mail will be missed. This next week will be very full as we leave on Tuesday for Monywa. It will be hot, but I don't care a cuss now I can be off with Freddie! Lots of love mother dear. Freddie is shaving and has murmured to tell me to send you his love. And now I must get up for my trip.

Monywa (Undated) June 1923

On the ferry to cross the Irrawaddy to Segine, there were a Captain and Mrs. Barker, a small boy and a Captain Fowler. It took all evening to Monywa by a train with one small carriage which was waiting for us. However, by much wrangling and many threats another carriage was tacked on and Freddie and I had one to ourselves all the way. The journey to Monywa was pretty awful; fearfully hot. We arrived at 2pm in the heat of the day. The Barkers gave us a lift in their gharry as Monywa seems to boast only about two conveyances. We met Mr. Mills of the B.B.T.C. and had tea at his bungalow and all our troubles began to fade. Since our arrival on Wednesday the days have been pretty hectic trying to straighten up and make the bungalow look nice. We are right on the banks of the Chindwin River and get a very strong breeze off the river all day, which all the other private bungalows miss. The noise is rather terrific and pictures and lampshades have a chorus all day to see which rattles the louder! How different a small station is to one like Monywa but I'm sure I shall like it. It is hot but we are lucky to arrive just as things are beginning to improve and it is anything over 90° during the day now. Last night Freddie and I faced the club for the first time. Only about six others were there, but all very nice. Mrs. Barker and Mrs. Slack are the only two ladies, the latter is busy with a new baby and the former about to be so. I better see what I can do! I wasn't so fearfully tired after the journey, the last few evenings. I have played a few holes of golf and felt better for the exercise. This place I think will do my rheumatism some good. At Kalaw I could scarcely move some days. It is still uncertain about my going up to Mahamyaung with Freddie who has to be back at his district about the 15th. I do hope I'm allowed to go. I don't fancy remaining here alone and I do think Freddie will do much better work if he's allowed to have me with him for a change! We want very little in life once we are together! This is quite a nice little bungalow, one large room, which we use for boxes downstairs and then stairs leading up into a good sized drawing room, with dining room and two bedrooms leading off it. It has large windows with Venetian shutters all around, and shutters down below the windows so we have all the breeze and air there is. All our goods have arrived safely and nothing broken and Freddie is very pleased about it as he did all the packing himself. There must have been very heavy rain up country because the river this morning is well up and thick with rubbish. We are quite near the bazaar. We went there yesterday and returned feeling like grease spots. There is not much peace for letter writing; men dashing about all round and there is so much to do I feel I must do the same. Yours of May 6th arrived yesterday dear. Well dear I must be up and doing something before it gets too hot. Freddie has gone to the office. Lots of love. I wish Ethel would write, the lazy so and so. I have heard nothing of her version of the journey home though I have from another source. P.S. The candle shades arrived last mail and are most awfully pretty.

Monywa, Saturday June 16th 1923

Gosh this is a hot spot. Wednesday I spent in bed, the one consolation about this heat is that my rheumatism is better and I don't think I mind the heat at all now I'm fit. Everything one touches seems to burn and there is no treat in changing into fresh clothes because they all feel like they have been kept in a hot case. The breeze seems to have gone and the punkah does its best during the day to keep us cool. Freddie feels very sceptical at taking me up to the Jungle next week and we are still waiting for the decision from Rangoon. I shall wilt altogether if I have to spend another long time alone. Last night we risked giving a dinner with Messrs. Mills and Pringle (B.B.T.C. men). I dreaded it because we have only Freddie's Jungle cook and an absolute fool of a Butler. I made the sweet, a cream thing and left the freezing to the Butler. When I came in at 7.30pm the cream was reposing on a piece of ice about two inches thick and the Butler was surprised it hadn't set. I dreaded the time for the sweet to appear, I can tell you, expecting to see a sloppy mess, however, the extra ice packed round the mould did the trick and all was well. We played bridge afterwards and Freddie and I seemed to hold all the luck and the others did not play a hand even. It was my birthday yesterday but at my age we don't talk about such things. Your letter of the 23rd arrived in the morning but you didn't mention anything, so probably next week's will bring your blessing. Thank goodness next year's will be spent at home. I'm not feeling very fit which makes me long for a sight and feel of Old Blighty again. In spite of all the bad accounts of the weather I take your friend Kruschen Salts every morning but that does not seem to rid me of the rheumatism and the injections given at Kalaw were no good at all. I'm so glad dear your general health keeps good. That is a great thing because it would be awful if you felt sick or had headaches etc. The mosquitoes in this house are pretty awful and I can never sit without a Joss Stick burning; which are splendid things at keeping them away. Joss Sticks smell rather like incense burning. Freddie and I went to the jail here the other day to order some wicker work. There is quite a big industry carried on by the prisoners. The little man who showed us round was determined we should miss nothing, even the gallows and three condemned men in their cells, which we did kick against gazing at. We have had several very big storms and Chindwin River is well up. The Burmans go down in troops to bathe and do their washing just in front of the bungalow and there is a terrific noise all day. Reminds me of Margate Seashore and then being near the bazaar we have dog fights to relieve the monotony of a wakeful night. Having just unpacked we now begin to repack. Freddie is doing his Jungle things but I won't touch a thing until the wire comes from Rangoon to say I may go. How awfully nice to have Mary rolling in to see you. You must love seeing people, poor dear, as you are kept indoors so much. It won't be long now before you have us to bother you. This is an extremely dull letter I feel but I'm feeling that way inclined. Next week will be better where I shall be quite happily away with Freddie or resigned to my fate of remaining here alone. Cheerio Mother dear. Our very best love.

Mabeyakan, Sunday June 24th 1923

Since sending my last and very scratchy letter we have had some very exciting if uncomfortable experiences but here we are two days after arrival at Freddie's headquarters and none the worse, golly! I was thankful to leave the boat as it was most terribly hot and although we landed at Maukkadaw that day the breeze on land was most refreshing. We caused a great deal of stir and excitement and while Freddie saw about the kit I sat under a tree and felt like passing the hat round for a charge to the crowd for gaping at me. No doubt I am a queer looking individual and I'm glad so many people find me so. At last the seven bullock carts were loaded and we started off through the village for about a mile and half to a small bungalow facing miles of marshy land on the banks of the river. Here Freddie had a lot of men to see, who came in loaded with all sorts of presents of fruit, milk, and one man gave us a packet of osprey feathers. Ospreys are very easy to get in these parts although the paddy bird is not allowed to be shot. Feathers are picked up in the fields after the breeding season which is the only time the male paddy bird grows them. I am collecting some to take home. And if I escape the twenty rupee fine for importing them you should have some when we come home. Thank goodness the pest of mosquitoes is better here than in Monywa. We had to be up at dawn and the bullock carts were soon creeping along their way. Very hard fat sandy land and often crossing dry sandy creeks beds. After about an hour we reached the point where the wonderful Ford met us. It seemed so queer to see a car (if you can call it so) away out in the Jungle many miles from any sign of civilisation. We had to wait for the carts to bring the small amount of kit we were taking along with us, the worst bit being fifteen thousand rupees, mostly in silver, and which was very difficult to heave up. We soon got away with our four boys clinging on as best they could on the top of the kit. Freddie and the driver and myself plus the dog faring better on the front seat which had some sort of padding. The back is just an open wooden arrangement. I take my hat off to an old Ford car after our drive on Wednesday. We went along a track in the Jungle just cleared of trees and stumps and that's all. My heart was in my mouth and my one hand clutching Freddie's knee and the other the dog, as we buzzed along missing trees at the side by a hairs breath. About three miles off a fearful knocking brought us to a standstill and the worst was feared. However it was discovered to be only one back wheel nearly off. The screws were quite loose and that was adjusted and we did fairly well for a bit. Except for the disturbance of Freddie and the boys at the back having to pop out and shove the lorry up any steep slope our difficulties were increased by running into an awful thunderstorm - which means a torrent! This made the road into a soft sandy stretch and I can't tell you the times we were buried almost up to the hub of the wheel and then had to be dug out and shoved over the spot. If we once got out of the rut the car skidded and did most blood curdling feats. It was a nightmare to Freddie because if anything happened and we couldn't reach home before dark we had no bedding provisions or shelter for the night. And eighteen miles is no joke to be away from any hope of civilisation in the middle of the Jungle. At one spot we were stopped by some road men who said the road a mile on was impassable, water rushing down, up to the knees and it was still pouring. So all we could do was to get under the workmen's hut and try to get some comfort from half a cold chicken and a loaf of bread. All three worked wonders and with a cup of tea we felt we could storm through even if the car failed us. Off we went and down through the stream. Except for more pushing and digging out we had no more excitement until near home when we met six carts with logs being pulled by buffaloes. The beasts were terrified and one or two bolted very nearly upsetting the two ton logs and the man perched on top. We were all very pleased to get in and take off our sopping wet clothes. Mr Streicher, the engineer, was here and stopped the night. He is out about twelve miles and in charge of the tractors etc. This is quite a nice little bungalow, quite flat country but Jungle near. There is a huge pile of logs just outside the compound, having being brought in by the train on the small tram-line drawn by a tractor with caterpillar wheels. These logs will remain here until all are extracted from the Jungle in this part and then the line will be uprooted and re-laid from here to the floating stream about eight miles away. All this extra work and expense on mechanical transport is owing to there being no creeks in this area. All our water has to be carried miles by cart each day. A Mr. Bawdwn is at present staying here with us. He belongs to the forest department and his men inspect the B.B.T.C. men's work in the Jungle, so that no logs are left behind or burned. Both are offences carrying heavy fines. Freddie and Mr Bawdwn both went off early this morning inspecting some place. Freddie is very sick of this man arriving now as there is endless office work to do after being away with me. This place is much cooler than Monywa. I prefer it more altogether in spite of the loneliness. My tummy is gradually righting itself but it has left me feeling pretty rotten. I don't believe I shall begin to get fat until I get home! There is no mail in yet. It takes a long time to get out here. Freddie will soon be in I hope, not that I feel lonely because there are lots of odd jobs to do. I'm not awfully fit yet and all I want to do is lie on the veranda, enjoy the cool breeze and have Freddie to look after me, which as you know he does jolly well. It's nearly worth being ill with Freddie to take all the fag of doing things for me. I tell you I'm being thoroughly spoilt!

Mahamyaung, Sunday July 1st 1923

Yours of May 30th arrived last Monday just as my home mail had left. I'm so sorry your rheumatism is so bad other than your knees; how you do suffer poor dear. I think it is a hopeless thing to have and often wonder if I shall be like you one day. I am quite sure I shan't be like you as far as patience is concerned. What miserable weather you are having at home. I hope we shall have more luck next year. Pouring every day won't upset me very much though so long as we are in Old Blighty. Time is getting on, at the most we have only eight months before we sail and Freddie has great hopes of getting an extra month and leaving this country earlier. Mr. Milton arrives out here to take over this district again early in January and there will be no need for Freddie to remain.

I suppose there is no chance of your returning to Hereford? I still hope to hear from the Macs at Netherwood. We'd so love to come and stay there but will come to Ross of course if the Miss Macs will have us. The newcomers don't sound any too exciting. But still even an old lady of eighty can lead you astray so be careful. Poor Connie, she does not have much luck with her servants, I get to hate them out here at times. Burmans are so lazy and we have to have seven out in the Jungle to do what two would do at home! The boys are settling down better now but at first everything was at sixes and sevens. Freddie's head boy (and quite good) is still down with a bad foot, the cook with sore eyes and the others have a grouse of some sort. All due to returning to the Jungle after kicking their heels in Monywa. My young Lugaley Bar-Tai is as faithful as ever and runs the whole ménage. He's a splendid kid and is getting on splendidly with his English, so my Burmese suffers consequently and I know next to nothing. That's my grouse, not being able to chivvy these people or go out to the kitchen to either see to things or do them myself. I'm finding our primus stove very useful and I make all sorts of things up on the veranda. This cook is quite hopeless for puddings. It is jolly difficult to think of food for meals with no meat of any description. Mainly chickens and eggs but not too many and no fresh milk . We try to keep from using too much tinned stuff. It's so expensive and not too good for us. So my brain is racked each day to think of dishes for two meals based on chickens. There are hundreds of cows all skin and bone but no one ever dreams of them. We were trying to buy one for our own use. We did have one and the first morning the man brought half a cup full and said the cow kicked him and he wouldn't do it anymore! Freddie is threatening me with an elephant and see if I can't get fat on her milk. I wonder if you have seen anything of Ethel yet. I have had no news of her since she went home and am wondering where Dorothy is now. Last Tuesday Mr. Bawdwn (the Forest Inspection man) left and we were thankful to see the last of him. He was alright but I wasn't feeling fit and I worried over work and servant disturbance and for two nights Mr. Streicher, the engineer in charge here was in, so there was a lot of extra work. On Monday Mr. Streicher drove us out to his place about 9 miles off in the old Ford car. No breakdowns but we got a good old bumping along the fearful road which runs parallel to the small tramline which brings the logs down. These huge logs are loaded on to the bogeys and the long line of logs is drawn by a tractor with caterpillar wheels which goes along the road. At the top of any incline the cable is unhitched from the bogeys which go tearing down with the load. Accidents often happen and no men are allowed to be on the bogeys going downhill; of course lots do and a fool had to pay for it with his life the other day. There are no breaks on the bogeys and at one place they tear down at thirty-five miles an hour. Should there be a faulty bogey the whole lot swing off the line and there is the deuce to pay. We're still very lucky with the weather. It's supposed to be raining hard each day but we have had a break of fine weather since our arrival. Freddie is kept very busy in the office still and except for meals I don't see him all day at times, but still he is get-at-able which is better than most of our time. And in the evenings I take my sewing and sit in the office. I think he's beginning to see daylight but to me the work seems endless and Freddie has only two quite untrained clerks. Well dear I must now write some other letters for the mail which leaves tomorrow.

Lots of love dear and I do hope this next letter will say you have been outside the house for a bit. I must write to Dorothy for her birthday this mail. We have brought her two rather nice silver Burmese bracelets. I have not heard whether she ever received my Christmas present. Since Miss Holmes left no one ever writes.

Mahamyaung, Sunday July 15th 1923

The mails are coming late now and I only received yours of June 13th on Thursday. Another mail should come today and I see in the paper our home letters missed the connection at Bombay so will be a week late. During monsoon time the boats are often held up. I had letters from Aunt Bea, and B. Child too. The former always has interesting bits of news as they gather many folk around them at Dilwyn. I'm so sorry Aunt Helen is still so bad, but I hope like with you that warm weather will see you both out of doors. Dear I know you have not forgotten my birthday really! Having to think a month ahead is always a trial. It will be your birthday soon. You must feel quite young and sprightly compared to your new lodgers. I love the descriptions you give of them and must find the old maid an awful trial. I do hope Mrs. Barker will remain on and keep you company. We are still extraordinarily lucky with the weather. This is supposed to be the middle of the monsoon, and except for a couple of thunderstorms in the evening no rain has fallen since the day of our arrival. This warm weather is doing my rheumatism the world of good and my fingers and wrists have no pain now and my late grievance 'Trots' has departed now. I'm glad I stuck it out with Freddie and didn't return to Monywa. The poor dear was so worried having me ill for five days away from any sort of help. However chlorodine[43] and a very low diet has done the trick and I'm more or less ok now. I believe I shall feel fit one day again. I often long to be what I was before and during my hospital days, and our months at home together next year will bring me near to those days. You have no idea how good and careful I have become! I watch Freddie eat the most luscious pineapples and fruit of all sorts and don't touch a thing. In fact soup and

---

[43] Morphine.

poached eggs has faced me at every meal since I came here but when I feel as fit as I do now, it's worth it. The sand flies have been dreadful lately and the little blighters seem to get through the net even. We have a moveable grate and burn as smoky a fire as possible every evening now, which does help. Servants are being a perfect nuisance as usual and we cleared the cook out one day last week as he was making so much mischief with the others. The matey[44] now carries on but scarcely knows the difference between boil and roast. The man is a criminal I'm sure judging by his evil face but, with all that, he is keen on his work and I have him up on the veranda and show him how to make certain dishes on my primus stove. He was awfully bucked at the successful cooking of some buns or 'bums' as Bar-Tai insisted on calling them the other day. We have Mr. Streicher here for the weekend. He is the engineer in charge here and a jolly clever man. He, like many other Jungle men, gets horribly depressed and worried over the work so we insist on him leaving it all and coming here for a change. I do my best to keep both Mr. Streicher and Freddie from talking shop because their minds are on it the whole day long and it's no use having the same talk in the evenings and night. Besides its so dull for me after a bit. The small girl who asked me to teach her embroidery is very bucked at a white muslin coat which they always wear and on which I drew a pattern of daisies and she embroidered in yellow. The Burmans love a splash of colour. A cow has at last been produced which will consent to give milk. It is a great joy to have it and a great help with cooking. There is no news this week dear so forgive a short dull letter. My life is awfully quiet, writing or sewing all morning. I read or sleep on my bed all afternoon and take a walk with Freddie after tea until dark, a late dinner, and then under our sand fly net as soon as possible. I don't mind the quiet life though, especially while not feeling too energetic. I can't imagine Mary and Stookey or many other people leading this life all the same. I'm just about to have my Horlicks milk, a nip I have every morning. Lots of love dear from us both.

Mahamyaung, Sunday July 22nd 1923

Such a nice long letter from you this last mail which I so enjoyed dear. Your writing is wonderful and does not seem to trail off at the end of the letter which with your rheumatic hand I should have thought was bound to happen. So glad Ethel and Sammy were over to see you. I envy them their car. Is it a two-seater with a dickey? I'm sorry Ethel feels I'm on her conscience. She hasn't achieved it so get her writing anyway. I hope we shan't cross with them on our way home. I'd like to see Ethel at Colombo. George looks very plump in his photo in The Hereford Times. I'm so interested to hear your description of the Rosslyn kids. Where is Will at school now? It is a pity that you are out of Hereford. You'd so love to see your grandchildren as at Tupsley. Poor old Ian he has had a rotten time trying to find a better life all these years. He was always so optimistic and cheery too through all the failures. Aunt Min will miss him going off to sea again. Tupsley did awfully well in their presentation to Mr. Ledger. The parishioners must be thankful to be rid of him by their donations. He did one quite good job in his life by helping to marry Freddie and me, because there has been no grousing from this side as yet. We are really having a taste of the monsoon now. Heavy rain and the compound is a swamp. I expect it will keep on steadily now as we have been very lucky in escaping rain so far. I hear Monywa has had none so far and that awful hot wind is still blowing. Golly! How thankful I am not to be there. Freddie isn't awfully fit and is just getting over a bout of low fever. I hope the change to Monywa next month will buck him up and help him to get through September and early October which are supposed to be bad for fever in this district. Mr. Streicher was in for tea yesterday. He dashes in the old Ford lorry and comes and makes a perfect whirlwind here. He's very keen on his work with tractors and

---

[44] Cook's help.

worries his young soul out if things go wrong. His camp is only six miles out now and he is always sending frantic chits into Freddie upon some grievance in connection with the labourers. Streicher has only had a couple of years dealing with the Burman and trusts and expects too much of them and so comes a cropper at times. The Burman is a wily dog and will diddle one whenever he can.

Monday July 23rd 1923

I gave up trying to write yesterday morning because I couldn't see straight so I sewed and slacked in a long chair instead. Freddie's better now and I religiously do mild physical jerks every morning after my bath as one gets very little exercise out here. I shall lead up to skipping gradually. Such a surprise mail arrived last evening. I can't think how yours of June 27th came through so early. Mary also wrote. Her life is a busy one looking after house and husband. I will write to Jack this mail and forward your enclosures from Edith and also your last two. We take the weekly Daily Mirror in now and send it on to Jack in case they don't see it. I heard from Mrs. Cleaver yesterday she's coming home on our boat in February with a nurse and two children. Mr. Cleaver has to stay out another year and Mrs. Cleaver is related to the Johnstons our Burra Sahib in Rangoon. He (Mr. Cleaver) and Freddie are great pals and we hope in the Cleaver's last visit to the Johnstons he will keep Mr. Johnston up to the present arrangements that Freddie takes over the Madaya District when we come out to Burma again. That will mean Maymyo as headquarters and a very nice house where the Cleaver's are now. I can't say whether I have any faith in the two injections I had for rheumatism perhaps two are not enough. Some doctors have more belief in them than others. I see in the papers the Americans are supposed to have found a serum to cure rheumatism. I think a regular course of injections would do you good and prevent rheumatism becoming worse anyway, but I don't think one course sufficient. A new cook arrived yesterday thank goodness and I have just struggled with him for the fodder for today. He only speaks Hindustani but with young Bar Tai my faithful boy we get through alright. I don't know what I should do without Bar-Tai he is exceptionally bright and smart compared to other Burmans. He lords it over all the other servants whatever their age may be and waits on me hand and foot. At night when I'm ready for my bath he bustles about holding my dressing gown for me to slip on and I believe he would come in and bath me if I allowed him! You need not fear all this tends to make me lazy and expect to be waited upon. At times I yearn to kick them all out of the way and let me do the job myself, but if one pays for the wretched boys I fail to see why they can't be made to earn part of it at any rate. Freddie wants to pay for Bar Tai to go to school while we are at home and then return to us. Eventually Freddie means to train him up as a clerk. It is wonderful what strange and unexpected people roll in to see you. Fancy Nellie Hale. I'd forgotten she was my godmother and wondered at her remembering my existence. How very nice to hear Aunt Helen is out and about once more. I do hope she is able to get over to see you one day. I expect Jeff's wife is busy having another baby and that is the reason for her silence. (You notice I write each mail). Freddie is kept very busy in the office still. He has only two very incompetent boys as clerks who give notice directly they are told off in any way. Well dear old mother there is no more news (not that there is any so far but so long as I get off two sheets to you to pass away a short time in the reading I don't mind). Anyway dull though it be to the best of my knowledge I have told you no lies. Lots of love mother dear and from Freddie .

Mahamyaung, Monday July 30th 1923

No mail in yet but I may get one this afternoon. Two came so near one another last week that I fear I shall have to wait a little time for the next. I'm rather stuck for news this week; no letter to answer and mighty little has happened here. There is the weather to talk about of course but that won't carry me far! We are having our usual luck. Except for thunder and rain at night we have had nothing. By the look of the garden one would not think we had had that much. Freddie says he has never known such a district and there is a lovely cool breeze all day and some nights a blanket is quite acceptable. Now my days here are coming to an end. Freddie wants to get away about the 8th and I shall be sorry to leave with the prospect of Monywa and its heat before me.

Tuesday July 31st 1923

I have just received yours of July 4th for which many thanks. I'm so glad you have been out in the garden but sorry to hear no different chair can be had for you. I should have thought one with lighter wheels could be found. I'm afraid there is no likelihood of me liking Monywa as much as Maymyo. The latter is the Sports Place of Burma, but with luck Monywa will see very little of me. I'm so pleased to hear Mrs. Barker is much better. You have not mentioned her for so long I feared the worst! Give her my love when she comes to see you. I don't blame her for agitating to return to India as soon as possible. I hear they are having lovely weather in Maymyo and everyone enjoying the bathing, tennis etc. Mrs. Grant and the Crumps (Doctor) are going home in October. I'd like to go up in September and see them before they go. The Crumps have a cottage up at Grasmere in the Lake District and want us to go and stay in the summer. Freddie has never seen that county and of course I'd love to so I hope the trip will come off. What we'd like to do during our leave would cover years instead of months but we shall put in all we can, you bet! As far as I can make out Freddie has never had what I call a decent holiday at home. He has never done anything much with his time because of his people being so busy and Freddie is one of these silly people who thinks no one wants to do anything with him! Well dear there is naught to say so I won't attempt to waste your or my time. I'm still very busy sewing undies, I shall want plenty to last me until I come out again, don't suppose there will be so much time for sewing at home as out here. Lots of love mother dear from us both.

Camp, Monday August 13th 1923

I am a cheap piece of goods! Here I have to write and say I have been ill again. Last Wednesday I woke up with awful rheumatic pains all over me and feeling generally rotten, stayed in bed all Thursday and by the evening I had a good old temperature and fever on me. Next two days I went on much the same and I remained in bed to try and rid myself of the aches and pains. Yesterday I really felt better and lay in a long chair in the bedroom. About six o'clock on came the fever again when I shivered and shook and nearly blew the house in! Then I got burning hot and sweated furiously. I think the fever is really out of me now though. I sweat an awful lot still and naturally feel dickey after such a high temperature. Freddie thinks it's a touch of Malaria as the fever returns at such regular intervals. My rheumatism is really an awful worry and we shall certainly take it in hand very drastically when we go home. My terror in life is not being able to stick this country and yet rheumatism is supposed to be so rare out east. That part of the world has been my downfall in life anyway; as regards health I mean. Poor Freddie has been fraught, poor dear. He is wonderfully patient and in spite of his many outside duties he finds time to wait on me hand and foot and he gets scarcely a wink of sleep at night and gets up at my slightest movement. In fact it is almost worth being ill to have him! Freddie threatens never to bring me out to the Jungle again but will send me home and goodness knows what other threats but it won't take me long to recover. Though five days in bed living on next to nothing is going to set me back once more from my wish to be a buxom wench! Oh dear it's difficult to keep one's pecker up at the rate I'm going on. 1923 hasn't brought me much luck so far. We had to postpone our return to Monywa in any case. Mr. Streicher suddenly decided to come in from his camp lock stock and barrel for the yearly overhaul of machinery which takes about two months. Freddie did not hurry away the next day so here we are and we start off on our travels in five days time. Freddie will be thankful to get me in. We have had scarcely any rain so it's not the damp of the Jungle which has laid me out. We shall do the journey in very slow stages and a bullock cart for me if I want to take things easy. Thank you so much for yours of July 18th with its enclosures. I always enjoy a letter from Aunty Bea. How clever of Mary to snuffle the first prize for John's fancy dress! A haystack is very original, if hot. This camp is very full up now with all Streicher's work people. The small Bates machine brought the whole lot bag and baggage piled up on the bogeys. On the morning of the departure three desperate fathers presented themselves to Streicher to ask how their wives and babies of five and ten days old were to come in here. Streicher never knew that sort of problem would be given him. However, he bundled mother and babes into the Buzzer without the engine and the whole lot was pushed along the line. I won't write more this week mother dear; the quinine makes my head buzz, but I wish my eyes and ear-drums would drop out to relieve it. Lots of love dear and I do hope Mary gets fixed up soon to come and stay with you. S.S. Shellong, Chindwin River

Thursday August 23rd 1923

Here we are once more on the move going down the Chindwin River to Monywa. It seems years since we left Mahamyaung and we have certainly put in much during the time. We postponed our trip so that I might get over my go of fever, which is quite gone now and temperature popping up to 105°. All our kit in seven bullock carts left Mahamyaung early on Sunday morning last. We stayed on and had breakfast with Mr. Streicher. We didn't start much before 9am and hoped to get over the ten miles to the first stop in a dry spell, but no such luck. It rained as though it had never rained before and of course we were soon soaked. Freddie walked but I had a pony and in spite of that and a big umbrella I soon felt the water trickling down me, but we kept warm which was the great thing, and the boys had everything unpacked and ready for us when we arrived just before dark. Our abode for the night was a funny little thatched hut with a mud floor with huge tarpaulins and a carpet on top. So we were soon cosy, especially with a log fire burning in the corner around which we hung all our dripping garments. The roads were in an awful condition with all the heavy rain. The bullocks can only go along at about a mile an hour. Fortunately the road is practically flat, but the wheels sink into the soft sandy soil which makes things more difficult. We had to be up at the crack of dawn to enable the carts to get away. Freddie and I stayed on in the hut for about a couple of hours after their departure so that our kit would be ready for us at the next stopping place. With books we soon passed the time away and did the next march of six miles in dry weather. Another night in a similar hut and the same programme of hustle and then a long wait the next morning. That morning (Tuesday) was not so fortunate and we got in for some very heavy rain. All through this Jungle the house flies are so dreadful and the poor pony was a bleeding mass from bites. Tuesday was a long day. Seven miles to a small bungalow where we had a scratch lunch and a change, and after a two hour rest for the bullocks they started the four miles to Sannahbin the last stage of our journey. A night there and then three miles to Maukkadaw on the Chindwin where we joined the boat. A long weary day had to be got through. First we went up to the Civil Bungalow and had our picnic lunch and then a long wait expecting the boat at any minute but which did not arrive until 5pm. It took a bit of doing to get our six boys and all the kit on board I can't tell you how many packages we had! But they were a good number, all our camp kit, bedding, food etc, etc. We are the only passengers, quite a nice Captain and the same boat as the one we came up on. Several heavy storms have made things rather uncomfy as the water streams down the deck as the one and only saloon to the front of the boat is all open. We are due in at Monywa in about six hours time. The Captain tells us it is still hot there. Monywa is in the dry zone and gets none of the rain such as we have had up the river. I shall yearn for the Jungle if it is very hot in Monywa. Mrs. Barker the only other woman in Monywa is still away and only about four men in. While Freddie is with me all is well of course but I rather dread life towards the end of September when he returns to the Jungle and leaves me behind. However, all the weeks help on towards February and we shall be on our way down this river preparatory to going home before we know where we are. The thing I look forward to most of all in Monywa is the dhobey and to get rid of our endless dirty clothes which have accumulated since we were up in Mahamyaung, and everything gets to smell so musty with all the damp. There is a lovely cool breeze as we go along and I breathe in to make the most of it and only wish it could be bottled for future use in Monywa. Well dear time is going on and I must end. Lots of love dearest.

Monywa, Saturday September 1st 1923

You say in yours of August 8th that no mail from me had arrived. That will be because of the breach in the line during the second week in July. I'm afraid last week will be the same dear as mails missed the boat at Rangoon for Bombay owing to a serious breakdown due to floods all along the low lying ground on the Rangoon line. Our mails yesterday were two days late. This sort of thing happens each year at about this time. How nice to have Connie over to see you again. You have no idea how much I'm looking forward to coming next year but disappointed to hear you can't face drives in the car now. We still hope to get one and would so love to buzz you around the countryside. You never know and perhaps you will be better by the time we come. What will the Miss Macs charge per week for two, eight guineas sounds rather a lot. We landed up at Monywa about midday on the 23rd of August, and I like this place and the bungalow better than on my first arrival, when it was so terribly hot. It seldom registers above 98° in our drawing room now and I hope that will continue. With the breeze off the river life is not so bad. Poor old Freddie is laid up now and is now lying with his leg up on a chair with a huge swelling from a kick he got playing in a footer match yesterday. There are six Bombay Burma men in from the Jungle and a team was scraped together to play against one of the many Burman teams which flourish in Monywa. All our men are very out of practice, of course, some only having played rugby and were most amusing to watch. However, the match ended in a draw which was jolly good as the Burman is extraordinarily fast and nippy. Freddie was playing a very stout game on the outside left and had against him an awfully fat Burman, who believed in fowling on every possible occasion, and a hefty kick got Freddie on the leg just above the ankle. It bowled him over of course and a murmur of applause and amusement went up from the thick crowd of Burmans watching. Freddie got up only to go sprawling again to even more applause. All the strength and feeling had gone and Freddie was helpless. Much to his annoyance he was carried off the field, and of course that was the climax to the crowd. Had Charlie Chaplin appeared in all his glory and long feet he could not have pleased the Burmans more than Freddie did by being hoisted up and carried off. And probably the feeling was mixed with one of heroism for the man who gave the kick. A huge lump on Freddie's leg swelled up at once and the doctor (an Indian) would allow no more play. The match over, we all returned to Mr. Mills' house (B.B.T.C. man) for well earned drinks and then the doctor drove us home. He, the doctor, says Freddie must lay up for at least three days as he fears the blood won't disperse a clot possibly forming. The skin is not broken but the place looks thoroughly nasty. A Captain Barker and Mr. Williams came in for dinner last night. After discussing all the football news we played bridge until after midnight. Consequently we were not ready or dressed when the doctor called at 9.30am this morning. The ménage is just about settled down now. You have no idea of the worry one has with servants, especially when settling down to a routine. Jungle boys hate knuckling under the Butler, who is a nice Madrassi. Well I've sacked the cook who came in with us from the Jungle and got an excellent man in his place. I have an awfully nice large storeroom down below the bungalow. My primus stove is fixed up there and I muddle round making all the cakes and sweets. Leading from the stores room is another large room where Freddie does his office work. I wish he could always carry on like that and none of this rushing away to the Jungle, which he will have to do about the 20th of this month. We have played golf several times but heavy showers have prevented tennis. I'm feeling much fitter and have no return of fever so do hope nothing will crop up to prevent me from getting up steam and getting fit for our leave next year. With Captain Barker we are out to dinner tonight and are off to the Slacks. (He is Deputy Commissioner here). Quite nice but they never go out of their compound. She has a new baby and is terrified to leave it. From having no exercise both of them are getting enormous and we have been warned as to the dinner we are likely to have tonight as the table fairly groans with food. We are fixing up a carrying chair for Freddie and I shall probably cuddle in with him coming home, my legs having failed me! It's awful the amounts some eat and drink out here. Mr. White, B.B.T.C. manager living in Monywa, is an awful soaker but one would never think it to look at or be with him. He has a half bottle of champagne or sparkling wine of sorts, whiskey and sodas all day long, and yet he is able to play games jolly well and do a long Jungle tour without turning a hair. I thought of you on your birthday. Dear Freddie's was on the 28th and we spent it the nicest way by having a peaceful time at home. Although we are quite near the club we don't go very often. It is such a fag to turn out after a bath and change. I am always the only girl there and about a dozen men, on whom I feel I put a curb on to their conversation by being there. I managed to push Freddie off there the other evening and he went with all good intentions to be home soon after 8pm for dinner at 10pm and the dinner still waited until about 10.15pm when he appeared full of apologies and very little else! All the men start bucking together oblivious of time, not one of them with a nagging wife awaiting them at home. Of course Freddie got very nagged when he discovered the late hour. Freddie has gone off for his afternoon snooze and I must do likewise. Very best of love dear.

Monywa, Wednesday September 5th 1923

There are still several big breaks in the line between here and Rangoon so I am sending my letter several days earlier this week in hope of catching the mail. I'm very much afraid last week's missed it again. I don't suppose I shall receive yours until the end of the week. We have at last got blinds up in front of the drawing room windows which makes life much more comfy. The glare was dreadful before as we look straight on to the river. The breeze is nice these days but it gets very hot at times. Nothing much has happened and I'm afraid you must find my letters very dull. The doctor comes to see Freddie's leg each morning and he said today he was writing to Rangoon office to say Freddie was no good for Jungle work yet. I'm jolly glad in spite of Freddie's leg being the cause so I hope now he will be in Monywa until the end of this month. That makes it four months being together, the longest consecutive months since we have been married! Nothing drastic has happened yet and I think we are likely to last the time without violence. Except the short distance to the club Freddie has done no walking yet. The doctor is afraid the swelling which is still there will cause blood trouble or an abscess. Freddie works in the room down below the bungalow, and it is so nice to know he will appear for meals at any rate. I have played tennis two evenings at the club and thoroughly enjoyed the games and felt none the worse except stiffness in my hands. The game always consists of three men and myself as there is no one else. Just now we get good games but all the men depart into the Jungle again soon so I shall have to content myself to lonely golf. There has been a lot more rain up country which makes the Chindwin right up to the level with the road in front of our house. The boats in these parts are very pretty; huge wooden things rather the shape of a gondola with enormous sails generally in a rust or brown colour. The boats fairly dash up with the wind blowing the sails full out, and then the current is strong enough to bring them down. Burmans believe unless one man in the boat sings or whistles the wind will fail them and then the boat won't get a move on, so every boat passing one hears a regular concert going on. Our drawing room looks so pretty now and it's nice to have it to ourselves of course but I would like someone else in the station. Helen's lampshades are still going strong and make a difference. We can't use our nice candle sticks now because the Punkas are too much for the candle but with luck we shall have Maymyo again someday where Punkas are not even put up in the house. Mrs. Cleaver and her kids and nurse are going home on our boat on February 28th. She's awfully nice and her husband is staying out another year. Mrs. Grant (the one I stayed with in Kalaw) took her small kid home last month and we hope to meet at home. Well mother dear I must send this off with my other mail letters. Best of love from us both.

Monywa, Saturday September 15th 1923

Such a lovely fat mail for us this week. Aunt Bea, Annie Bowden, Stella, two from B.B.T.C. people and Emma Turner and not forgetting yours dear with its enclosures. I have yours of Aug 15th and 22nd to thank you for. The mails are going through alright now and I do hope you have had a letter from me each week. Though mails are uncertain these days you couldn't look forward to my letters any more than I do to yours. Freddie always rags me at my excitement each mail day. I think Nora did the only thing by bringing Michael home. Its fearfully hard on them both but for separation for any length of time in a foreign country is quite hopeless, especially when it's a matter of health or a kid to be thought of. There are numbers of cases out here of ex-officers having to ship their wives home in the hope of finding a job out East after being axed from the army. Thank goodness Freddie has a job, we are lucky compared to many in spite of the rather trying life in the way of separations. Poor old Johnny! He hasn't had much luck and I do hope all will turn out well before long. I'm glad we shall see young Michael and Nora next year. The former was such a sweet kid. Nora I suppose will make her home with her mother. I'm so glad Mary got to Ross after all, you must love having a bit of your family with you for more than a day. I can't quite remember what part of Ross Ashfield is. Anywhere near the river? Wherever you are I'm afraid there will be a hill for you to tackle. I'm not surprised at Aunt Mary leaving Herefordshire, are you? She misses her garden etc. and I don't suppose Mrs. Parry-Jones is exciting as a neighbour. I wonder if we shall see anything of Aunt Min next year. Emma Turner always writes me such awfully kind letters and insists on our going to Fayre Oakes when we arrive home and to use that as our headquarters. We shall both love it and a great help to know there is some spot where we can sit and look around when we first arrive. Annie Bowden writes that she is going to spend next Easter holidays on a trip to the Ardennes and wants us to join her. It would be topping if we had longer at home but six months is all too short. We intend dividing that time as equally as possible. Two months with Freddie's people, two months with mine and two months touring around. It doesn't sound much does it dear but of course all my share will be spent with or near you. I daren't stop to think about it but this time next week I shall be alone once more. Freddie leaves on the 21st and I hope it will be only about six weeks before I can join him. I have written to ask a Mrs. Heath to come and stay with me for a bit. Her husband is in the B.B.T.C. up at Mawlaik, about four days travelling up the river. I always find lots to do so won't be lonely but to go the whole day with not a soul to talk to is trying for any length of time. At home it would be all so different with one's own kind around. Natives all around one makes loneliness felt more keenly. One never goes out during the day as it's too hot here, but after tea what Europeans there are turn out like worms after a storm and congregate either to watch football or if possible I get a tennis-four or a game of golf. The new Pubic Works Department man arrived up the other day in all his glory on a government launch which tied up within sight of our house. Mr. Hughes is blessed with a Burmese wife and he himself is an awful little pup, so not much use as my nearest neighbours. Mr. Haffenden his predecessor is such a nice man and we shall miss him. Major Gordon Smythe and Captain Bullock are the two new military police officers and are both fearful nips. Not much fun for me to go to the club. The latter was told off by the Secretary of the club and threatened with a fine for using bad language the other night! Captain Barker the civil police officer is nice. His wife returns next week so I shall have someone but I doubt even she will get me to the club in the evening. I love my game of golf or tennis after tea, after which it is essential to come home and change at once and then all I want is to stay quietly at home and have a comfy evening in my dressing gown! Those who return to the club seem to roll home for dinner at about 10pm which I hate doing and I must say cooks are rather marvels out here. If one is two hours late the dinner arrives as though he times it for that hour even though I may have ordered dinner for only ourselves and then bring two extra home, there is heaps to go around. (Shows what the servants have for themselves when we are alone). It has been awfully hot in spells and then a terrific storm will come along and cool things a bit; 100o in our drawing room is often registered. The other morning Freddie saw two men carrying a leopard on a stick past the bungalow. They were going to the Police Office to claim the twenty rupees for having caught the animal in a trap that morning. Freddie called them in and as the skin was in good condition offered them the reward of 55 rupees extra. They were quite pleased and there and then skinned the beast in the compound and we sent the skin round to the jail to be cured. The animal was taken with much glee and no doubt the men had a good fat feed. The leopard is not a very big one and Freddie wants to take it home to see if it will make up into a fur for me The markings are very fine. Any wild animal caught or shot and the man who shoots it can claim a reward. We shall be able to reclaim the twenty rupees from the police. Last Saturday we had a regular night of excitement, for us, in Monywa. The staff of the PWD gave a party as a farewell to Mr. Haffenden, to which all the world and his wife were bidden, to say nothing of including all the scallywags in the town. It took place about 50 yards from our house so we got the full benefit of the fearsome noises produced from tom-toms and the many queer instruments that the Burman's go in for. They are hospitable, if nothing else in this country, for an entertainment lasts for never less than twelve hours! And in some cases it goes on for days; the same two or three performers the whole time. Freddie and I arrived at about 4.30pm and found the other Europeans consisting of about eight men already sitting round a large table laden with the most ghastly and repulsive looking sweetmeats and cakes you can imagine. Mr. Haffenden the honoured guest was slowly but surely becoming green from the sickly smell from the many garlands hanging round his neck. The pi-dog is ever in evidence and for once we blessed him to help us get rid of the eatables we had to take for politeness sake. A plate of petit-beurre biscuits saved us as we all nibbled at those in pretence of eating something. In the mean time two boys were doing quite a good juggling and balancing show with Chinlone Balls. Chinlone is the Burmese national game; the ball is light bamboo, plaited in and out with square holes left and with strands of bamboo going all round. These boys had performed before the Prince of Wales and are going home to the Wembley Exhibition next year For the Chinlone game the boys stand in a circle and with a knee, foot or hand, toss the ball to one another. A simple sort of game, and footer and hockey are fast taking its place. After this performance we went on a Peve, a musical performance. Oh Ye Gods the artists! There were five girls and three convict looking men, the former wore the old court dress of a very long lungey, which is really a thick piece of silk wrapped tightly round them from the waist to the ground all the way down the sides are safety pins so as no leg or foot is to be seen. The bodice is very tight fitting also with long muslin sleeves and funny little kick-up bits and this shape wound round the waist.

Masses of cheap jewellery and a fan completes the kit. You will gather the skirt part allows for no bally dance touch. So the dancing consists of a series of wriggles from the hind quarters commonly called in the best of circles the bum. They use the hands very well and could give actresses at home many hints there. I'd love to dress our Dorothea up as a Burmese dancer. She is so like a Burmese girl in features and I am quite sure she'd excel in the wriggling part though she is about twice the size of these snips of girls. The less said about the singing the better - puts my teeth on edge to think about it and by special request one girl sang *Clementine* (the only bit of English she knew) and Oh My Darling was bawled forth in her grim cracked voice. Huge excitement from the crowd when Captain Bullock got up and started conducting the song! The men's part seems to be chiefly vulgar remarks about the girls and I believe it was just as well I understood nothing. We stayed on until about9.30pm and then a Mr. Mills and Mr. Richards came home with us for pot luck and we had the pluck to return to the Peve until midnight and that was only half-time. Freddie and I went to sleep to the noise which went on until 4am. Well I seem to have shouted a lot about a small bit of excitement but it may help to pass a little time away for you and I must send this down to the post now. Lots of love mother dear and keep cheery though that is not a necessary thing to tell you.

BOOK 3
Monywa, Friday September 21st 1923

I am sorry my birthday letter did not arrive in time. Your letters can now take quite a week longer. I ordered bedroom slippers to be sent here but they have not appeared yet but you will certainly have them. This is a new book for my letters to you. My last carried on for exactly a year as the previous one did. The tracing paper does not allow me to write on both sides of the paper, as I tell you everything as life goes along I find it quite useful. Your letter of August 29th is full of interest; so many people having been over to see you. I heard also from Aunt Mary. I am sorry she is leaving Nunnington, for our sakes, but I'm not a bit surprised and to be amongst her own people is very natural. I wonder if we will see her next year. It is so sad to read from all home letters about poor Aunt Helen. It is dreadful for them all at Dilwyn but must make Aunt Helen happier to have so many of her family around her. Well here I am once more on my own. Freddie went off early yesterday morning. It seems ages ago. Instead of sleeping the night on board he arranged with the staff to take his boat at 4-30am and start at 5am. Soon after that a regular blast started including the searchlight full on. We could do nothing but obey the summons and get up. Freddie sent the Durwan down to the boat to tell them to 'shush' or we would get sworn at by the whole community. The Butler got up and made Freddie some tea and then he departed. I watched the boat pass our bungalow and I could see him waving in the lamplight so I sent flashes back on the torch. With luck we should only have a month's separation this time. Freddie's boat is tying up at a special place to enable him to tour up a creek which has to be inspected and will save him a thirty mile march. Had Freddie no touring to do I would have returned with him but a woman makes it such a business during the rains so he will do it all over this month and I will join him at the end of October. I expect you will remember my mentioning a Mr.White. He is head of the B.B.T.C. Ltd., in these parts and has charge of an awfully nice launch for rafting inspection all the way down the Chindwin River. Only B.B.T.C. men are allowed to travel on her but to my delight Mr.White, when dining here for the night, proposed a trip for me. He says the launch is at my disposal from October 11th when I can do the week's trip up the river right on beyond Mawlaik and Homalin where the ordinary steamers run and on up the Yu Yu river where the snowy peaks of China can be seen. Mr.White goes up as far as Kalewa where we stop the second day. My regret is not sharing such a treat with anyone outside the B.B.T.C. for I can ask no one as there would be a fuss from Rangoon. Mrs.Cleaver is the only one but, as there are only two cabins in the launch, difficulties might arise while Mr. White is travelling. Our plan is for me to go up and then get off at Maukkadaw on the 20th on my way down, and Freddie to meet me and go to our Jungle home. Isn't it a pity Freddie can't do the trip with me? But to leave his work for a pleasure jaunt after having been in Monywa a month would kick up a bit of dust and fuss. However, I shan't feel lonely with *me dawg.*' I shall have the scenery which I believe quite puts the Irrawaddy into the shade. I am awfully lucky to see so much of the country. I have to take my own servants, crockery, etc., so shall soon be packing up our goods here and shan't see them again before February when we do the usual packing for home. Time is going on, isn't it dear? And we shall be home quite soon now. Last Sunday I had some good tennis at the club and in the evening Freddie and I dined with Mr. Mills. Except when the Wesleyan padre takes our evening service we get no church. There is a little English church here but the padre only seems to have time to get around about every two months. I have played tennis most evenings and get very good sets with three men. Even if I feel like overdoing things we can't play too much tennis. It is too hot to play before 5pm and we can never get more than three sets in before it is dark. On Monday evening Captain and Mrs.Cartmell and Captain Barker dined here and I played bridge afterwards. I love a game so we always have an odd man out as Freddie is not keen. At least he is keen enough but shy of playing from want of practice. A Mr. Cooper and Mr. Lett came in after dinner so we had plenty to choose from for a game. Next night (Tuesday) Mr. Cooper, Lett and White dined here and they enjoyed the dinner. Mr. White is very trying and aggressive at times and especially when he takes a dislike to anyone, which he did thoroughly obviously to Mr. Lett, a young pup only two years out from home and wants squashing badly. Only Lett took a dislike to Mr. White and both believed in showing it. I must say Lett was horribly rude and when we sat down to bridge White and Lett were drawn together. White said something to rag Lett who lolled back in his chair and gave a forced yawn to show that he had no use for whatever Mr. White might have to say. White was peeved by this time and I said I thought it quite time Lett went home if he felt so weary, after which he sat up and took more notice. We bought some liqueur glasses from a man who was leaving Monywa and at dinner Mr. White said he couldn't put his nose in such a glass, so had a pint glass instead. In handling the glass the stem snapped off in Mr. White's hand. He was very apologetic but of course we didn't mind. Freddie said: I wonder if this one is the same and 'blowed' if his glass didn't break. We were tickled about the whole show until suddenly we caught sight of Mr. Lett's face. He was absolutely glowering and shaking his head at me as much as to say for goodness sake 'shut up.' Seems he was superstitious. Anyway he was thoroughly rude. Well that's a lot about nothing isn't it. Freddie's leg was well enough to play tennis just before he left and we had good games against White and Mills. Freddie is pretty nippy despite advancing years. The same might apply to me. Mr. White is a great cricketer and he used to play against Herefordshire when she could boast a county team and when in Herefordshire Mr. White stayed at Bryngwyn, when the old Sir Rankin was alive. Last night I dined at Mr. White's and Mr. Mills was the only other there so we got bridge. I keep having to stop writing to kill mosquitoes and scratch where the blighters have bitten. They are dreadful in this bungalow. Lots of love Mother dear. I was so glad you were able to get out a bit and see Ross.

Monywa, Saturday September 29th 1923

Yours of 5th of September was the only letter by mail I received this week. I had one from Freddie at the same time. I lack nothing dear. Before I forget, when you enclose letters would you tie a piece of string around the envelope. The ones you are using seem so weak around the edge and the last ones arrived with their innards exposed. I hope you are still looking out for a nice comfy chair for yourself. I have written Mary to do so. Freddie says he will give a share towards the expenses if you are not fixed up by the time we come home. We shall have to nose around and try our luck. We hate to hear of you living bumped along in that chair you have at present and I am sure you would get out more often if you had a chair that was easier to push. So don't refuse if you hear of one you like. Money will be forwarded for it alright.

George is like a Hereford bull himself. So which I suppose is natural when he has so much to do with them. They always say dogs grow like their Masters. Do you remember how we used to tease old Arthur about 'Top' his precious dog who had a habit of heaving one leg up behind him as he ran along and Arthur did exactly the same, in our time. There is a bit of a breeze this morning which is quite a treat. I'm used to hearing thunder around in the last few days and the air is stuffy. The breeze shuffles around from the south to the north showing that we are getting to the end of the rains. I wander round the bungalow and sit where I can find enough of a breeze that will bring some cool air. The end of the rains is always a trying time when most people go up to Maymyo for two or three weeks. Mrs. Cleaver has cousins staying with them, but I'm sure she would have me if I wanted to go. I don't feel the need of a change a bit, besides I would not miss my trip up the Chindwin River for anything. I am taking my small camera and will get some good ones to send you. The enclosed is our bungalow here in Monywa. This time up in the Jungle I am going to stick all our Burma photos into a new book so that we can show them to anyone interested at home. I expect we shall do a lot of photography in the evenings in the cold weather. The great difficulty in the Mahamyaung is the water for washing the negatives and prints. There is no running water at all in Freddie's present district. All comes out of a dirty old pond in which rain is collected. Many photos Freddie has had spoilt by a splotch of dirt. This last week has been quite busy with one thing and another. I never find a day drags. I write letters in the morning. As a rule it is cooler and my hand doesn't stick as later in the day. In the summer I always keep a tin of talc handy and at any sign of stickiness of the needle I powder my fingers. That is the only way to enable me to sew at all. If that were denied me I would be lost. I have had only one evening dress made up by a dressmaker since I have been out here. I have kept myself going in everything so far. One evening dress I made some time ago has come to its end. I had it on when dining at Mr. White's the other night. In the middle of a game of bridge I looked down to see an enormous white lining showing through. The underneath silk had split. It's too hot to wear a petticoat. I managed to hide things in the folds and with my bag but you bet I was nippy in saying my farewells and going away in the car. Except for tennis last evening I have played golf all week. Mr. Rider stayed with Mr. White for four days. I played each evening with Mr. White against Mr. Rosie and Mr. Mills. The latter and Mr. White are B.B.T.C. We had a very good game but there are only five holes to our course, but in any case there is not time to play more. It is too hot to play before 5pm. and dark after 6pm. This place is wonderful for sunsets of which we get a full view from the golf course which also overlooks the racecourse and the football field in the middle of that. So much is done in the one clean flat space in Monywa. Our golf nerves are always put to the test at the three last holes which run by the football field, where a game is nearly always being played. Half the crowd wander off and surround us and nearly bowl us over. What with the shoving, smell and the other day one man had violent hi-cups and each time I attempted to hit the ball a loud hic would make me jump. I see a lot of Mrs. Barker the Superintendent of police's wife. She is just back from spending the hot weather at Ooty. She has a small boy of three and is to have another in December. They are both very proud and the sort who drop in on you at any time, as I do to them. It is nice to have another woman in the place. There is also Mrs. Gordon the Wesleyan padre's wife who is a nice little thing but she does not do anything in the way of games and never comes near the club so we don't see a lot of one another. The only possible time to go out is after ten when I feel the need for exercise in the day or tennis. Last Sunday I went to tea with Mrs. Gordon. She has two dear little dogs and then on to her husband's church. We rarely have a padre here so Mr. Gordon occasionally takes a C of E service which chiefly consists of singing hymns. On Tuesday I had a quiet dinner and evening at the Barkers'' and on Sunday dined at Mr. White's. On Wednesday morning Mr. White called for me in at 7-45am and drove me along to where there is good quail shooting. He was the only gun and we wandered over muddy fields where he shot a quail. We went out the next day too so I have been eating quail for breakfast and dinner for some days - very nice too. I am going out with him today again and my Cocker Spaniel 'Spiker' is also cordially invited and comes in useful. Freddie had a good trip up on the boat and was landed at a special place at the mouth of a creek he wanted to inspect. From there he had difficulty with his kit as for the first six miles there was no possible cart tracks for bullock carts. So about 40 coolies were procured and he marched along with a regular cavalcade. I am so glad he has managed to do this tour. He is forced to sit tight at our headquarters now and directly the weather is possible I can join him. I think that will be about October 22nd when I come down from the river trip. And now I must awa' Mother, dear. And I do hope the pain and discomfort are not worse.

P.S. Please enclose my letter to Mary in your next one to her. I have written her a letter and you will want to send her out a Weldon's fashion book with patterns.

Monywa, Saturday October 6th 1923

Yours of September 10th was the only English mail for me this week and it was late in arriving yesterday. You must not worry about my health dear. I am really much better now; more so than I have been for a long time. Perhaps I did wrong in telling you. [Editor's Note: Writing becomes indecipherable but concludes she feels quite young and that home leave is the best cure for her ailments]. I am glad you have a nice man to take you out in your chair now. You must go out whenever the weather permits. How much do you give him per trip? This is the first I have heard of Tiny still driving the car. When I left home she was horribly nervous. No I have had not a line from Dorothy. I do think Mrs.'Tiddleypush' with whom she lives might see that I get an acknowledgement of my parcels. I don't know if both bags I sent last June ever arrived but I'm glad you say Dorothy got the bangle. What a good thing the kid is going to school. She will be far happier and a much nicer girl in consequence. I always hated her being with the Browns as I am sure Dorothy never had a look in. Next year I must try and get her to stay somewhere with me for the holidays. You need never fear that your letters are dull dear. I look forward to having them tremendously. Just to know you can write is enough. I have had one letter from Freddie since he got back to Mahamyaung . Endless office work to catch up with and he is kept pen pushing until late every evening but he never objects to having plenty to do which is the best way of hurrying along the days. He had a hard time up the creek and there was no proper road track and the man took him well out of the way before he discovered he was on the wrong path. However Freddie is pretty wiry and the twenty two miles on the march did not seem too much for him. We had rather heavy storms last week. I do hate it when we get the fearful thunder and lightning at night. It is too hot to hide my head under the bed clothes. The weather is always cold at the tail end of the rains until it settles down to long cooler fine weeks. I quite forgot to enclose the photo last mail and do so now. If we were not so near the bazaar with the everlasting noise I'd like this bungalow very much. The position is lovely; right on the river bank. At night I sit out on the balcony at the side with a bright moon shining on the water and the coconut trees. Most romantic it sounds doesn't it? And none of it is lost when Freddie is here to enjoy it as well, I assure you. I often long to sleep out too but it is much too public and from what I can gather those who do sleep out have very disturbed nights this stormy weather. I have had several late nights this last week dining out. I enjoy the dinner parties more than in Maymyo I think. At Maymyo they were always such big shows but here one generally finds four or eight and bridge afterwards. Last Sunday our padre was here on one of his rare visits and I wanted to go to the evening service which I thought to be at the usual hour 6-30pm. Knowing there to be plenty of time I accepted an invitation from a Major Gordon Smythe to go out with him in his car to a place nine miles away to inspect a sheep farm in connection with the battalion. It was a lovely evening and a pretty run. Coming back we had a puncture but that was only a matter of seconds to put right. Major Smythe drove me up to the church door just after 6-20pm and to my horror I found them busy with the hymn immediately before the sermon. However, I wasn't going to be put off and squeezed in a back pew but of course there was a general gaze round from everyone. I felt awful but I did put in an appearance and the two rupees collection money no doubt was acceptable. That evening Mr. White and I dined with the Barkers. Monday they played Slippery Sam, an awful gambling game with counters. Mr.Hughes went down seventeen rupees, another man twenty rupees. I only lost two rupees. One is either rich or ghastly poor if one goes on too long. Mr. Hughes who is in the Public Health Department has a Burmese wife and she was there in all her fine silk and jewels. She speaks English and is extraordinarily nice. Mr. White has just been here this morning. He took me down to look over the B.B.T.C. launch on which I do my river trip on the 14th. Mr. White goes up tomorrow and is dining here tonight before he sets off. The launch is called The Chindwra and is a 'topper.' It is the fastest boat on the river and the others won't beat it for steam. The river has gone down a lot lately this year. Rafts and logs come past Monywa. Well Mother dear I must stop and pack. This next week the packing cases must be stored until March. The place is full of white ants and they leave few things intact. They are most destructive once they get into anything.

Monywa, Friday October 12th 1923

Yours of September 19th arrived today for which very many thanks you dear old thing. You never fail your Liza with a letter do you? I'm so sorry I scared you about my go of fever. It was certainly awful at the time but I have had no other attack so I'm sure the old germ has left me; coming home so soon now it will disappear altogether. It must be a treat for you that I have not groused about my health for quite a long time now. A Mrs. Hacker who has just returned to Burma tells me not to despair about getting fat as she has put on over a stone during the six months at home. Both Freddie and I could well do with that much extra. It is still hot down here; in fact very trying sort of weather with a good deal of rain and heavy thunder storms; the usual sort of thing towards the end of the rains. I am sitting under a punkah which is necessary for ones comfort these days. Have just finished my lonely dinner and want to get my letter off early as the next two days will be full of packing and plenty to do. I do hope last week's mail got there alright. I heard afterwards that due to the rain there was a breach in the line so the mails may not have reached Rangoon in time. I'm hoping that the two Miss Macs are kicking against their part of the bargain in running the Ross establishment and that they will return to Hereford, you with them. I would so love you to be near friends during the winter months. I'm afraid you will be more isolated than ever. Only four more months now before we start home. It is too lovely to stop to think about. I have never felt homesick out here. Freddie is too sweet for ever a thought like that to come to me but the best and nicest of husbands will never blot out the yearning to see and be with my own folk again. We mean to have a car and will certainly take you out for some runs. We will manage it somehow. How perfectly wonderful to hear about Aunt Helen. I'm so glad and hope your thoughts will come true and the internal trouble will go. Sammy does not sound fit to come East again and I cannot think how Ethel can allow him to do so. For a few extra hundreds Sammy may have to suffer all his life. So often I have heard men saying 'no thank you I have got my health which I may not have if another chukka is put in.' Both Freddie and I agree we'd rather live on £300 a year in a cottage than double anywhere else. Freddie feels no go in him after slogging away out here. I never want to see Freddie full of fever. He has bouts of it even at home. I do hope the injections will do you good. It's dreadful to think of you suffering so much pain. I hope it will keep off and help you to bear the confinement to the house, which is bad enough. There is nothing much to tell you this week. I'm afraid my packing is well on its way and tomorrow all the china and silver put away. The former only to storerooms. Freddie will pack some silver, when we come in February, and I will pack one box and send it to the office. You know these Louis stands you gave me for dinner parties. I always use them for sweets and desserts. The pair has always been admired; several men saying that one day they are coming to bag them all. From what I've seen in other houses I sport quite as nice a table as anyone, thanks to the many nice things you have given me including the long table cloth. I hate dismantling the house. I have been very happy here and the position overlooking the river could not be beaten. There was a very feeble race meeting here yesterday. Mr. Barker felt it our duty to put in an appearance and I managed to lose the large sum of two rupees. I am dining at the Barker's tomorrow and the next night they will take me down to the boat where I sleep before we start off at the crack of dawn. Dear don't be alarmed if no mail comes for you next week. I shall be travelling further away from lines of communication each day and may miss the mail but of course I will do my very best. Good night Mother dear, it won't be long now before you're with Freddie and me. He is very fit and full of work. Lots of love.

S.S. 'Chindwara' Sunday October 21st 1923

Yours of the 7th arrived. This letter will not catch the mail but with my warning last week I hope you weren't worried. Ever since I left Monywa last Saturday we have gone further and further from civilisation and impossible to post a letter to reach Rangoon in time. Although only a week tomorrow since the river trip started it seems ages. The days have not dragged in the least but being on the move from dawn until dark, and seeing so much, the week seems longer. I hope you can borrow a map which will show you my travels and follow up the Chindwin going from Monywa to Homalin just where the River Uyu Chaung runs into a creek. I hoped to go up but owing to the water being so low we could only go up about a couple of miles where there is a log rafting depot and where logs are made into rafts for taking on to Rangoon. After staying about a couple of hours at this village we turned round the sharp bend into the Chindwin again where we finished up at Homalin. I took 'Spiker,' the dog, for a walk but it was a bit hot so we soon got back to the launch where there is always a breeze off the water. Besides that we didn't get much peace; what with being stared at and all the pigs and cows in the neighbourhood coming after us. 'Spiker' is a Cocker Spaniel. He isoften made fun of with his long floppy ears. He is a wonderful companion and I wouldn't be without him for anything. After a riotous evening dining at the Barkers' last Saturday they came on to the launch where I slept preferring it to getting up so early to be on board by dawn. Apart from the usual noise in starting I slept well after we left Monywa and liked to find mists all round and quite cold and I thoroughly enjoyed pulling on a blanket after not wanting even a sheet at Monywa. I was thankful of a slack day after the last two in Monywa, packing and fussing with the odd things that accumulate at the last moment. On the Saturday afternoon I left the servants to struggle with the moving of my kit and went off to the races with the Barkers and returned after tea to see all was serene. The Butler is quite a nice man but goes to bits when there is something out of the ordinary to be done and he is quite capable of taking all the wrong boxes and leaving those which I want. The first part of the Chindwin is not very pretty. We went the whole day long and tied up after dark at Intha. A lot of coolies were on board being taken up and dropped at various rafting places. Directly the launch stops at night they are all off in a flash and busy. Soon numerous camp fires are burning and these the men squat around on their haunches cooking curry rice. This is done with infinite care and trouble and one would think they would wish to linger over such a repast instead of stuffing it down in handfuls as they do; nothing else but fingers used. And then they seem content with life and squat around the fire sucking their huge cheroots about seven to eight inches long and about two inches in diameter. One often sees one cheroot doing the rounds for several men, each taking a huge puff and passing it on. Women and children are as great at smoking as the men. Washing up plates and pots, clothes and themselves all goes on round the launch but no thought of that is given when any man wants a drink. In the mornings it is dreadful and is the only fly in the ointment during the trip. Every one of the men seems to have a deep hacking cough and the concert which goes on first thing makes me hide my head under the clothes to avoid the choice sound which invariably follows the cough. The first morning we were late getting off owing to the thick mist and soon after the start we tied up for firewood. Huge logs of wood and always carried on board by women and girls. They are wonderful at balancing. They carry everything on the head with a piece of cloth rolled round to look like a pill box hat and to act as a pad. They seem capable of carrying any weight. In spite of the heavy work the Burmese women are most awfully cheery and great laughing and joking goes on. The same when we turned up later to unload a lot of stores for one forest. They had to be carried across a raft alongside which we were anchored and however the girls kept their balance with a weight on their head that took two men to lift, I can't think. At 2pm we stopped at Maukkadaw where the clerk came on with a letter from Freddie. From Maukkadaw the river gets prettier and the country on either side is broken up by great high cliffs straight out of the water. The pampas grass is very pretty too; miles of it standing about fifteen feet high and the white feathery flower is at its best now. The third day we reached Kalewa one of our headquarters. It was early when we tied up, so I went ashore with 'Spiker' and had a look round and to my surprise I met Mr. and Mrs. Cantwell who were on tour. Perhaps you may remember about me telling you about them. They passed through Monywa a short time ago and dined with us. It was nice to meet someone I knew as I did not like to go far alone. I dined with them at the Dak bungalow which made a change from the boat. Very often a halt is made in the morning when I am still in bed with awnings only half-way down. The crowd on the bank can see right on the deck. However when I am caught napping they can only see a bundle in the bed and I curl myself well up but I feel like passing the hat round for a collection when we tie up and I am having tea in my dressing gown and even any other meals when I'm clothed. For them I'm certainly the centre of all interest. Wednesday about 4pm we arrived at Mawlaik, quite a big place and the headquarters of several of the B.B.T.C. men, and where we were to go before Freddie was sent to Mahamyaung. Mrs. Heath was the only B.B.T.C. woman and so I walked along to their bungalow and met her for the first time. She is awfully nice and of course made me stop for dinner. Her husband was in bed with fever so Mr. Hughes from his bungalow in the next compound came over. The first time I'd met him too. He is an absolute topper and so witty; one of the senior men. He goes home next year where his wife is already. I don't mind meeting strangers who are in the Corporation because we can always start off talking shop. Everyone in this show seems so awfully nice. Higher up the river there are quantities of fish and every place we stopped the men stopped off the boat and in about five minutes they caught quite a basketful in a large net. They certainly get a reward for casting out their net. And now here I am a day later and getting every minute nearer Maukkadaw where my old Freddie will meet me with a grin on his old 'physog.' He couldn't grin more than I do with pleasure at the thought of three months together. I love meeting people and always manage to have a cheery time wherever I go but much of the gilt on the gingerbread is taken when we are separated. In spite of the loneliness of the Jungle I don't dread going back a tiny bit. There's lots to do and when Freddie is not busy in the place we have lots of rags together. I've got Freddie really quite going and frisky when together, although some think he takes life too seriously; only in connection with his work over which I think he is far too conscientious and does a bit extra for which he gets no thanks. However, he does not mind swallowing that when I am there to help him digest it. Last evening we did not arrive at Maukkadaw before 7pm. Luckily there was a good moon or we could not have done it as this launch has no searchlight. I went straight to the Heaths. Mr. Heath had gone out to the Jungle. Mrs. Heath and I dined at Mr. Hughes where a Captain Donnely made the fourth. Mr. Hughes has a most lovely gramophone which he played after dinner. The two men saw me back to the boat and I fear they must have had a soaking going home as we had a heavy thunderstorm. I must see about my packing now dear. Lots of love. I'm so looking forward to reading my mail when I reach Maukkadaw.

Mahamyaung, Monday November 5th 1923

It was a sad mail last week and Aunt Helen's death came as a great shock after hearing that she had been out in the car but it was a great blessing to her and all at Dilwyn that there was no great suffering at the last. It is an extraordinary thing how I wrote to Uncle George and Aunt Helen and each letter arrived in the mail after their death. I wrote Aunt Helen because Aunt Bea had mentioned how she looked forward to letters. Yes, I think Uncle Fred will want to retire now. I do wish Ethel and Sammy would settle at home now. It would be a great trial to Aunt Bea if she is left to look after Uncle Fred. As to Dotty and Pat Armstrong, I do hope he makes her happy. He is a good sort but very difficult to manage as he is such a spoilt boy and unless he is carefully handled will be very selfish. I suppose everyone has that in some degree. However, I am awfully glad our Dotty is to marry. It is sad to think that the two great attractions in the shape of Uncle George and Aunt Helen are gone, and we will miss Dilwyn and Nunnington too when we are home next year. I hope Aunt Bea and Ethel will be able to get over to see you soon dear. You will see by the date on the enclosed cheque that it should have been sent two months ago. I am so sorry dear I quite forgot it until too late to enclose. Freddie sends it with the hope the money will help with your new treatment. We are watching the exchange which has gone up a bit. I hope to catch it right to send our money home for next year. We have decided to go across from Marseilles so should be in dear old Blighty a day or two earlier. I don't know what we shall do on arrival yet but expect Freddie will want to see about a car before leaving London but you bet I shall get down to Hereford as soon as possible. Time is getting lovely and short now and we are both as excited as can be. I am taking citrate pills which I think are doing me a lot of good. I don't look and certainly don't feel as washed out as I did. It is so nice not to feel a worry. It is getting quite nippy already. I go to bed with a hot bottle and blankets and a fire burning to say nothing of 'Freddie' keeping my back warm. These Tayan bungalows are not too warm. Tayan is planted strips of thin bamboo which after a time shrinks and so plenty of breeze sets through. Saturday we had our first storm and were very worried in case the rain proved too much for our garden with the seeds all coming up so nicely like. The sun shines so we smile once more. Every evening we spend our time poking about and so far we hope to have lots of vegetables in the cold weather. Mr. Streicher and the two Eurasian engineers all expect vegetables from this garden and so there is a lot to do. Our coolies do the actual work and watering of course, but they are quite mad at anything else. I forget if I told you the last time I was up here that two pigeons appeared in the compound and we induced them to live in a coup Freddie built and then two more appeared so another house had to be erected. The pigeons are called Jack and Jill and Sue and Sam. Poor Sue was bagged by a hawk. But great excitement! Jack and Jill have produced twins and Freddie spends most of his time gazing at them through the field glasses. Jack and Jill are so tame and are now sitting on the rail of the veranda, before me, as I write. Out here in the Jungle the excitements are nil and it is extraordinary the interest one can derive from even a couple of pigeons. Mr. Streicher is still away as he was ordered up to Maymyo. Streicher goes home on leave most years and Mr. Steven will go out to their camp about nine miles off where the work of felling logs is now in full swing. On Friday Freddie had to go out to see about road making through new Jungle, so I went with him in the buzzer and read until he had finished the two mile walk in the dense Jungle. Poor dear came back swarming with ticks and has scratched ever since. At night it is dreadful for warmth seems to make the irritation worse. A nasty accident happened on the line the other day. One of the bogeys caught a piece of wood and turned right round and off the line. One man got his leg pinned underneath and was carried in here in a bad state, leg broken and skin badly cut. He was patched up and sent in on a bamboo stretcher. Freddie shot a gye (barking dear) one evening. It is topping to eat and as there is plenty of it his boys are equally delighted for they have their share. Mrs. Barker writes from Monywa that life there is quicker than ever; the joy of it goes a long way, and she sends me magazines out which is nice. Mrs. Jackson arrives at Monywa with her husband and new baby soon, so Mrs. Barker will have a companion. Mr.Jackson is in the B.B.T.C. and both are very nice. She has travelled twice on the same boat as Ethel. Freddie's new clerk is a great success and is an enormous help and so relieves Freddie of work and responsibility. Well mother dearest I must write more mail letters now. I do hope we shall hear the new treatment is doing good. Lots of love from us both.

Jungle, Tuesday November 13th 1923

What a lovely surprise to get yours of October 11 yesterday. I was very lucky as last Thursday brought me the mail of the week before. I do wish you could get into Hereford again. I don't like the sound of your two Miss Macs at all. Do you think Emma Turner knows of any place? She is a very likely one and she would do anything at making enquiries and Mrs. Baker may hear of someone in the Garden City. That's where she is going to live but do ask her. It's dreadful to think of the family you have and all the friends in the old days and not one able to do much. Of course it is very easy for me to talk when I am so far away but we must have you fixed up comfy like. Last mail I sent a big bundle of letters to Jack; yours and from several other members of the family. I expect Jack is like me and doesn't mind how stale the news as long as he has letters. Poor Nora! Mary's account is too pathetic. I can quite understand how she feels about the Rosslyn atmosphere. I used to be the same if I happened to be out of a job in the old days. Connie, kind as she may be in some ways, is so bitter and can never hide her feelings lest any of George's family dump themselves on her. She has estranged George from us all and I honestly don't see how her life is harder than anyone else. I'm so glad to hear the letter arrived about the treatment dear. If only the doctor can do something to relieve pain and enable you to shift about easier. You mustn't hesitate to take whatever cure he recommends dear. The money will always be forthcoming somehow and to see you walking about a little again would be worth all the pounds we can scrape together. It is fortunate I am able to be out in the Jungle as it is our only chance to save. I have my work cut out at times to keep Freddie's pecker up as he has had such bad luck with his rubber shares. If he had not been so busy getting engaged to me in 1920 he would have made a lot of money whereas the chance was lost and now we want a favourable opportunity to sell out. Everything is down at present so we hope for the best. The exchange has crept up to one shilling and fourpence three farthings. I am not at all surprised to hear about young Denis but feel so sorry that two such possible boys should be spoilt. Of course since a youngster Denis wanted very careful handling, which he didn't get and the RAF will do him no good either. He is bound to meet a lot of 'wrong uns.' Shove the boy off to the so. Then I would, if I could see her. One is always sorry for anyone with worries, but if Edith Colonies to do some real hard labour, would be the best thing but we mustn't tell Edith had taken a firm line from the beginning and done a job her boys would have benefited and been a darned sight happier. What an awful shame George should have such a rotten start in life. What became of the £100 Uncle Sid left him? You mustn't worry about Edith dear she has, and never will, take any notice of anyone bar herself. We must try and see her on our way home. The work here is held up with the Bates (the locomotive which brings the loads of logs) having broken down. It is ridiculous to think that the whole of this important work depends on one small machine and costs the Corporation about three hundred rupees per day with all the labour being idle. This district has cost a fabulous sum to start and run already, and they won't see their error in refusing to have another locomotive. A lot of money will be lost in clearing this area which government has marked out to be worked. Another firm (Steeles) would have stepped in and said: 'We'll do it' which would have lost us our sole right to the river. The Irrawaddy has a conglomeration of firms but Steeles and B.B.T.C. are the only ones to work teak. All last

Thursday Freddie was inspecting work and I spent the day alone but I was able to be out in the 'buzzer' with him the next morning. We went about ten miles to Penive and watched the tractors load logs. When we arrived there men were busy mending the gantry which lifts the logs. In trying to lift a huge log, green with much leaves, the gantry broke dropping the log right across the line. Green logs are not properly dried by the time they are felled and have to be left on the bank of the creek for another three years. (Green logs will not float.) Mr. Steven arrived on Saturday. He is to relieve Mr. Streicher. Mr. Steven is such a nice man. I'm sorry he has departed to Penive this morning but he will be back often. Like the 'buzzer' and Ford car it is easy to get in. Freddie took him out there. The weather is delightful now. Not a lot of heat during the day and decidedly chilly at night. Our garden is doing well and much against Freddie's better advice I have already picked some lettuces. He means the lettuce to have a heart and the lettuce and I are not much good without one. But my tummy rules out all better feelings and the lettuce does look so luscious and tasty. Seeds grow so wonderfully quickly. Everything pops up after three or four days. Cheerio Mother dear. I want to write to Aunt Mary now. Lots of love and I'm awfully fit so you must not worry about me anymore. Freddie is too, though beside Mr. Steven's browning sunburned face, straight from home, Freddie wants more colour. But he is very nice as he is, bless him.

Jungle, Monday November 26th 1923

I am so sick that I did not remember that last week was the Christmas mail Dear. I am so sorry and it was only as I was going off to sleep last night that the fact took me 'all of a heap like.' Perhaps it will not be too late even now to send you our very best love and wishes dear. I do hope you will have a comfy day, at any rate, but I'm afraid you must feel rather sad and lonely with not one of your family with you. Oh dear, I wish and long that we could be there. We're not likely to ever spend a Christmas at home as our leave always comes during the summer months, which really is as well of course. You must buy something you want with the enclosed. The snaps are some Freddie took the other day with our small camera. The buzzer is the little car which runs on the train lines and is successful for popping along to the various camps in all sorts of weather. One of me standing by a log will give you an idea the size teak can grow to. This is only a third of a tree. The other two logs are about the same length. On the top of the log you will see my beloved dog '*Spiker.*' Mr. Stoner the man in charge of the engineering part here is standing by me with his kit on hand ready to go out to the camp. Our compound and thatched house you can see in the distance. The weather is simply glorious now; sleek bright sunny days and nippy at night. Good for my rheumatics which is very much better. My hands are always painful. I simply must have them put right. I have no brains but I reckon I'm not so bad at doing things. No English mail in yet. The messenger is already a day late and may be due to the boat being stuck on a sandbank. The river gets very low from now onwards. Mr. Milton returns from leave January 4th so should be up here to relieve Freddie by the 14th, which should suit us well and might see Freddie finished with this place and so give us a clear month to pack up. Time is getting wonderfully short now and I can scarcely believe that by the time you get this we shall be nearly home. Our garden is simply splendid now and we get a nice lot of vegetables each day; enough to send up to Mr.Stricher and Stoner. Both of them have been in for breakfast, a midday meal. I'm out testing the old Ford car which isn't going well. In any case the roads make it impossible to use a car. These two often pop in suddenly which means a meal as a rule so it is just as well one has large amounts of stores in the Jungle always so we can dash for a tin of fish or sausages. Yesterday Freddie lent his gun to a coolie to try to get us some game or anything eatable. He returned with a couple of monkeys strung on a pole; a huge Gibbon standing about four feet tall, its baby one clinging to its neck. The man saw the big one at a distance and shot not knowing what it was. It was a horrible sight; a big ungainly animal looking so human like. The grey short fur skin so very nice and we are having it cured to see what we can make of it. There is absolutely no news dear so I will get on with a letter to Aunt Bea and ones to the other two I want to write. Lots of love and from Freddie.

Jungle, Sunday December 2nd 1923

We are on tour for a couple of days and six miles away from Thabeyhaw which place we left yesterday. Bullock carts with kit left early in the afternoon and we followed later and found everything unpacked and comfy on our arrival just before dark. We are camped in the village of Zayat in a shelter built by villagers for the use of any wanderers. Zayats or pagodas are built as a rule with the idea of gaining merit in the next world. This particular one is exceptionally clean so we hope we will not go away with more friends on us than we came with. Freddie left early in the morning for a six mile tramp to inspect work and won't be back much before noon. It is such a treat to come to a place with open spaces, up and away from the thick surrounding Jungle, which we have at Thabeyhaw. There are paddy fields here and in the evening we hope for some Jungle fowl shooting. We were a bit late yesterday but I managed to get one dove which did for our first course at dinner.

It is getting colder and colder and all the comfort Freddie gives is that it goes down to 40^0 and that it is warm now compared to what we shall have. It is an effort to leave my comfy bed in the morning now so I dread to think what will happen by the time I have to act as a hostess to Mrs. Phillips. We are having a little thatched house built in the compound and are generously giving over the bungalow with all its rats and mice to the Phillips. Lunch, tea, and dinner we shall have with them in the bungalow but chota is looked upon as a solitary and private meal by everyone in this country. Jolly good idea too. Thank you for your letter of October 31st, dear, I always enjoy the enclosures. Mrs. Baker sounds such a kind sort and I can quite understand how much you must miss her. Let's hope she will soon tire of being her daughters slave and return again to be your companion. Netherwood sounds so nice and cheery with the various people going there for tea. How I wish we could get you back there again. So our Dottie is still vulgar is she? I don't think Pat Armstrong will be able to curb that for her. I must make Dottie some undies towards her trousseau sometime. We shall leave something as a wedding present on our way through Colombo. At present I am sewing my own clothes for all I'm worth. How clever of you to still be able to knit socks for Jack. Are you wondering when we are going to ask you to knit some baby's vests? Your Ross doctor seems to be having more success with the treatment than Mr. Cuthbert. Do you think his partner is the better man for me to consult when I get home? I tell Mary that she and I had better decamp somewhere for a cure. I am now wearing the white sweater you made me and the grey scarf. You have no idea what joy they are to me these cold days. If you have time and the inclination you have no idea how much Freddie would appreciate a pair of socks made by you and given when we see you next year. We will pay for the wool of course. Don't mention it in your letters if you make them. Keep it as a surprise. He hasn't a very long foot which may be a consolation. Well dear there is no news, not even any to make up on, so will stop. Lots of love dear I shall have your mail when we return tomorrow but this must be off first.

Thaybeyhaw, Monday December 10th 1923

Your very welcome and cheerful letter of November 6th arrived last mail. It is splendid to think you may be able to walk again before long. You can't possibly look forward to my letters as much as I do yours and when it holds such good news, as that had; it makes all the difference to life out here. I do so hate to think of you boxed up in the house and everything so difficult for you. It may be a great blessing that all circumstances made you go

136

to Ross. The doctor is so nice and has certainly done a lot of good already. I've a good mind to leave Mr. Cuthbert and go and see your new man when I am home. My finger joints are getting pretty rotten and my right thumb makes writing, sewing etc., very difficult at times. Sad to say our leave has been postponed for another month. So we shan't be home until the end of April now. It is a great disappointment of course but we shall still have six months at home and perhaps landing in April will be nicer than March. It is more of a strain on Freddie than on me because that one extra month makes all the difference. So much work with the whole of next year's working plan to be made up. Mr. Milton has his month's extension on account of health. We shall go to Monywa for ten days in January. Freddie has to fetch more money and a break from Jungle life will give us a nice change. I shall return here with Freddie of course. Monywa is not much fun alone and poor old Freddie loathes Jungle at the best of times and would get very fretful alone out here. Besides we have a chance to save money away from civilisation. I'm awfully sorry not to be travelling on the same boat as Mrs. Cleaver. She has just been doing a lot of shopping for me in Maymyo. She is always so willing to do anything. Freddie and Mr. Streicher have just gone out to try the Ford car and I am alone here and in an awful fit with two men in the compound fighting like *'billy oh.'* I went out to them at last when they started at one another with sticks, plates and finally knives. Wish to God Freddie would come back. Burmans have fiendish tempers and nothing stops them once worked up. I hate them all and shall be truly thankful when we see a good old buxom wench at home once more. Annoying as they may be life and housekeeping in headquarters is of course very much easier than in the Jungle. Here we can only have raw boys but the Butler takes most of the responsibility at headquarters and if things go wrong he gets it in the neck especially if stores disappear. I have to dole everything out daily here otherwise it would be bagged. I suppose life can't be all beer and skittles anywhere. We start on tour for Maukkadaw tomorrow to meet the Phillips on the 14th. It will be a relief when their visit is over. An inspection gives Freddie a lot of stick and worry and if the wife is bored with life here they go away with a nasty taste in the mouth, which might reflect back on us sometime. Freddie is back and he in his turn kicked up a fuss and sacked the two men, so now perhaps we may have peace; very sickening just as we are going off on tour and want servants while the Phillips are in here. However more are always forthcoming. Yes, I get *The Hereford Times* and regularly enjoy reading all its various bits of news. I suppose the St. Giles Chapel is really doomed now after the motor bus accident. All such dangerous spots should be rectified these days of ever increasing motor transport. The road must be pretty thick with cars now as the prices are going lower and lower. We still busy ourselves most evenings in the garden which is doing splendidly. Freddie does so love what I call frittering and will be another Uncle Fred in his old age. Freddie is never as happy as when there is a job to be done and he longs for the time when he can return and have a settled home. Yesterday the head clerk here presented me with the most lovely silk parasol that his wife bought for me in Monywa when she heard I was going home. It is dreadful to let them spend so much money on me but one can't refuse the gift. I must away and think of packing a few things for our trip. Lots of love Mother dear, I do so hope you will be able to go on giving me such good news of yourself. Best of love from Freddie too.

Jungle, Sunday December 23rd 1923

Yours of November 30th came last mail for which many thanks dear. I do so enjoy reading Aunt Mary's letters. She is so sweet to send such nice messages to me, but like all home letters I never get all the information I would like. Not to be wondered at as the little things which interest me would not be worth the writing. It is sad that Aunt Joan has to give up Birchwood. I think it wiser as Helen will never live in Malvern, which she hates, and James is more likely to work in London, but as in your case it is such hard luck that Aunt

Joan has none of her family with her. Ethel never writes so I don't know her news. Does she intend staying in England for good now? Now Aunt Bea and Minnie are free you will see more of them. It is a pity Miss Mac's charges are so high. Perhaps Aunt Bea. and Minnie would stay with you sometime for treatment since it sounds very helpful and so long as it is doing you no harm in any way I should certainly carry on with it. My last letter was from Sannahbin, the last stop before Maukkadaw on the river. The Phillips were fixed to arrive on the launch on the 14th. So we went down to meet them. Freddie has made the four miles two days running and no sign of the wretched people. I was very annoyed because Freddie was having his fever all the time and would have been better to stay in camp. However Sahib must be treated like a little tin God and so Freddie puts his own likes into the background. The third time of asking, on the 16th, Freddie had more luck and appeared back in camp at 11am with Madame Phillips riding a very slap up pony. She is very nervous riding. I very much doubt her sticking another six weeks Jungle after this. I like Mrs. Phillips very much indeed. Luckily she enjoys the peace of this life and has no use for the social duties of Rangoon. Of course this Forest is easy, for with no travelling elephants a later morning start does not matter. I wonder how Mr. 'P' will enjoy getting up at dark for the elephants to be off. I didn't enjoy the first few days very much. Freddie is not too fit and has a thousand and one things to be responsible for, not knowing whether Phillips would like his camp etc., etc., and what fussed me was that they brought up their Rangoon cook, who is good of course, and our miserable Jungle man is quite hopeless in comparison. We take alternate days for cooking and with endless lots of tinned stuff we have done fairly alright. We got so weary of doing short marches that we left the Phillips on the third day and got ahead with a small amount of kit on the Ford car. Mrs. 'P' has the most wonderful long leather boots which prevent her walking much. So riding six miles is about all she can do. We did not leave them until early afternoon. The car went so badly we were not home before dark, a distance of only about fourteen miles. The road is terribly sandy and the wheels seemed to lose all grip. Anyway Freddie did not think it advisable to send the car for them next day so they had to remain another night on the road, for which we were truly thankful, asit gave us a breathing time here and could get things ready for them. Thursday they finally rolled up and were charmed with their little thatched hut in the garden. We made it as comfy as possible so that they would prefer to sit down there and they have caught on beautifully. A fireplace completed the comfort so they disappeared soon after dinner, which is a relief. Mr. and Mrs. 'P' have been married only a year and I am as sure they are as pleased as we that they should have solitude. Freddie and I have sympathetic understanding of that if in no other. Mr. and Mrs.'P' both know Herefordshire well. Mr. 'P' has a brother living at Whitfield in the Clives old house and another brother Ledbury way and I think it is his old mother who lives still at Bacton. His brothers are very keen on Hereford cattle and I expect known George. Yesterday we all had a long day out at Kwaythay where Mr. Steven is in charge of the work. Mr. Steven came up for the 'Ps' on the buzzer and Freddie drove us out on the Ford. The driver was ill so it had to be done. I must say it was particularly delightful on fearful Jungle roads with just room and Freddie unaccustomed to driving. We got to our destination which is about all I can say. I was thankful when we all came home on the buzzer. Freddie and Mr. 'P' left early this morning for more inspection work. We start off on tour again on the 26th and they join the launch on the 3rd. We go by a different route as a creek is to be inspected. Mr. Steven and Mr. Streicher will come in for Christmas Day so we shall be a party of six in the morning. We are all motoring six miles for a shoot. There is still no news about our passage. I shall be horribly sick if they postpone it for too long and do hope Freddie and I will not dread returning to this country after our six months leave. Most do, especially the married men, for the separations become more difficult to put up with as the years go on. I only wish it were possible for us to retire now and Freddie be able to run a small place at home. Our garden is still producing the most wonderful vegetables and the salads are so delicious. Yes, I had a nice long letter from Edith. She has popped up once more. I do hope things will go more smoothly for them. We may see her in Paris on our way through if her work takes her there. I had a long letter from Mrs. Carol last mail. She says Mrs. Cox has built herself a wonderful little house in Fleet. It is so wonderful, in fact, that there is no money left for anything else. Peter, Mrs. Cox' son, who has a hideout in Champery has turned out to be an utter rotter. Babs has a family and she and Mrs. Cox fight as much as ever when together. Lots of love mother dear from us both.

Thaybehaw, Saturday January 5th 1924

I was frightfully disgusted at having missed the last mail. I hope you weren't very disappointed or worried dear. We were out in camp with the Phillips and depended upon the incoming mail and messenger to arrive in time to take the home letters. Of course the messenger was two days late and Freddie had no spare man to send. Such an influx of letters when mails did turn up and I had a lovely fat bundle which always thrills me more than anything. I shall have a nice lot to forward on to Jack which I do with any letters coming my way. Your dear little calendar is very much appreciated dear. It was the first on the scene here and settled many disputes we had here as to whether 1924 was a leap year or not etc. Yes my letters from up here are bound to take longer for I have to send a week previous in order to catch the mail at Rangoon. Your last letter of December 5th with Mary's electioneering letter arrived this week. The newspaper cutting is most amusing about Stookey. I don't think much of the caricature. I could do a better one of Stookey representing a lop eared bunny. Do you remember in the old Edenhurst days how wild Mary used to get when we teased her with the magic lantern of the lop eared rabbit. Perhaps she would be hurt now but I don't think so. Your treatment sounds more drastic than I care to hear but worthwhile if you were able to stand it again. It would be 'topping' to see you walking again though I have missed seeing you through your worst time. Tell your doctor man that your first exercises must be up and down steps the height you need to get into a car, for we mean you to get around in our bus when we are home this year. It is wonderful to say this instead of next. We have not been given any definite date of sailing yet. I heard from Emma Turner, Aunts Minnie and Mary, and actually short letters from Ethel and Dottie. They both thought the other would tell me all the news so I fell between two stools and got no news at all. Mrs. Carrol is also very faithful in writing and of course Stella and Dorothy Brooksbank. The latter is in Cheltenham teaching some very riotous children in a family of nine. Oh dear! I am so glad that it is not my lot now; though to turn my hand to any other sort of job does not appeal to me in the least. My last letter must have been written just before Christmas. Christmas Day was quite jolly and was a party of six. We started off early in the morning Mr. Phillips and Streicher riding and the rest of us crowded on to the Ford lorry and went about six miles to Yawdaw where there are good paddy fields and plenty of Jungle fowl. We had Burmans going through the thick Jungle to drive the birds. We did not reach back home before 3pm so were ravenous and ate quite as one should on Christmas Day. We had no sooner finished and it seemed we had to consume an enormous Christmas dinner with dark green peas out of our own garden and tinned Christmas pudding, which was excellent, to say nothing of the brandy butter Mr. Phillips excelled himself in making. Both the Phillips were very jolly and I so enjoyed the cheery time all sitting round the fire after dinner feeling content in every way. I assure you Boxing Day was rather hectic. We started out packing and getting our kit off and Freddie did a hundred and one things in the office. It was some rush. However, staff got away early afternoon in the bullock carts which were travelling alone at two miles an hour. We always try to arrange our kit goes ahead so that our camp is ready on our arrival. We did not arrive here before 4pm. Mrs. 'P' and Freddie and I went in the car and the others rode the six miles to Yawdaw which was our first stopping place. It was most awfully cold and we were glad of the big camp fires which were burning outside our tents. We dined with the 'Ps' that night, in fact we did each day, and we gave breakfast, as the carts always went ahead over night, so that breakfast was awaiting us. The 'Ps' are not uncomfortably early in the mornings so there was none of the before dawn rising which is our usual rule but with Mr. 'P' who does not do much of the walking or riding, we had to have short marches. From Yawdaw we did about six miles to a very nice camp under thick trees. On our way the men folk had another shoot sothat we did not get in until late. It is the first time I have done the route, which is very much prettier than the monotonous flat sandy road to Maukkadaw. This route to Chiningzone is being opened up with a new line of seventeen miles to carry the timber on down to Chiningzone Creek, which is the nearest and only possible way of delivering the logs to the Chindwin river. We went as far as Moodike with the Phillips and left them to do the last two miles to the Chindwin alone. The B.B.T.C. launch was to pick them up there to go on up to another district. I was sorry to say goodbye as both are so nice, but I must say it was somewhat of a relief to be alone. I suppose Forest Inspectors don't earn their fat pay unless they find fault with their various districts and I was on pins and needles lest more stick and worry cropped up for Freddie. Today Freddie has gone out to the working area for the day. Since Mr. P's visit the standard of logs has gone up considerably and many Freddie would not have rejected have now to be turned down. There is a fearful slump in timber and they only want the best stuff down in Rangoon. Well mother dear I don't think there is anything else to write about so I will switch off. Lots of love dear and don't get downhearted about your treatment it will all be forgotten soon when you are able to walk a little.

Jungle, Sunday January 13th 1924

Yours of December 12th arrived last mail for which many thanks dear. The mails are coming through quickly now and take a week from Rangoon to reach me here. I am so glad Ethel and Dorothy have been over to see you. Dottie must be on the high seas by now. I do hope she will be happy with Pat. She will find Wigton a very different place to Watawalla where they are on the main road and very central. Wigton is a grind of about six miles from the main road and during the rains very difficult to reach. But still where and when one is happy there seems to be ample to keep one employed. I must have inherited the gift of keenness for sewing from you, a thing I can't be too thankful to possess in this life. I never tire of it and wish more could be done, for I find there is very little time to make anything for anyone except myself. But as I have had only one evening dress made (and that I embroidered) since I came out to this country you can imagine how my time is filled up. You have no idea how quickly cotton frocks and undies go to bits out here. Poor Dottie would have a rush to finish her things and get off with so many in the house for Christmas. I have only had one short letter from Ethel for ages. She seems to have lost her old keenness for letter writing, to me at any rate. It seems such a pity that Sammy should return to Ceylon when he is not yet fit. Do you know when he is going to return? He will be very pleased if they can buy their old house back at Eardisland. It is splendid to hear of you moving about a little now dear even though it is only to shuffle along holding on to the dining-room table. That is the beginning and I am looking forward to taking you for walks when we are home. You mustn't give up heart whatever you do. So much depends on one's own efforts and pluck anyway. I know you have the latter but when it gives so much pain it is bound to dishearten us to make the effort and to do exercises. It is becoming hotter every day now and is sad to think of the fogs of the cold weather passing. I dread our packing in Monywa when March temperatures can be anything over 100^0 and I don't suppose we shall feel comfy or dry from the day we leave here until the boat takes us away from Rangoon. This extra month out here is going to make all the difference. Thank goodness it does not mean a month out of our leave at home. Mr. Streicher is here today and goes home on February 28th on The Yorkshire, which was our original boat. After handing over all the tractor work etc., to Mr. Steven we have had Mr. Streicher here with us. He is an absolute expert engineer and it is perfectly wonderful how quickly he detects and adjusts anything wrong with the numerous mechanical devices under his charge. Mr. Streicher is seeing about a car for us. There is something of a scarcity of cars this year owing to an influx of visitors to the exhibition. We do not want to be landed with nothing. Our choice is between a Morris Oxford, Citroen or a Standard four seater. We mean to do all car travelling or the bus and shall want space for our luggage, to say nothing of passengers. Friends returning to this country on leave have all done around about five thousand miles and had not entered a train once during their six months. Both Mr. Steven and Mr. Streicher were here last night and we had a farewell dinner for Mr. Streicher. We ate our last Christmas pudding. There is always more excitement over the brandy butter I make than anything else. Mr. Steven is a very good keen shot. He has lent me a little rifle of his which I use for potting at doves or any old thing in the evening. We are not going into Monywa for money after all as Freddie has so much work to do but on Thursday we start to go down to Maukkadaw to meet the special twenty thousand rupees which is coming up on an Irrawaddy boat. We shall make the tour as short as possible by going in the car. Well dear there is no news so fear this letter is dull. Write the one mail after you receive this letter and if we go by the boat in middle of March I shall receive it all right. We can't possibly go by the earlier boat. Lots of love dear

Camp, Monday January 21st 1924

I received yours of December 9th on our way to Maukkadaw to fetch the money and we are now at the last but one stopping place on the return journey to Thabeyhaw. This is a very weary monotonous march becoming heavier going each day in the many carts churning up the sand and making deeper ruts. Bullock carts can only do about a mile and a half per hour so you can imagine the weariness of driving twenty four miles at that rate. We send two carts ahead over night with tables, chairs food boxes and the cook and our other servants so we can go ahead next morning and arrive at camp to find a bath, change and food all waiting. Our other carts with the remaining kit come crawling in about three hours later. Freddie doesn't get too far ahead this trip as one never knows when some blackguards may attack the cart men in charge of the money. Twenty thousand rupees is no small amount to lose. As this money is mostly in silver you can imagine the weight of the box, which is a load in itself. The boat was a day late in reaching Maukkadaw so we have been kept out longer than we expected. It is really exciting to think that the next time we come along this road it will be for the last time of asking, and we shall have started on the long trail for home. Golly that seems too good to be true. We were disappointed at the last minute on this trip in not having the old Ford car to help us over seventeen miles of the way. The car had been out to the workshops for repairs and the fool of a Burman driver, in their usual harem scarem way, drove the car into a tree with the natural result of a bent radiator. Mr. Steven is evidently having trouble with her otherwise we should have had the car by now to meet us. The sun is already very hot in the middle of the day and I rather dread another trip in a month's time. I will let you know our boat directly we know ourselves. Do write in answer to this one dear, just in case we don't go until the last boat in March. I shall receive the letter in Rangoon then. It will be such a very long time to wait for news of you otherwise. I do hope you decide to take another course. Apparently this one has helped you a lot and one more may do the trick and get you on your legs once more. Do be guided by your doctor dear. I'm sure he would not advise more treatment to the detriment of your general health. I'm afraid my writing goes rather to bits at the end of a page as I am scribbling on my knees before a fire which is still needed at nights, though the sun makes things very hot during the day. At Sannabhin, our last stop, we had some good pigeon shooting, crowds of them in the evening all roosting in the trees. Mr. Steven lent me his nice little rifle which gave me some sport though it's really difficult to get anything with only one shot to depend on. I like Freddie's shot gun best which gives one much more help. I do hope Mary spent Christmas with you. She's like me and hates to think of you being without a member of your family with you. Don't worry dear about getting the Miss Macs to charge less for our rooms when we come to Ross. Three guineas is a lot per head but we must pay for the charming society within their gates.

There seems to be every possibility of another general election so perhaps Stookey will gain his seat this time though personally I think his own seat deserves a good whacking for fighting as a Liberal. When they and the Labourites are in power it will be interesting to see what steps they take to reduce unemployment. At present the papers say nothing as to how that will be done. I can't understand how the members stand the expense of so many elections. I heard from Jack last mail, poor old dear seemed down on his luck still, but glad to be back on the land. Glad to hear that too; because one can stick so much when one feels fit. He can't bear being without Nora and Michael and I do hope luck will favour them sometime so that they can lead a love life together. I know how much harder it is to put up with things when one is alone. Aida Barton (the girl who stayed with me at Maymyo when she had her baby) is back again in Burma and wants me to go and stay before I leave for home. Pakokku where she lives is only a day's trip on the river from Monywa so shall do my very best to go down. She is an awful dear and but for her husband's serious illness last year which entailed them going home earlier, we should have gone together this year. I do miss girl pals in this life. Of course Jungle is 'topping' but with Freddie out or in the office so much I long for a cheery girl to keep me company so that we can wag our tongues and say as much as we like. I don't know how we are going to fit in everything while we are home. An extension of leave is the only thing to enable us to see everyone we want. Stella, Dorothy, the Brooksbanks, Mrs. Carrol and the Crumps all seem to promise to be our life's enemy if we don't go and stay with them. A weekend is as much as they will want I expect. We do not know where we shall go yet on our return to this country. I hope Maymyo in a way, but it has its many drawbacks. It is much more expensive for living with its necessary amount of entertaining and I would have to bring out more glad rags than if we were posted to a quieter station. We are both out to economise all we can out East. Freddie is very fit now but much perturbed by the rate his few remaining hours are coming out. He is fast getting an island on his top-knot. You know the sort with a little patch in front, the rest on top a shiny bald pate until the ring around the head comes. I don't wonder he loses his hair with me attached to him. I'm sure I must be a fearful trial and apparently Edith warned him I was of a very independent nature (before we married). However much is patched up by saying 'Purr purr' (like Mary used to you) or 'Bow wow', after some long discussion, when ten to one I get heated and Freddie doesn't turn a hair! Lots of love Mother dear,

Jungle, Monday January 28th 1924

Many thanks for yours of December 24th. What a killing letter from young Geli he seems a splendid boy. I do hope the Lad will be able to settle at Miss Louise's as he is very young to make a start in life though he is made of the right stuff. I wonder if young Tommy is as his letter leads one to think, but sooner or later the sportsmanship in Charlie and Nell is bound to come out in him. He sounds the 'prig in a Boy's storybook' but I am sure he is not really. It is such a pity the boy can't come home. How splendid that Mary and young John were with you for Christmas. I am so glad and I am sure their company made all the difference to you. I have been so busy all the morning and left my mail until afternoon, which is most unusual. So as per usual I shall not send the letter I always intend writing. As it is

142

Monday I thought it appropriate to have a washing day. Having come down to my last frock it is none too soon. I give nothing to my boy to wash if I can help it. The clothes seem to come back more grubby and smelly than when I gave them to him. I find undies are quite nice to wear un-ironed, also most of my frocks made of strong cloth. So it is not much of an effort to do all my own things. Sam Pay, Freddie's boy, does all his shirts etc., also table cloths etc., and very well too. My chief and only grievance is that washing and wringing afterwards that I find difficulty in doing anything for a bit. Writing is pretty hopeless too and it is rotten to stretch out my fingers after holding the pen for any length of time. However, I have every hope of being put right when we are home. My last letter was written on our return journey from Maukkadaw. We, as well as the money, arrived in quite safely, and it is nice to settle in the bungalow once more. Leaving for only a few days our doves have two more eggs to hatch before the family is able to fly off and give more room. They give me no end of amusement and interest from here in the veranda where I sit most of the day. I'm glad to say the old ones have wisely turned out of their original cot and are now hatching the third never risen above doves before. A Jungle cock is like a Bantam cock in colour and much larger. Jungle hens are like our hens, dark grey. They are awfully good to eat, and in this weather after hanging about three days are excellent. I never go out shooting alone, because if I happen to get anything I can't bear to pick it up. Freddie has to do the dirty work! There is a lot of game of all sorts all around here now water is drying up in the Jungle and the animals come for water. This morning a man was out after a pig, or anything to eat, and came face-to-face with a small leopard, which he shot and brought in. There is a reward of twenty rupees for all leopards and tigers. The skin is sent to the nearest District Commissioner's office and the money given, also the skin is returned. Any good skins Freddie gives five rupees to the man and gets the reward for him. This one will make a good pair with one we got at Monywa. Tigers are an awful nuisance round here too and in the last fortnight two bulls have been killed. I wish I could tell you our date of sailing, but so far have heard no news. They can't keep us in suspense much longer. Lots of love Mother dear, and take care of yourself. If you can get hold of a book called: *In the Middle of the Road* by Philip Gibbs I think it will interest you.

Jungle, Sunday February 3rd 1924

Here we are in February. It must be next month we go home. Nothing definite yet and we fear the date will be given us at the eleventh hour, which will make everything the most awful rush. However, you bet we shall catch the old boat alright. Many thanks for yours of January 2nd. It arrived last Thursday. I was so pleased to read Edith's long letter. I send all home letters to Jack, including yours in case you forget to tell him some little odd bits of gossip. Without Nora and the Reddie I expect information interests him. Am afraid Nora will have departed ere we reach Home and that will be a great disappointment. I forget dear if I told you that your letters arrived intact lately. The envelopes seem stronger and *The Hereford Times* is most beautifully packed. You all seem to have done yourselves very proud on Christmas Day. You must have loved John and Mary being with you. Sorry there were no drinks. Freddie sent his boys a £1 for Christmas on condition a bottle of booze was bought and nothing else. They spent part on a bottle of Burgundy. We have heard that Freddie's sister Norah, married and living in Canada, is coming home for two months this year. Like many others, her husband is struggling for an existence on a ranch in British Columbia and bad luck in many things has made them hard up. Freddie and his brother Harold have combined forces and will pay Norah's expenses. I'm so glad we shall see her. Norah, the youngest in the family, is a great favourite apparently. It is most disappointing to hear you have stopped the treatment. At one-time it seemed so helpful. Doesn't the Doctor advise you to continue with the injections? You must try and be brave dear and carry on with the exercises. That alone will be disheartening sort of work. Even to walk up and down stairs and out in the garden will seem a great joy to you I expect. We quite intend staying in Paris a few days, if Edith is there still. I'd love to see her again, and she is such a splendid one to trot one about. Freddie and I both think that in Paris we will feel too much like country cousins to do any sightseeing on our own. I am forwarding your Daisy......... letters which you must not repeat after her strict injunction –that what she infers about Brian's treatment of Dorothy is stale news. I always felt that he was left out of things. Where she is now there cannot be so much favouritism. Poor old chap! He is getting a bit too long in the tooth ...Freddie and I were out all day yesterday. We started early in the car with our lunch and did not return until tea time. I started off in the Jungle with Freddie who had to go all round the place inspecting logs but I turned back on discovering the place was pretty thick with ticks. So I sat in the shade behind a log and read. It is becoming really hot in the day now. The Jungle is looking burnt up with leaves thick on the ground. Fire protection of all logs has to be done now, which is difficult and very responsible work for there is a dickens of a row if any logs get burnt. Elephants also have to go to their next camps at the approach of hot weather. Water and feed are getting scarce. I still sew all my days. I am so often held up and can't finish a dress for the want of something or other. It takes at least a fortnight to receive an answer from Rangoon. Am enclosing a few snaps. The small leopard is the one I told you about last week and which was killed quite near our camp but Freddie thinks he looks like Mr. Lloyd. The other shows how we grow marrows. Freddie suggests the size of the marrow is similar to that of a tick after it has spent the night with him. The little photo is part of the zone here. Off to the right is looking towards our bungalow. We do photography nearly every evening now and hope to have a nice collection by the time we get home. We intend waiting to buy a book in England. Lots of love Mother dear, keep cheery,

Camp, Sunday February 10th 1924

Please excuse a pencilled letter as Freddie has gone off with the key of the office box and I can't get at the ink. Many thanks for yours of January 9th received in the last mail. Also Edith's with her postcard. I am deeply flattered she thinks that the fair damsel is like me. Freddie seems to think the salon worth a visit to second Edith's opinion. So perhaps we shall see for ourselves when in Paris. Edith is a wonderful India rubber ball isn't she? It never seems to affect her for long however many kicks she may have when her luck downs her, and directly her luck is turned she bobs up again at once. I am so glad there is a chance for her to make some money and she will probably regret not having got down to it a long time ago. There is nothing nicer than the feeling of the pay coming in when it is a case of having to shift for oneself. Who is the Peggy she talks about having too much of a hold on the young Denis? It is a great pity if he sees too much of Freda Masters too. You will love having Edith with you. She will back you up a lot. The Miss Macs have quite a lot to thank you for. You certainly attract a good many visitors to their house which all helps with the expenses. Aunty Bea wrote that she hoped to get over to see you once the excitement of Sammy and his departure was over. Ethel has quite given up writing. She is probably kept pretty busy during the holidays. How topping for all the Dilwynites to be given the Eardisland house to live in. What it is to have wealthy and generous in-laws, isn't it? You have the latter but, none of your family seems destined to collect money in any way. Sam will be delighted at getting his old house back again. I expect he always hated parting with it. I wonder if there is any chance of Ethel coming out East again about the time of our departure next November. Very jolly, if we could travel out together. We are still hanging in mid air waiting for a definite date for sailing. We are pretty certain it will be either March 13th or 24th. In a way I hope the latter. The 13th means such a hopeless rush for our packing in Monywa at which time the heat will be pretty terrific. Yesterday we left Thabeyhaw for our new camp at Kwaythay; about fourteen miles from Thabeyhaw at the end of the train line where all the Jungle work is at present being carried on. Our logs with our tent etc., left on the return journey of the Bates. (The motor engine which brings in the load of logs) After a scratch lunch with Mr. Steven, who had motored in, we left in the car for Kwaythay going along a new road first, which is being opened up for the work later on. I've had the most hairy ride. Mr. Steven is a most beefy harem scarem don't care sort of gent, and along these Jungle roads it is pretty nerve racking to motor slowly, so from the start of the trip until he had the sense to give up to the Burman driver I was in one long breathless state of wondering which tree we'd finally smash into. Poor Freddie suffered from me hanging on to his leg and had considerable difficulty in keeping the leg of his shorts being pulled above the height of respectability, The steering of the car is all wrong to add to our miseries and our journeying is nothing but a sharp wriggle all along a road, which only just takes the car. However, we lived through it all, which is the main part. Freddie went off at the crack of dawn this morning leaving me still comfy in bed. He is very worried about his side of the work here; which is responsibility for the timber side of this job. Burmans are so unreliable and fearfully lazy and awful liars. All this to be contended with adds no end of extra stick and worry. There are four hundred logs and trees missing. As the work is supposed to be finished in this area the tractors and the Bates should really move off to another part but Freddie naturally fights against that until all the lost timber is accounted for. So he has come out here himself to arrange and supervise search parties as a Burman is not at all above lying that every area is searched and nothing is to be found. Jungle fires will soon be starting and logs lying at stump more than likely will be burnt and, if found by the Forest Department later on, there is a dickens of a row. All this Jungle work is now a fearful trial – the place is alive with ticks and we are both still suffering from the day we had lunch out last week. Fortunately for me ticks don't bite me much but Freddie is a mass of irritation. We had quite a heavy thunderstorm one night last week which is unusual this time of year but the rain freshened up things considerably. We dined with Mr. Steven last night and he will be with us tonight. He is a most awfully nice man obsessed with thoughts of shooting and nothing else. The work is very much a second consideration. Very different to Mr. Streicher, his predecessor, who if anything, was too much the other extreme. I love being out in the camp at this time of year. In front of the tent we always have a bamboo structure on which is a tarpaulin and where we feed and sit with the fire near enough as safety permits. Last night we had a Jungle pheasant which is so good, and Mr. Steven has given us a Jungle fowl for tonight. All a topping change to our proverbial chickens. I drink a good deal of stout these days, which I think is helping to fatten me up. Freddie accuses me of being an awful boozer and complains that I giggle too much after a bottle of stout. I blame the fact that I am following in your footsteps. Bees buzz all round the place. In fact, any part of the Mahamyaung District is noted for honey. Cheerio Mother dear. Lots of love,

Jungle, Sunday February 17th 1924

Another week gone and one nearer to coming home. We have had no further information re passage from Rangoon so there is probably nothing doing for the boat at the end of March, so we are pretty certainly for the *Warwickshire,* sailing March 13th. She is the boat I came out to Burma on, the oldest and pretty rotten. I really don't care so long as she lands us at Marseilles. Okay, I am writing Edith this mail. We would like to stay a few days at her digs. She seems to think they may not be good enough for us. Which is all wrong. We have no more money to splash about than anyone else has. Mr. Milton lands at Rangoon today and apparently is to come up here at once. We shall be in Monywa before the end of the month and then the fun begins. Our packing here is practically finished but is very little compared to all the china, pictures etc., in Monywa. We hear it is stoking up there in Monywa, which I can quite believe, as it is bad enough here in the middle of the day though we still sit round a fire in the evening. I had such a nice mail last week and was so pleased to get yours of January 15th A letter from Edith is enclosed. How 'topping' for her to have a family gathering. Michael sounds so sweet. He was always an attractive baby. Our Nora was prevented from taking him to Hereford. Connie unconsciously does not exactly entice people to Rosslyn. She is so touchy when any of the family do not go to see her and George but she looks on them as spongers more than ever. Then she might think members of the family only take notice of her and George when money is wanted. Perhaps I should not write this but I'm sure Connie will not be one to read this letter. I am writing this making buns at the same time. By dint of much swearing and bad temper on my part I have got the cook to bake cakes fairly well. I wish I had brought my Perfection stove in up here. There is mighty little news dear. This is the land of work and naught else. Freddie is busy in the office most of the day and I am left to amuse myself. But I do bar the office claiming him after tea when we generally go for a walk and then come in to do photography as a rule. Freddie took some very good ones when in the camp at Kwaythay. I will keep all photos now and show them to you when we get home. Mr. Steven has come round for the night here. Friday being Sunday there is no work so instead he has gone out for a shoot. I longed to go too but Freddie said it was too hot for me. The everlasting office work keeps him here. Whole lot of game fowl to be had now. The Jungle is drying up and the birds congregate around where there is water. Fire protection has begun and all around here it is thick with smoke. Always seems to me to be such a waste to burn the topping wood which lies on the ground. A Mrs. Wroughton has written from Rangoon asking us to stay with them before we sail which saves us a lot of bother in making other arrangements. Mr.Wroughton is head man in our Shin now, both very nice. I got to know them up in Maymyo where they took the bungalow next to ours for the hot weather. Mother dear I expect you're longing for the warmer weather to come along. We must get you out a bit in your chair when Freddie and I come to stay at Ross.

Sannabhin, Sunday February 24th 1924

Excuse a short letter this mail dear. I must tell you the topping news first of all. We really and truly do sail on March 13th on the '*Warwickshire.*' We have had a very hectic time the last few days. Freddie suddenly made up his mind to quit Thabeyhaw and get down to Maukkadaw to catch the February 26th boat, otherwise the next one would not get to Monywa before March 4th which would leave us so little time for our packing. So with our fifteen carts containing kit we left our old Jungle headquarters on Friday. The carts went off the night before and we left early the next morning in the old Ford which took us the first twelve miles to Pugamah beautifully. We decided to get the car to take us all the way to save trudging the twelve miles to Sannahbin in the heat and along the sandy roads and across the dry sandy bed of a creek about seven times. The car went like a bat for the first three miles and then the most awful noise went on in the innards and we came to a sudden stop and the car was still. Fortunately for me Freddie in his usual careful old way had arranged for the Syce to follow with the pony. I did the remaining miles in comfort and Freddie got a good sweat up walking. Much to our surprise we found Mr. Milton here before us. He had been rushed up from Rangoon directly he arrived out. All the rest of yesterday and all today he and Freddie are up to their eyes in work talking outside in Mr. Milton's tent. Tomorrow we go into Maukkadaw to catch the boat which gets us to Monywa the next day. It is decidedly hot here midday so goodness knows what Monywa holds for us. I have a lot of letters to write before the mail goes tomorrow dear, so will end. So pleased to get the letters from you yesterday dated January 23rd. So yes by all means dear do try to get someone to fix you up in Hereford for the Summer. We'd love that but if that fails we will be perfectly happy with you in Ross. Perhaps Emma Turner could arrange something. Write back.

Postscript

Mully and Freddie remained in Burma with the Bombay Burma Trading Corporation until they retired to England in 1935. That year Mully's mother Alice died. Their first child Rodney was born in Hereford in January 1925, and his brother Deryk seventeen months later. The boys spent the first seven years of their childhood in Burma, with happy memories of riding on elephants, before being brought back to England to their preparatory school, Winchester House, in Northamptonshire. Later they both joined the Royal Naval College, Dartmouth.

Photo Vivian of Hereford

Deryk and Rodney

Mully died in 1947 at East Bergholt in Suffolk, at the early age of fifty-five. Deryk died, aged twenty-two, a year later, in a flying accident. For Freddie and Rodney trauma surrounded both tragedies.

The Ipswich Evening Star reported Mully's death on Friday 8th August, 1947:

"RADIO CALL DID NOT REACH SON IN TIME
An S.O.S. message broadcast by the B.B.C. on Sunday evening after the ten o'clock news, failed to reach Lt. R. Bowden., cruising in the channel on the yacht "Planet" in time for him to return to East Bergholt, to see his mother Mrs. Muriel Eliza Bowden, before she died. Mrs. Bowden, whose home was at "Sparrows", East Bergholt was seriously ill and unaware that the S.O.S. message had been sent. She was fifty-five years of age. In the village of East Bergholt where Mrs. Bowden had taken an active part in the life of local organisations during the ten years she had been resident, her many friends were extremely sorry to hear of her serious illness. She had been treasurer of the local branches of the Woodbridge Women's Conservative Association and the Church Missionary Society. Also a member of the Mother's Union and Women's Institute, she was a keen worker for all local organisations with which she had contact. A greatly respected resident of the village, her presence will be greatly missed. She leaves a widower and two sons both of whom are serving in the Royal Navy. A memorial service will be held at St. Mary's East Bergholt, on Friday."

In June, 1948, the *East Bergholt Parish Magazine* reported to the tragic death of Lieut. Bowden when his Seafire crashed into the sea near Fraserborough, Aberdeenshire on Tuesday May 18th:

"By his death the Fleet Air Arm loses a keen young officer who loved his profession - his death is part of the great price which has to be paid from time to time, in peace as well as in war, by the great Force to which he belonged in fitting itself for its dangerous work. To his father and brother the sympathy of the whole village and to his wide circle of friends will go."

The Ipswich Evening Star reported details of the Memorial Service held for Deryk:

"Relatives and many friends attended the memorial service in St. Mary's Church, East Bergholt, on Wednesday for Lieut. D.G. Bowden, of the Sparrows, East Bergholt, who was drowned at sea while on a naval exercise last week. The service was conducted by the Rev. Mervyn Young of Ipswich, who was godfather to the deceased. During the service the hymn "Eternal Father strong to save" and Psalm 23 were sung. An address was given by Mr. Young who spoke feelingly of the shock the village had sustained and the loss to the family. Throughout the service the casket which contained the ashes was draped with a White Ensign. The ashes will be scattered at Ipswich Crematorium in the near future." After the death of Mully and Deryk, Freddie remarried and went to live in Telfont Magna in Wiltshire. Freddie died there at the age of eighty in 1966. His son Rodney enjoyed a distinguished career in the Royal Navy:

The Daily Telegraph of 5 November 2004 published Rodney's obituary following his death in June 2004:

"Captain Rodney Bowden who has died aged 79, helped to rescue a group of Norwegians twice in 1945; first from the Soroyar Islands of north Norway, where they had been living in caves after the German army had destroyed their homes; and then several days later, from two lifeboats after their ship had been sunk off the North Cape.

Bowden was a junior officer in the destroyer Zambesi when it made a high-speed dash into enemy held fjords. The sight of the White Ensign prompted what seemed to be a trackless amphitheatre of snow to erupt, as hundreds of men on skis followed by their families on snowshoes made for the rescue boats. Some 525 men, women and children were taken off, while 180 of the fitter men folk remained to resist the retreating Germans and advancing Russians, Zambesi carried them to Murmansk where a baby in arms was among those transferred to the American liberty-ship Henry Bacon, which then encountered some of the fiercest Arctic weather of the war. The 60ft waves and blinding horizontal snow protected them from enemy attacks, but their convoy was dispersed. Henry Bacon then broke down and, after being spotted by a squadron of German torpedo-bombers, was sunk. The American crew placed their passengers in two lifeboats while they took to makeshift rafts. When Zambesi came across them, the survivors were too weak to help themselves. The waves were level with Zambesi's deck, and as her thrashing propellers were exposed several men were sucked under the stern and killed.

Unhesitatingly Bowden tied a bowline round his body and leapt into the water to rescue two unconscious sailors. When he was ordered up, he was so frozen that he could not clench his hands and had to be hauled up sitting on a grapnel. Back on deck he was unable to stand. But he was encouraged by seeing, among the moving bodies of those he had rescued, some whom he recognized from the first rescue. It was typical of Bowden that he mentioned the incident to few of his family until he was invited to California in 1992 to meet one of the survivors.

Ian Rodney Bowden was born in Herefordshire on January 2 1925 and taken by his mother to Burma where his father was senior manager in the Bombay Burma Trading Corporation. Young Rodney attributed his enthusiasm for the sea to his being offered ice-cream at 11am each day on the ship carrying him home to prep school, aged seven. He did not see his parents again until he went to Dartmouth six years later. His younger brother Deryk followed him two years later but was killed in a flying accident, aged 21.

Bowden recalled that when he navigated Zambesi into Bergen shortly before VE Day the boarding pilot had burst into tears; Bowden had then entertained some pretty blondes with white bread, corned beef and bottles of newly-liberated champagne labelled "Reserved for the Wehrmacht". His first post-war appointment was as a specialist navigator in Surprise, the dispatch vessel of the C-in-C, Mediterranean. Once when entering Malta, Bowden advised his Captain to slow down. On being ignored he warned: *"Sir, if you do not go astern now I will leave the bridge and accept no responsibility."* When Surprise hit and sank a floating galley, Bowden was exonerated. Bowden had a dry sense of humour and he could seem reserved; but he was a natural leader.

He went on to command the frigate Llandaff and conduct Exocet missile firing trials in the destroyer Norfolk in 1975. Yet it was in appointments requiring his gentle diplomacy that he excelled. He was commander of the Royal Yacht Britannia during a particularly successful period, 1966-7. When nut-smeared Pacific island chieftains sitting on the royal veranda for a kava drinking ceremony, left 18 buttock-shaped stains on the white teak deck, he and the Queen Mother agreed that they should be left "as marks of respect". At Tonga, Bowden organized for the yacht to be listed over seven degrees so that the heavyweight King of Tonga could embark via a stores hatch. As the king made his way slowly to the royal apartments, Bowden had the yacht righted so that the dining table would be level. Nor was Bowden fazed when the Queen Mother was invited to the wardroom for drinks, and she led the way to the galley in long dress and tiara to cook bacon and eggs.

In 1971-2 he commanded the ice patrol ship Endurance, landing Commander Burley's Joint Services Expedition on Elephant Island in the Antarctic. Four months later he re-enacted the cry "Are you all well?" which Sir Ernest Shackleton had made when he returned after making his epic journey to South Georgia in 1916. When the Chilean navy asked if he could catch and transport some reindeer from South Georgia to an island in the Beagle Channel, he persuaded incredulous officials at Portsmouth dockyard to build stalls in the forward hold. In 1971, Bowden in Endurance rendezvoused with Chay Blyth, who was circumnavigating the globe in the yacht British Steel sending him a carton of matches and a bottle of whiskey. Endurance undertook her share of survey work, and a previously unmarked pinnacle in the southern ocean is now known as Bowden Rock. A keen recreational sailor, and later a member of the Royal Yacht Squadron, Bowden was on the staff at Dartmouth in 1957 when he sailed one of the college yachts in Cowes Week, afterwards entering the Royal Ocean Racing Club's Channel race in what he called "very dubious weather". Two other college yachts retired with storm damage, and Bowden's was the only one to complete the race. He devoted much care and attention to his own yacht Sky High, which he sailed around the seas off the West Country and off the northern French coast. He later bought a motor boat Clara Blue, to give his grandchildren some sea-time."

Rodney Bowden had been interested in young people since he was boy's training officer in his first ship, and appropriately on retirement he became Captain of the Sea Cadet Corps and then President of the Gosport Sea Cadet Unit. He was appointed a Lieutenant of the Royal Victorian Order in 1967. He is survived by his wife Ann, their daughter Sally, two sons Mark and Nick, and seven grandchildren Katherine, George, Frances, Laurence, Christopher, Alexandra, and Marina.

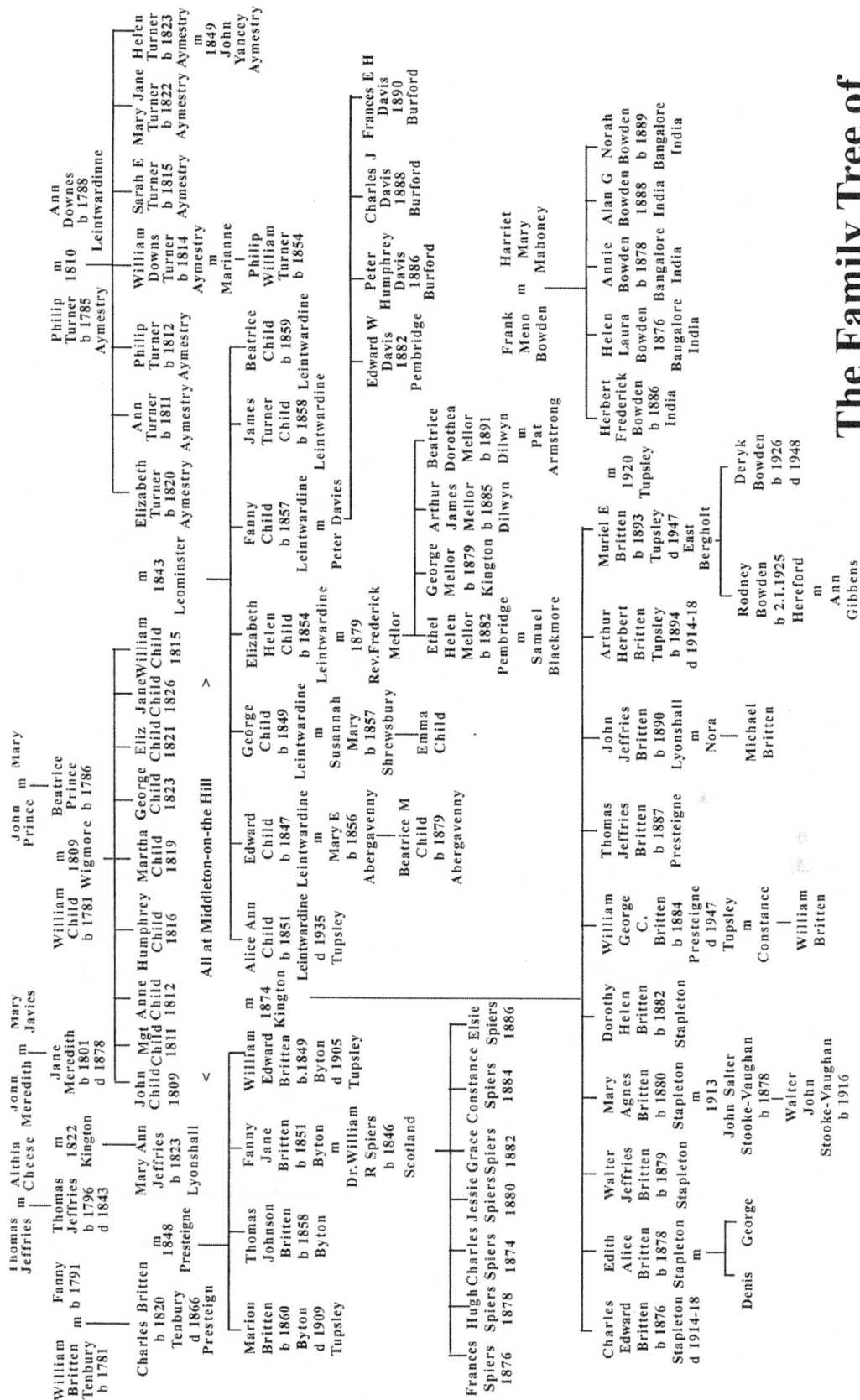

The Family Tree of Muriel Bowden

Thomas Jeffries m Athia Cheese

Jonn Meredith m Mary Javies

John Prince m Mary

Philip Turner m 1810 Ann Downs b 1788 Leintwardine
Aymestry

William Britten m b 1791 Tenbury
Fanny b 1781 Tenbury

Thomas Jeffries b 1796 d 1843
Jane Meredith m 1822 Kington b 1801 d 1878

William Child b 1781 Wigmore m 1809 Beatrice Prince b 1786

William Downs Turner b 1814 Aymestry m Marianne
Philip Turner b 1812 Aymestry
Sarah E Turner b 1815 Aymestry
Mary Jane Turner b 1822 Aymestry
Helen Turner b 1823 Aymestry m 1849 John Yancey Aymestry

Ann Turner b 1811 Aymestry
Elizabeth Turner b 1820 Aymestry

Charles Britten b 1820 Tenbury d 1866 Presteign
Mary Ann Jeffries b 1823 Presteigne m 1848 Lyonshall

Humphrey Child 1816
Martha Child 1819
George Child 1823
Eliz Child 1821
Jane Child 1826
William Child 1815 m 1843 Leominster

John Child 1809
Mgt Child 1811
Anne Child 1812

All at Middleton-on-the-Hill

James Turner Child b 1857
Beatrice Child b 1859

Fanny Child b 1858 Leintwardine m Peter Davies

Elizabeth Helen Child b 1854 Leintwardine
George Child b 1849 Leintwardine
Edward Child b 1847 Leintwardine

Edward W Davis 1882 Pembridge
Peter Humphrey Davis 1886 Burford
Charles J Davis 1888 Burford
Frances E H Davis 1890 Burford

Marion Britten b 1860 Byton d 1909 Tupsley
Thomas Johnson Britten b 1851 Byton
Fanny Jane Britten b 1851 Byton d 1905 m Dr. William R Spiers b 1846 Scotland
William Edward Britten b.1849 Byton m 1874 Kington
Alice Ann Child b 1851 Leintwardine d 1935 Tupsley

Susannah Mary b 1857 Shrewsbury m 1879 Rev. Frederick Mellor
Mary E b 1856 Abergavenny
Emma Child
Beatrice M Child b 1879 Abergavenny

Ethel Helen Mellor b 1882 Pembridge m Samuel Blackmore
George Mellor
Arthur James Mellor b 1879 Kington
Beatrice Dorothea Mellor b 1885
Mellor b 1891 Dilwyn m Pat Armstrong

Frank Meno Bowden m Mary Mahoney

Herbert Frederick Bowden b 1886 India m 1920 Tupsley
Helen Laura Bowden 1876 Bangalore India
Annie Bowden b 1878 Bangalore India
Alan G Bowden 1888 Bangalore India
Norah Bowden b 1889 Bangalore India

Muriel E Britten b 1893 Tupsley d 1947 East Bergholt

Arthur Herbert Britten b 1894 d 1914-18

Rodney Bowden b 2.1.1925 Hereford m Ann Gibbens
Deryk Bowden b 1926 d 1948

Frances Spiers 1876
Hugh Spiers 1878
Charles Spiers 1874
Jessie Spiers 1880
Grace Spiers 1882
Constance Spiers 1884
Elsie Spiers 1886

Thomas Jeffries Britten b 1887 Presteigne m Nora
John Jeffries Britten b 1890 Lyonshall

Michael Britten

Charles Edward Britten b 1876 d 1914-18
Edith Alice Britten b 1878
Walter Jeffries Britten b 1879
Mary Agnes Britten b 1880
Dorothy Helen Britten b 1882
William George C. Britten b 1884 Presteigne d 1947 Tupsley m Constance
Stapleton Stapleton m

William Britten

Stapleton Stapleton m 1913 John Salter Stooke-Vaughan b 1878
Walter John Stooke-Vaughan b 1916

Denis George

151

Rangoon
12th March 1924

My Yu Win,
Monywa MHM

Dear Sir,
I have stored the following in the Monywa Chummery during my absence on leave:

Packages all numbered from 1B to 54B excluding 53B
Packages numbered 1 to 40
Total packages 93.

Please check and inform me whether the above are in order.

I will also be glad if you will instruct the Durwan to pile the kit away from the wall so that when inspecting he can be more certain that white ants are not attacking the packages.

Yours faithfully

H F Bowden

Letter Showing Requisition for Stores

C/o The B.B.T.C.
Rangoon

Messrs Barrett Bros., Ltd.
Rangoon.

Dear Sirs,
Please send the following to me c/o B.B.T.C. Ltd., Monywa, Chindwin District. The R, M/R or R/R to the Head Clerk, Monywa, as usual:

2 bottles of Scrubbs Ammonia,
2 tins of Evap. Apple rings,
2 tins of Evap. Peach rings,
5 lbs. of Bacon,
3 tins of Borwicks' Baking Powder,
4 tins of Heinz Baked Beans in Sauce,
2 large bottles of Bovril,
1 tin of Cafe Noir Biscuits,
2 tins of Digestive Biscuits,
2 tins of Ginger Nut Biscuits`,
1 tin of Bombay Duck
1 tin of Pepper Drums,
2 four and a half pound tins of Polson's Butter,
3 large bottles of Capers,
1 bottle of Cayenne Pepper,
1 small tin of Chocolate Powder,
6 bottles of Chutney (assorted Indian),
6 tins of Pelley's Coffee,
6 bottles of Ginger Beer Essence,
3 tins of Cornflour,
3 tins of Tapioca,
2 tins of Sago,
3 large bottles of Curry Powder,
1 2lb. tin of Dripping.
4 tins of Hops,
1 bottle of Ellimans' Embrocation,
4 bottles of Essence of Celery,
2 tins of kippered Herrings,
2 tins of Bloaters,

2 tins of Fresh Herrings,
2 tins of Haddock,
6 tins of Sardines (in oil),
3 tins of Wholemeal Flour,
50 lbs. Flour,
1 bottle of Sultanas,
1 bottle of Rasins,
3 tins of egg Plums,
2 tins of Peaches,
1 pkt of Gelatine,
1 tin of Golden Syrup,
1 10lb Ham,
1 bottle of dried Parsley,
1 tin of Blackcurrant Jam IXL,
2 tins Gooseberry Jam,
2 tins of Greengages,
1 tin of Red Currants,
6 tins of Marmalade,
12 tins of Lard,
1 case of half-tins of Ideal Milk,
2 large tins of Colman's Mustard,
1 bottle Foot Oil,
1 bottle of Rangoon Oil,
4 quart bottles of Salad Oil,
2 bottles of White Pepper,
4 bottles of Pickles (assorted),
1 pot of Bloater Paste,
1 pot of Anchovy Paste,
2 tins of Quaker Oats,
2 tins of Salmon,
3 tins of Cerebos Salt,
2 bottles of Sutton's Anchovy Sauce.
The remainder of the items on the list are unreadable.

Bibliography

Arnold, Sue, Burmese Legacy, Hodder and Stoughton, London, 1996.

Larkin, Emma, Finding George Orwell in Burma, Penguin Press, London, 2005.

Macaulay, R.H., History of The Bombay Burmah Trading Corporation 1864 -1910 . London, 1934.

Orwell, George, Burmese Days, Penguin Books, London, 1967.

Pointon, Arnold Cecil, Bombay Burmah Trading Corporation 1863-1963: The Millbrook Press. Southampton 1964.

Pointon, Arnold Cecil, Wallace Brothers,University Press, Oxford, 1974

Webster, Anthony, Gentlemen Capitalists: British Imperialism in South East Asia 1770-1890. (London: Tauris Academic Studies. 1998)

Williams, J.H., Elephant Bill. The Reprint Society, Bungay, Suffolk, 1951.

Map of North Central Burma 1909

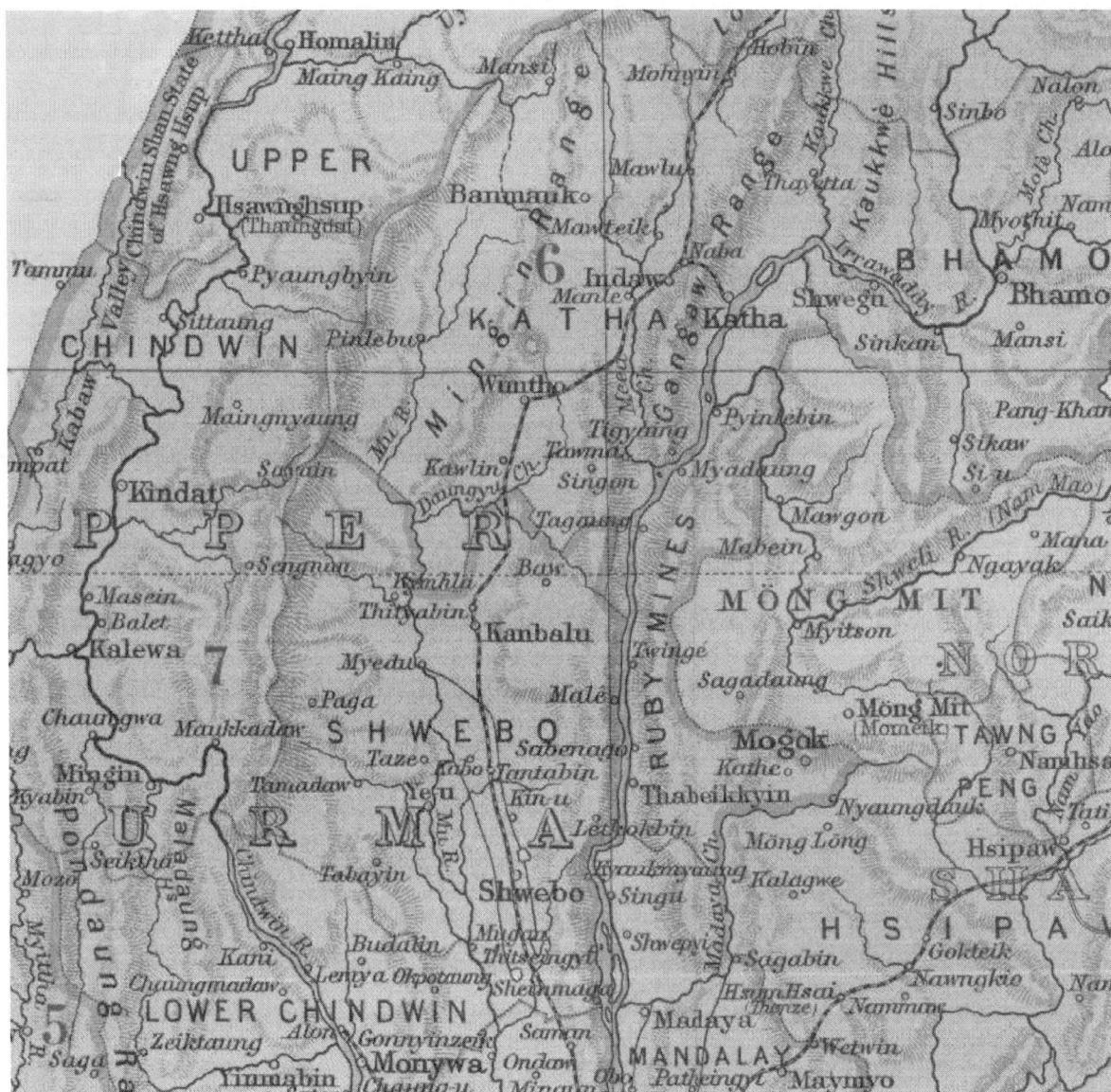

Index